D1169178

West Texas

EXPLORER'S GUIDES

FIRST EDITION

The Countryman Press
Woodstock, Vermont

this is for you and I to continue our journey together

Copyright © 2012 by Judy Wiley

Explorer's Guide West Texas: A Great Destination

ISBN: 978-0-88150-920-5

Interior photographs by the author unless otherwise specified
Maps by Erin Greb Cartography, © The Countryman Press
Book design by Joanna Bodenweber
Composition by Eugenie S. Delaney

Published by The Countryman Press, P.O. Box 748, Woodstock, VT 05091
Distributed by W. W. Norton & Company, Inc., 500 Fifth Avenue, New York, NY 10110
Printed in the United States of America

10 9 8 7 6 5 4 3 2 1

For my mother, Gwen Bonner—my favorite West Texan

Explore with Us!

THIS BOOK IS DIVIDED into five chapters that cover different segments of West Texas. Introductions cover highlights and, in some cases, history, and are intended to give you a general grasp of the area. The beginnings of chapters may also include Guidance—places to go for information; Getting There; Getting Around; Media, which lists local media; Medical Emergencies information; and Tours, where pertinent.

Recommendations and listings follow, with the name, phone number, Web site and address of each place, days and in some cases hours of business, followed by a brief description and/or recommendation. All information has been checked as close to publication date as possible, but prices and hours can change quickly, so it's best to confirm ahead of time. In some of the smaller towns, businesses open and close irregularly, so I've suggested you call for their hours.

For easy reference, generally listings are organized in alphabetical order, not in order of preference. For the most part, I do not cover chain motels and restaurants (you'll see exceptions). I understand that you can easily find a familiar chain if you need to, so this book is geared to giving you information about less-familiar, more local establishments—after all, the joy of travel is in learning and new experiences.

PRICES

Because prices change, I've rated them according to range. Especially in the case of restaurants, you still may find an unexpected price for a meal, as more and more establishments are using changing, seasonal menus. I've noted where credit cards are not accepted, but otherwise, assume they are. I haven't made special notes about children, because they're fine in most West Texas restaurants—but if you're not sure about an upscale location, call ahead and ask. As for pets, I've noted a few places where they're definitely not allowed and suggested ways to find lodging for them in the area.

I didn't include detailed information about pets because of the distances involved—I'm assuming most people won't want to fly their animals to a location and then continue with them on a long car trip—and also because policies seem to change frequently. If you do want to take a pet (and I know they're hard to leave behind), check ahead with the hotel or motel.

Restaurant prices indicate the cost of a meal for two without drinks, tips, or tax. Lodging prices indicate the cost of a double room or its equivalent per night.

Price Codes

	Lodging	Dining
Inexpensive	Up to $80	Up to $15
Moderate	$80–140	$15–40
Expensive	$140–200	Over $40
Very expensive	Over $200	

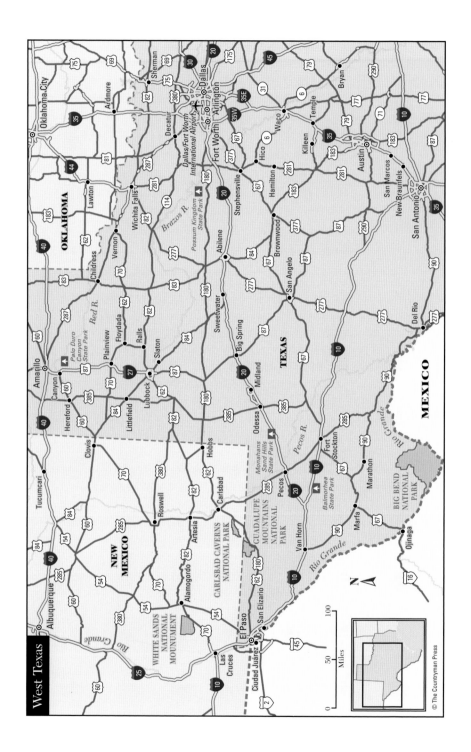

West Texas

8

Contents

Acknowledgments

A LOT OF PEOPLE helped make this book happen. Visitors and convention centers in the cities and towns were an invaluable help and resource. Friends who live in some of the locations put me up during research trips and helped me stay current after I left. Still more friends of the editing persuasion looked chapters over in draft and final form. Others took care of my dogs while I was gone, helped me get where I needed to go, and listened to me talk endlessly about the project. Some of you didn't even have to be physically with me to cheer me on and listen—you were there on Facebook or email. My current boss and a former one were kind enough to give me time off for trips and to write over the past year and a half. Food critic and author June Naylor passed along the word that Countryman Press wanted a writer, encouraged me all along the way, and finally wrote an essay for this book. Kim Grant, my editor at Countryman for most of this process, was incredibly patient and endlessly helpful.

And then there's my family. My mother, Gwen Bonner, to whom this book is dedicated, was born in Ranger, Texas, and showed me all her life what it means to be a hardworking, determined West Texan with that inimitable, dry sense of humor they all seem to be born with. She, along with my brother and sister, read over chapters and gave me their thoughts. My daughter, Sara, put up with my distracted, slightly crazed state of mind as the deadline drew nearer—and so did her wedding.

To all of you and anyone I've left out: Thank you. I appreciate you more than you know.

Introduction

MY FIRST MEMORIES of West Texas were as a traveler, a child riding through the night in the back seat of the family car. Once a year, we made the eight-hour trip from our home in New Mexico to Ranger, a town near the end of a vast, mostly open stretch of plains across West Texas known as the Big Empty. I remember crossing the state line at Hobbs, New Mexico, and hours later seeing the twinkling lights of Sweetwater after we swooped down to the interstate, more than halfway there. My mom's voice always softened a little after that. She was coming home.

My grandparents lived on 5 acres at the edge of Ranger, and their property seemed a wonderland of trees and grasses and flowers to me, a child of the desert.

Our way of life was different during those visits because it was influenced by Texas traditions. We slept on beds under intricate, lovely quilts hand-pieced and painstakingly finished by my grandmother and great-aunts. We spent hours playing music—me or my mom or aunt on piano, my grandpa on fiddle, uncles on guitar or banjo, my aunt on accordion, all of us sweating in the summer heat with no air-conditioning, drinking sweet tea and lemonade. We ate fried okra and snacked on bread-and-butter pickles my grandma had canned.

Years later, in college at New Mexico State University in Las Cruces and later, working in northern New Mexico, I became an avid Texan-hater. Noisy hicks with ostentatious belt buckles, I sniffed, even as vacationing Texans bolstered the economies of places like Ruidoso, New Mexico, and Santa Fe. *Dallas* had started its 13-season run, which firmly fixed Texans in the minds of the nation—and eventually the world—as a greedy, unscrupulous bunch of oil barons. My own scorn was an interesting conceit: My entire family had, in fact, picked up and moved to Texas while I was in college.

LEFT: If you're lucky, you might see a roadrunner at Palo Duro Canyon.

When I visited, I flew into Dallas–Fort Worth Airport, and we drove two hours to towns like Hico, on US 281 amid rolling hills and trees. I gave up my snobbery long enough to absorb some of the real Texas, the kind with fairly normal belt buckles on everyone except rodeo champions, and guys who automatically say *ma'am*. I saw staggering stretches of wildflowers (part of the work started by Lady Bird Johnson in 1982); ate melt-in-your mouth barbecued brisket, cream pies with a good 3 inches of meringue, and Parker County peaches so ripe the juice ran down to your elbow on the first bite. So, for a long time, I experienced Texas as a kind of tourist—but one with the best guides of all: family and friends who had been in nooks and crannies of the state for generations. A journalist and therefore a skeptic by trade, I ignored the braggadocio and larger-than-life image, choosing instead to experience Texas as most Texans do—not at dude ranches, and not wearing cowboy boots and a hat, unless I intended to ride a horse all day in the sun. I gradually gave up my hardnosed hipster attitude and lived in El Paso, vacationed in Port Aransas on the Gulf Coast, and finally made a trip to see the Alamo. Eventually, my newspaper career brought me to North Texas to live.

In Grapevine, between the busy urban scenes in Dallas and Fort Worth, I got still another taste of the Lone Star State. The nightlife in Dallas's Deep Ellum district taught me a little about Texas music, and visits to a friend in Austin who plays guitar gigs (who doesn't, in Austin?) led me to a deep appreciation of its many genres. I became hooked on roots blues by the likes of Blind "Lemon" Jefferson, for whom there's a plaque in Deep Ellum, and learned that Stevie Ray Vaughan came from the Oak Cliff neighborhood of Dallas, just a few miles from Grapevine.

As a newspaper editor, I directed coverage of notorious criminals like the Texas Seven prison escapees and reveled in the Texas details, like the report that they drank Shiner Bock—a Texas beer—at their Colorado hideout. I covered the Cliburn International Piano Competition in Fort Worth and got to spend hours listening to the best young pianists in the world perform in Bass Hall, one of the best concert halls in the country. Our metamorphosis into actual Texans was slow, but I knew we were getting close the day my daughter announced she was "fixin'" to do something.

I really began to absorb the state in detail when I became travel editor at the *Fort Worth Star Telegram.*

The last in a long tradition of travel editors at the paper, I hopped around the state on short flights or drove into small towns for a night's stay, a day's shopping, and eating. My hope is that with this book I can deliver to you straightaway the joys and beauties and tastes and sights of Texas that

won me over. Besides, this is a huge state. I don't want you getting lost in
the Big Empty, asking "Are we there yet?" until you run out of gas. I can
show you where to turn.

WHAT YOU'LL FIND IN THIS BOOK

My favorite trips anywhere are partly planned and partly a kind of aimless
wandering. To that end, I often suggest must-see sights or attractions as
well as lesser-known gems found during my wandering—saving you the
trouble of any dead ends I encountered. First-timers will want to make sure
to hit the attractions marked DON'T MISS, while veteran West Texas tourists
may find new experiences with the others.

A note about lodging and restaurants: My aim is to open doors to singu-
lar experiences that give you a genuine feel for places. That might mean
an historic hotel or a new boutique, delicious taco stands or a Texas chef's
latest eatery.

The same goes for activities and shopping. Anyone can go to the mall
and buy a pair of boots. But I'll help you find craftsmen who will create a
pair just for you.

Search out the right pair, and I'll show you where they can take you.

What's Where in West Texas

ARMADILLO Be happy if you see one, because it doesn't happen all that often. But don't chase it around, shoot it, or otherwise fool with it—they have a limited immunity to leprosy and sometimes carry it, although the chances of getting the disease from the state animal are slim. The nine-banded armadillo is a tough creature; unfortunately one of its biggest predators is the automobile. Be really happy if you see one with her babies—they're the cutest little pink things. The other state animals are: mammal, Mexican freetail bat; dog, blue Lacy; bird, mockingbird; reptile, Texas horned lizard; insect, Monarch butterfly; fish, Guadalupe bass.

AIRPORTS AND AIRLINES Most major airlines fly in and out of most major cities in Texas. Dallas–Fort Worth International Airport is the hub for and headquarters for American Airlines. The home of Southwest Airlines is Dallas's Love Field, where President John F. Kennedy landed the day he was assassinated in Dallas. Southwest and American Eagle fly lots of commuter routes daily within Texas.

ART MUSEUMS Once you get outside Fort Worth and Dallas, the museums are largely historical, but don't miss the University of Texas Tech Museum in Lubbock, and the surprising Old Jail Museum in Albany for fine art.

ATTIRE Fine dining in the big cities requires the same attire as any other white-tablecloth restaurants. Even if you're not used to the heat, put on a sundress or a sport jacket. Some resorts also frown on caps and shorts, etc. In rural West Texas, you're fine in boots and jeans or shorts and sandals almost anywhere. A tip: If you're in Lubbock around springtime and have long hair, bring hair ties or you'll be fighting the wind all day. You'll see a lot of women in baseball caps for the same reason.

LEFT: Boots!

Visitors can spend hours at the Museum of Texas Tech University.

BARBED WIRE Barbed wire, actually invented in Illinois, changed the West. Before it existed there was no good way to keep cattle within the boundaries of large spaces. Ranches in the Panhandle were among the very first to use it that way, which spelled the end of free-range ranching. If you think you have to crawl through some—don't. It's there for a reason, and you risk getting shot at for trespassing. If you've lost something really important in the wind, it's best to drive to the ranch house, if you can spot it, and ask permission to be on the property. And don't let anybody convince you to stick your tongue to the barbed wire when it's freezing outside.

BASS That's the kind of fishing you'll find in most of West Texas. The lakes here provide good hiding places for big fish, and tournaments are frequent. Crappie fishing, which is fun for kids because of frequent bites, also is popular here. For more about licensing, etc., go to www.tpwd.state.tx.us.

BICYCLING With the exception of Marfa, where bicycles are everywhere, West Texas has only recently caught cycling fever. Fort Worth and Dallas are starting to install bike lanes. Mountain bikers can get their fix at most state and national parks.

BOATING As with fishing, www.tpwd.state.tx.us is a trove of information about locations and licensing, and also will tell you whether rentals are available at a given lake.

BOBCATS They're about twice the size of a housecat and mean as all get out. You're not likely to see one, since they're nocturnal, but get out your camera, at a distance, if you do.

BOOTS, COWBOY Entire books are written about this subject—how they're made, best ways to make them, fancy ones, plain ones, etc., etc. The best advice I know how to give is don't drop all your money on a fancy pair, because you might not wear them back home. Instead, get a good pair in neutral tones from one of the factory outlets mentioned in this book—many of them are in El Paso. You'll save money and be more likely to wear them later. Plus you won't stick out like a sore thumb everywhere you go, which you might if you opted for a crazy pair. In fact, if you run across a used pair, that's one of the best deals of all.

CAMPING The state and national parks have plenty of campsites, as do many lakes. Spring and fall are excellent times to pitch a tent. The lack of rain can be a blessing, but remember it's also a fire hazard, so follow the fire rules posted at campsites. For the same reason, haul plenty of water with you. Also, a word to the wise: Camping in much of West Texas in July and August is just plain hot. Unless you sleep well in heat, think twice about trying it. As with camping anywhere, if you're not sleeping near your vehicle, bring your valuables with you.

Film fans come from miles around for Marfa's annual festival.

CAR RENTAL I almost always get a free upgrade without even asking in Midland or Lubbock. They're small airports and usually happy to help. If the upgrade is not a gas-guzzler but is a vehicle with higher clearance than the original, take it. Especially in the Big Bend area, you don't want to be uncomfortable taking a dirt road.

CHAPS The correct pronunciation of the leather leg protectors worn by both cowboys and bikers is *shaps*.

CHIGGERS These pests will get you if you go walking off in the tall grass in the summertime, which is ill-advised anyway because of the possibility of snakes. If you get to your tent or room and find itchy welts wherever elastic was touching you—along the bra line, panty line, waistband, etc.—then you've been chigger-bit. Luckily, they're not dangerous, just wildly itchy. Calamine lotion and Benadryl will help.

CONVENTION AND VISITORS BUREAUS These are where you'll find hundreds of pamphlets and lots of cheerful volunteers who can point you to a local walking tour or a countywide festival or just about anything else. If you're not sure what to do in a given location, stop in to see them.

COTTON Especially around Lubbock, many of the fields you'll see stretching for miles around you are cotton fields. They're irrigated, which explains the big circles you'll see from the air. You may also see cotton gins in your travels—these remove the seeds from the cotton.

DEER The smallish whitetail deer is what you'll usually see, sometimes grazing roadside in the evenings. The state does also have the larger mule deer, prevalent in New Mexico. Landowners in Texas lease their property to hunters, who must have licenses. Details about hunting are at www.tpwd .state.tx.us.

DINING As in many Southern states, you may hear people talking about breakfast, dinner, and supper rather than breakfast, lunch, and dinner. That probably comes from the days when hardworking farmers and farmhands ate the biggest meal of the day at noon.

This guide is divided into *Dining Out* for fine dining and *Eating Out* for more casual venues. I've ferreted out non-chain local establishments, or regional chains, figuring you know how to find fast food.

DON'T MISS I've tried to make sure you see what's important with the *Don't Miss* headings in many sections. If you don't see one, that means I couldn't pick just one thing.

DRY COUNTIES As of the end of 2010, there were 26 dry counties and 44 wet ones. Dry means no alcohol is served anywhere in the county. Some counties do allow "private clubs" that serve liquor. You can buy a one-night membership to drink alcohol. The easiest way to tell if you're in a dry county will be the lack of beer at the convenience stores. Then again, some counties permit beer sales but not hard liquor. If you're desperate, drive on—the counties are small and everything could change in another 30 miles. The larger cities in this book have both liquor stores and bars, and sell beer and wine in grocery and convenience stores.

DUST DEVILS The swirling circles of dust you'll sometimes see by the side of the road in the desert.

EMERGENCIES Dial 911 from anywhere. I was pleased to find that nowadays, even on long stretches of remote highway, I almost always had cell phone signal. That doesn't necessarily mean help is close by, but I've included information about where to find it in some of the more remote regions. It's always a good idea to carry a first-aid kit in the car, and I can't say it enough: plenty of water.

ENTERTAINMENT Night-time entertainment venues have been opening and closing with some regularity the past few years, so I've listed a few in each spot and, where applicable, referred you to the local newspaper or entertainment magazine for current listings.

FOOD See June Naylor's excellent essay on West Texas food. She's a well-known Texas food writer, purveyor of food tours through her company, Texas Toast, and a member of Les Dames d'Escoffier International.

GAY AND LESBIAN SCENE Dallas has a thriving gay scene, predominately in the Cedar Springs area (the primary bars on the strip are JR's, S4, Sue Ellen's, and the Roundup, among many, many others), but extending all over town. Fort Worth's gay scene is expanding rapidly, with five bars, along with other gay-owned, gay-friendly businesses in the burgeoning South Jennings *gaybourhood* as well as a couple of nightspots on the eastside. There are a number of bar and business resources online. Lubbock also has a low-key GLBT scene. West Texas, except for Marfa, is a conservative part of the country, and the more rural areas aren't always accustomed to cultural differences.

GOAT ROPERS A somewhat derisive term used to describe people with hats, boots, trucks, but no cattle or any real knowledge about them, either.

HATS, COWBOY The cowboy hat is something of a sacred object in West Texas. Real cowboys don't wear them every day for looks, but for actual protection against the sun, except in the case of the dress hat.

The "work" straw hat for summer is worn daily until it's so greasy and sweaty you have to retire it. The "good hat," straw for the summer and felt in winter, is for wearing to church, dinner, or business meetings. You can get a decent Stetson for $70 or $80, but you'll really stick out if you get either a straw or felt hat and don't have it steamed and shaped. Luckily, many big Western wear stores have in-house steaming. If you really want to look like a tourist, buy one of the straw hats at a tourist trinket store with the brim curled up on the sides and a string that goes under your chin.

HISTORY See the History chapter (page 29).

HORSES Plenty of places will rent a horse for you to ride, especially if you're staying at a ranch. Rental horses generally are tame but stubborn, often insisting on going back to the barn before you're ready. Some general rules of thumb about horses: If you haven't been told a horse is tame, don't approach it, try to pet it, feed it, or yell at it. If the wranglers tell you it's OK, you may feed a horse. The way to feed a horse something small is to place it in the flat of your hand and offer it. That way your fingers won't be chomped. Also avoid standing behind a horse and making loud noises, because that can get you kicked, which is serious and can be fatal. If the rental horse you're riding seems bent on heading for a fence, stop him. Sometimes they'll

The Old Red Courthouse in Dallas is also the visitor information center downtown.

use the fence to rub you off, and then go wherever they wanted to go.

HUNTING Deer, wild turkey, quail, dove, and wild hogs all are hunted in Texas. For information about seasons, licensing, etc., go to www.tpwd .state.tx.us.

INFORMATION ABOUT TEXAS The best source of all-around information about history and most everything else is the Texas State Historical Association's Handbook of Texas Online, www.tshaonline.org. In individual cities and towns, check with the local convention and visitors bureaus. The phone numbers and Web sites are listed at the beginning of each chapter.

ITINERARIES See the separate Itineraries section of the History chapter (page 34).

LODGING The lodging you'll see reviewed in this guide is either non-chain or regional chain establishments. They're listed in alphabetical order. The rates in this guide do not include taxes, nor do they address various discounts that may be available (AARP, etc.). For the most part, I listed few bed and breakfast establishments because I feel as a travel writer I would need to stay a night or two in these private lodgings, and that was not always possible (the lodgings that are listed are those I've either stayed in or looked over closely). To explore the Texas B&B world, take a look at www.bbonline.com/tx.

MAPS You'll find good maps available, usually free, at most convention and visitors bureaus.

MINGUS This little town between Gordon and Strawn outside the Palo Pinto area has long been known as the only place that sells liquor for 50 miles in any direction. But Texas counties are changing yearly, so this may not hold true as you read this. It was named after a pioneer settler, not after jazz great Charles Mingus.

MOUNTAIN LIONS Take warnings about them seriously. I've never run across one, but park rangers keep track of sightings and post notices accordingly.

MUSEUMS See Art Museums.

NEWSPAPERS The small-town paper is alive and well in West Texas. You can generally pick one up at any roadside café or convenience store. Reading one will give you a feel for what matters here, whether it's cotton prices, weather, schools, or what the Legislature is up to. In Dallas, Fort Worth, Lubbock, and El Paso, the Saturday editions usually include entertainment and dining guides, which can help you keep up with what's new and which bands are playing.

Besides trailers, teepees are for rent at El Cosmico in Marfa.

NIGHTLIFE You're not liable to find a lot of it in the small towns, where people work hard and go to bed early. If you do, there's no reason to fear the honky-tonk. People are friendly and like to have a good time.

OPOSSUMS You may see them, with their prehensile tails, by the side of the road. Sometimes they're roadkill, but they might just be playing possum. As with any wild animal, it's best to leave them alone.

The road and sky go on forever in West Texas.

PETROGLYPHS You can see some at Hueco Tanks State Park near El Paso, and also at Big Bend National Park.

QUAIL See Hunting.

RAILROAD The railroad was responsible for a lot of West Texas towns' existence, and you'll still see a lot of freight trains on any trip West. Amtrak also runs trains from Dallas and Fort Worth to San Antonio. There are frequent stops, so it's not the route to go if you don't have a lot of time. On the other hand, it's a relaxing and economical way to travel. Just be careful about taking the trains during spring break, when families and college kids fill them up.

READING See the Recommended Reading section at the end of each chapter and the Bibliography at the end of the book.

RASPA A slushy, icy drink in a variety of flavors from pickles to popcorn to cherry limón that I've only encountered at the Murphy Street Raspa Co. in Alpine. Anything icy in West Texas in the summertime is a good thing.

SAILING Texas lakes are large enough to sail on—Lake Grapevine, for one, often is filled with sailboats on a weekend evening. Check with the marinas about rentals.

SHOPPING Every section ends with Selective Shopping, with entries in alphabetical order. Dallas definitely has the most overall shopping, with Fort Worth second. Because even mall shopping in Dallas is a little different than the norm, I've listed malls there. I've listed a few other malls, but tried to focus where possible on guiding you to local shops and boutiques where you might find something unusual to take home, something besides the usual T-shirts and shot glasses.

SMOKING It's outlawed even in bars in Dallas, and in some, if not most, restaurants in Fort Worth. Many hotels across the region outlaw it, but some in the smaller towns—as well as restaurants and bars there—do permit smoking inside.

SPEED LIMITS In places—stretches of wide, flat road—they are as high as 80 mph. Keep an eye on the signs, though, when you're approaching a town and follow the posted limits closely. If you're not on the Interstate, they'll go as low as 30–35 mph, and the local police do enforce them.

SWEET TEA Most of the time if iced tea is pre-sweetened with sugar, you'll be offered sweet tea. If you're watching calories, it doesn't hurt to ask.

SOCIAL MEDIA Many places in this book that have Web sites also have a presence on Facebook. If you're a fervent Facebooker, search for them and Like them—in some cases that page is updated more frequently than the Web site.

SPECIAL EVENTS There are listings at the end of each section. Also, the convention and visitors bureau Web sites have complete listings, and the state tourism Web site, www.traveltex.com, is a good resource.

TAXES Sales taxes vary widely across the state, largely because the Texas Legislature is loath to pass a state income tax. It will be printed on your receipt.

TIME ZONE Most of Texas is in the Central Time Zone, but farther West, including El Paso, is in the Mountain Time Zone.

TORTILLAS The farther West you get, and definitely in El Paso, you'll be asked whether your side of tortillas should be flour or corn. Don't automatically default to flour. Fresh corn tortillas are delicious, and lower in calories to boot.

TORNADOS Tornado season is March through June. Take the warnings seriously—a big twister ripped through Fort Worth and destroyed much of Downtown in 2000. A tornado watch means one is possible. A tornado warning means one has been spotted and you need to find shelter. Towns usually have a shelter set up—listen to the emergency radio station if you're on the road. If you're in a room, the safest place is usually the bathroom, away from windows.

A sky ahead with a greenish cast often means tornado weather, and hail is also a sign. Don't try to outdrive a tornado—you don't know what's ahead.

The lowly tumbleweed makes a desert decor statement in Alpine.

A radio station will be your best source of information if you're concerned, unless you have access to the Internet and radar maps.

Also: Storms with rain and hail will move rapidly over parts of West Texas in the spring, so sometimes your best bet is to pull over underneath something to save your car from damage, and wait it out.

TO SEE AND DO The attractions are listed in alphabetical order in this guide. I've included longer stories (sidebars) where more detail is needed, or when something is particularly interesting.

TUMBLEWEEDS There are some big ones, big as Volkswagens, out around Lubbock. OK, maybe not quite that big, but big. They won't hurt you, but they can stick to your car bumper or underneath, so it's best to steer around them.

WEATHER The saying goes, IF YOU DON'T LIKE THE WEATHER IN TEXAS JUST GO TO BED; IT WILL CHANGE BY MORNING. That's true to a point. West Texas is a huge area, so no one characteristic fits. Dallas and Fort Worth are more humid. Abilene is drier, and Lubbock and Amarillo have more wind. Anything north of Amarillo tends to be a lot colder than the rest of the state in the winter. A Blue Norther in West Texas is what happens when an Arctic front makes its way into the state. This typically means the roads are sheets of ice and the only safe route is to pull over and stay somewhere until it melts in a few days.

In the Big Bend/Fort Davis/Marfa area, you'll still feel the heat in the summer, but evenings can cool down to sweater weather.

El Pasoans love their city for the year-round warmth and low humidity, though it gets very hot in the summer, especially July and August.

WEB SITES If an entity or business has one, they're listed in this guide. Some statewide resources:

www.traveltex.com, Texas government state travel site;

www.texasescapes.com, stories by a variety of travel writers from Texas and elsewhere;

www.tshaonline.org, Texas State Handbook Online, The Texas State Historical Association's Web site, very easy to use and well-done.

WILDFLOWERS Lady Bird Johnson started the movement to introduce people to wildflowers, and now they brighten roadsides all across Texas. The first to bloom in the spring is the bluebonnet, the Texas state flower.

Bluebonnets are the first Texas flower to bloom in the spring.

History

WEST TEXANS ARE A HARDWORKING LOT, and almost unfailingly friendly, though not in an overly talkative way. The single characteristic, though, that stands out (if there can be one to describe so many people across such a vast space) is stubbornness—and if they've been here for generations, they came by it honestly.

Just survival even in a good year took a lot of work and luck, especially if a frontier family was farming for a living, and they often were. Add in severe, years-long droughts in a land having very little water to start with, and the result is abject poverty.

My own family's records from around the turn of the century show my great-great-grandmother in the Strawn area writing to a church back in Tennessee for money—any money—even just $1 or 50 cents. My great-great-grandfather was a preacher, and usually was paid in goods—a chicken, for example—so they were fed. But money for shoes and clothing was another story.

Wealth came to some who could afford cattle, or later, who struck oil. But the average West Texan in the early years of statehood and well before that had to be stubborn to stay. Why did they? Well, some didn't—they headed back East. Those who stayed were determined to make a better life for their children. Some were dreamers, some adventurers, but they all had a big streak of independence. Nobody bothers you much in the farthest reaches of West Texas, then or now. The big sky stretching from horizon to horizon and gorgeous with stars at night can be all yours.

LEFT: Indian Lodge at Davis Mountains State Park gets booked up fast every year in January.

Bear in mind that this history is about West Texas—so except for mentioning major events if they impact this part of the state, I'm not dwelling on statewide history.

HABITATION

Artifacts indicate the first Texans probably came into the state before 11000–8000 B.C. They must have had quite an interesting life—the bones of giant armadillos, mammoths, camels, and giant bears have been found at the Lubbock Lake Landmark site. One of the next indications of early man in Texas also was found in West Texas—Midland Man, a burial from 8000–7000 B.C., was discovered in Midland County in 1953. Rock art on cave walls dating to about 4000 B.C. was found in what's now Paint Rock, about an hour east of San Angelo, in Concho County. In 1500 B.C. corn farmers had settled near Presidio (outside what is now Big Bend National Park).

Early Europeans

Drought has always been a problem. Alvar Nunez Cabeza de Vaca came upon the corn farmers some time in the early 1500s A.D., and found it hadn't rained there in two years. In fact, they thought he was a god and asked him to have a talk with the sky about it. Some 20 years later, the first European on record as having come to the Panhandle was Francisco Vazquez de Coronado, who crossed part of it while he was looking for Gran Quivira. By 1598, Juan de Oñate and his expedition, along with Native Americans who lived in what is now the El Paso area, celebrated what some today call the First Thanksgiving (see sidebar in Chapter 5, Far West Texas). Oñate claimed the land for Spain, and Spanish missions to convert Native Americans to Christianity began with a trip in 1629 to present-day San Angelo. It was after the Pueblo Revolt of 1680 that Spanish and some Native Americans fled to El Paso and started the missions you'll see today on the Mission Trail.

Texas Independence

Mexico gained independence from Spain in 1821, and it was under Mexican rule that some Anglo colonization took place in Central Texas, under Stephen F. Austin. Texas adopted its declaration of independence in 1836, the same year as the battle of the Alamo. Texas was annexed to the United States in 1845. It was about this time that many of the forts you'll see in West Texas were established, to guard the frontier against Comanche and Apache raids. Fort Belknap, near Graham in Young County, for example, was established in 1854, and an Indian reservation was established in that

Fort Belknap State Park is just outside Graham.

area as well. In many cases, the towns that sprung up to support the forts with supplies, groceries, etc., became the cities and towns you see today.

The Civil War and Beyond

By 1859, Native Americans who had been moved to Northwest Texas reservations were moved again, this time to Oklahoma Territory.

The U.S. Civil War began in 1861, and Texas seceded from the Union. Some families from the East immigrated to Texas during the war, to escape the devastation in their home states. When the war ended in 1865, the word that slavery had been abolished after the war didn't make it to Texas until June 19 of that year, the reason the Juneteenth holiday is celebrated across the state.

During the Civil War, the military withdrew from the forts established in the 1850s, but settlers called for help as Native Americans began to exert control again. Texas Beyond History (www.texasbeyondhistory.net), a virtual museum operated by the University of Texas at Austin, gives this account of events that followed:

- The Medicine Lodge Treaty of 1867 was signed, setting up two reservations. The government was to provide the tribes with housing, food, supplies, and guns for hunting for 30 years, and also permit hunting south of the Arkansas River as long as the buffalo ranged on the land. Tribes agreed to stop attacks and raids, in return. But commercial buffalo hunters killed off practically all the herds in just four years, from 1874 to 1878, leaving the tribes to depend on reservation food and supplies.

- There wasn't enough food, and Native Americans couldn't understand or accept the reservation restrictions.

- In spring 1874, tired of starving, the Native Americans struck back at Adobe Walls, near the Canadian River in Hutchinson County, led by Comanche Chief Quanah Parker and leader and prophet Isa-Tai, They were overpowered. The ensuing Red River War of 1874 included 20 engagements. Quanah Parker surrendered at Fort Sill in 1875.

The Cowboy

The cattle business in Texas took off in earnest after the Civil War. With the buffalo hunted out and Native Americans confined, lots of land and wild cattle were available. Once the post-war need for meat became obvious, and rail transportation came West, the cattle drives began. The drovers, as young as 21 or 22, pushed herds of thousands for many miles to railheads in Kansas City or Abilene, Kansas.

But the earliest Texas cowboys were Mexican, often with roots in Spain, where the vaquero tradition began (the word *cowboy* is a translation of *vaquero*, which essentially means boy who takes care of cattle. *Buckaroo* is a mispronunciation of *vaquero*.) Through land grants, the Spanish owned huge tracts of land down along the Rio Grande and kept herds from Mexico.

Wild cattle, often the hardy longhorn, were there for the taking in many cases—this was before the barbed wire fences, so the cattle roamed the open range and flourished or suffered according to the weather.

Towns that had grown up around forts became rest stops and watering holes for the cowboys. The red-light districts with saloons, dance halls, and whorehouses were often called Hell's Half-Acre, but the one in Fort Worth was considered the wildest, and it became one of the biggest, at 2.5 acres and more. Outlaws like the Sam Bass gang reportedly hid out there, violence was rampant (although some Fort Worthians suggested it never was as bad as its reputation), and the whole thing eventually was shut down around 1889, with the help of Prohibition.

Between the 1860s and the 1880s, some 5 to 10 million head of cattle were driven from Texas, most of them longhorns because they were long-legged and hardy.

One of the worst droughts in Texas history took place in 1885–86, just after land in the western part of the state was opened and farmers immigrated to the area.

Detailed record-keeping is scanty in West Texas during this period, probably because those who stayed were living a hand-to-mouth existence and didn't have much time for writing.

The longhorn's time ended in the late 1880s, partly because of the advent of barbed-wire fences—open-range ranching was no longer booming, and cattle could be kept and bred for faster growth. Longhorns were crossed with other breeds, and by the 1920s were almost non-existent. They later were brought back, in part with help from oilman Sid Richardson, whose eponymous museum is in downtown Fort Worth today.

Oil

The first gusher in Texas was Spindletop, down around Beaumont in 1901, but there is and was plenty of oil production coming from the Permian Basin in West Texas.

The oil boom-or-bust cycle took its toll on places like little Ranger, near Strawn, which was a flourishing town in the early part of the century, reduced to a few stores and a library off the interstate today.

Oil still plays an important part in the economies of Midland and Odessa, where you'll see oil trucks (they're like flatbed trucks carrying lots of equipment) and pumpjacks nodding across the plains.

Oil drilling equipment is on display at the Panhandle-Plains Historical Museum in Canyon.

Another industry that took hold in West Texas in the 20th century was cotton farming, which shifted here from Central Texas as irrigation became more viable and cost effective. You'll see cotton fields all around Lubbock.

Farming made the most significant contribution to the economy in the early 20th century, but because of droughts, it suffered until irrigation became widely accessible in the 1920s. Lubbock began to grow, too, when Texas Tech began classes in 1925.

One of Texas' most famous politicians, Lyndon B. Johnson, began his rise with election to the U.S. Senate in 1948. The first Texas-born president, Dwight D. Eisenhower, who was born in Denison and attended Abilene High School, was elected in 1953. Women finally gained the right to serve on juries in Texas in 1954.

At Texas Instruments in Dallas, the first integrated circuit was successfully tested in 1956, a development that would change the world.

The nation mourned when President John F. Kennedy was assassinated in Dallas in 1963. Vice President Johnson was sworn in as president.

By 1988, Texas had another president, George H. W. Bush, who had raised his children, including George W. Bush, in Midland. His son was elected president in 2000.

Today, some parts of West Texas are unchanged by design—Big Bend National Park, for example, is preserved for posterity, but even there signs of acid rain and other pollutants have been observed.

Some towns and cities in the west have been almost abandoned, but West Texans tend to try to stay even when times get tough. Even little Terlingua, a ghost town, keeps going with its collection of outdoors lovers and off-the-grid types.

The recent recession has meant a lot of boarded-up buildings in cities big and small, but, on the other hand, people have started up businesses in the face of the economic disaster and succeeded in the past few years.

Tourism has also begun to reach West Texas, as wide, open spaces look more appealing to crowded city folk who want to get out of the rat race. The low real estate prices here also have had a hand in drawing people west.

Or course, a lot of independent souls who live where the land is flat and the rain infrequent would just as soon things stayed the same. Cut them some slack—they're just being stubborn, and yes, they came by it honestly.

ITINERARIES

In a place this size and one so plagued with stereotypes, you need to think about what you want out of your trip.

The view from the infinity pool at Wildcatter Ranch near Graham

If what you have in mind is a pair of boots, a Stetson, and a horse that won't throw you, we can do that. But that shouldn't be your entire goal. Whatever you're wearing, West Texas offers awe inspiring wide-open spaces, rolling hills, sophisticated urban scenes, and deeply ingrained diversity, via its proximity to Mexico in the south. You can't see it all on a week-long road trip, or even in two weeks. I'd suggest choosing your kind of experience and planning your vacation around it.

Here are a few ideas for weeklong trips.

Cowboy Culture

Fort Worth isn't called Cowtown for nothing. Spend your first night or two here, and then take in the Stockyards Historic District, also making sure to see Western art at the Sid Richardson Museum and the Amon Carter Museum of American Art. Eat some barbecue and spend an evening at Billy Bob's, reputedly the world's largest honky-tonk. Then drive to Weatherford. Stop at the Old Greenwood Cemetery, where the real cattlemen represented by the characters of Gus McCrae and Deets in *Lonesome Dove* are buried (their real names are, respectively, Oliver Loving and Boze Ikard). Continue on to Palo Pinto County and stay a day or two at Wildcatter Ranch, where you can ride horses, feed cattle, or just relax. Then hit the road for Abilene. There, be sure to visit Frontier Texas! to soak up history and background of cowboys and frontier life in general, and go to the Grace Museum, which includes a re-creation of the workshop of a 1940s bootmaker. Pick up a pair of boots while you're in town, and maybe a mesquite-base lamp. If you're traveling with a large group, consider booking a stay at Stasney's Cook Ranch, a working ranch that also is a nature retreat and a real taste of the prairie. The original ranch house sleeps 15–18, but smaller cabins are available.

History Buffs

You have several choices. One is taking the same trip as you would for Cowboy Culture above, but before you leave, order the Windshield History tour CDs from the Abilene Convention and Visitors Bureau. Put in the first CD and follow the directions on to Abilene. You'll learn about both military and cowboy life, gaze at places where battles with Native Americans took place, and take in historic forts. (There's also a CD for the return trip.) Detour outside Abilene to Sweetwater, and see the National WASP WWII Museum. If you were really ambitious, you could drive the Texas Forts Trail (www.texasfortstrail.com), but that would take a lot longer—it covers about 650 miles to see eight historic forts.

Latino Experience

With a population that's about 80 percent Hispanic, El Paso is your best bet for learning about both Spanish settlement in Texas back in the 1600s (in the form of the Mission Trail), and enjoying Latino culture today (amazing food, getting to hear Spanish spoken all around you, catching *folklorico* performances). While Juarez, across the border, is too dangerous for tourism these days, you can still get the flavor on a walking trip through Downtown

The National WASP WWII Museum in Sweetwater remembers the Women's Airforce Service Pilots.

A cactus blooms at the Chihuahuan Desert Nature Center near Fort Davis.

El Paso. (San Antonio has a strong Latino culture as well, but it's beyond the scope of this book). Fly to El Paso from DFW International Airport for a Mexican food fix, and be sure to visit the Chamizal National Memorial while you're there. Spend an afternoon on the Mission Trail. Once you've sated your taste buds (this takes several days, if you're an aficionado), drive to southern New Mexico for a different take on Mexican food and culture. A wonderful time to visit is around the holidays, when *farolitos,* paper bags glowing from candles set inside, light the plaza in Old Mesilla. (Some people also call them *luminarias,* but I'm not getting into that debate here.) Or, come in the fall during the green chile harvest, and take in the divine scent of chile being roasted. Area restaurants generally have fresh batches this time of year.

Desert Minimalism

The Big Bend is the Zen-like part of Texas, the place for solitude seekers as well as adventurers. You can easily spend a week here and still not see all the beauty. Make sure to set aside a night just for stargazing. You never knew there were so many. The chapter on Big Bend gives you pointers on how to get there. A good week's trip is staying one night in Fort Davis, taking in McDonald Observatory; the next in Marfa checking out minimalist art; going deeper into the remote reaches of the desert with a stay at peaceful and rustic Chinati Hot Springs; and then seeing Big Bend National Park mostly from your car, with a few short hikes. Serious hikers and adventurers probably already know where they're going, but local outfitters and park rangers have plenty of information to help. For a quieter trip with less driving, just book a week at Chisos Mountain Lodge and explore. Raft, hike, bike, or just enjoy the silence.

Sophistication, Texas Style

Dallas and Fort Worth have plenty of cosmopolitan art and dining, but if you stay put in the Metroplex that wouldn't really be seeing West Texas. Instead, take in the museums and fine dining there for a couple of days and then head out. There are a couple of choices here, and both involve some long distances. If you go west toward Abilene, about 150 miles, book a room first at Perini Ranch Guest Quarters, and make a reservation at Perini Ranch Steakhouse in Buffalo Gap. On the way, stop in Albany, and spend a few hours gazing at the Picassos and other fine works in the Old Jail Museum. Continue on past Abilene to Buffalo Gap and stay in one of the well-appointed guesthouses. Just for fun, drive back through Dublin and stop to see the Dr Pepper factory.

Get to Know Real West Texans

While you probably won't find a week's worth of things to do in Lubbock and Amarillo proper, it would be easy to stay at one of the cabins in Palo Duro Canyon for even longer (book a room in advance, there are only a few and they fill up fast). After arriving in Lubbock, make a relaxing stop at the Museum of Texas Tech, to see fine contemporary and Southwestern art as well as dinosaur and historical exhibits. Drive to Amarillo and see Cadillac Ranch (a famous row of Cadillacs stuck in the dirt as an art installation). Spray-paint your name on one of them, take a photo of it, and then go to your magical cabin perched at the edge of Palo Duro Canyon. Relax. Look at the stars from the roof. Repeat.

WEST TEXAS FOOD

by June Naylor

Nobody, but nobody, sets out for West Texas in search of great food. Oh, what a surprise, then, when the region delivers gustatory joys that boggle the mind—and palate. Of course, you expect to find a sensational platter of fried chicken at Allen's in Sweetwater, a magnificent steak at Perini Ranch Steakhouse, and the occasional toothsome chicken-fried steak or tendercrusted, freshly made fried apricot pie on some serendipitous stop at the random small-town café.

The little cabins at Palo Duro Canyon were built by the Civilian Conservation Corps.

To the astonishment of all, however, it turns out that the food landscape of West Texas is not limited to the Texas trilogy—steaks, barbecue, and Tex-Mex. In fact, I found myself gobsmacked the first time I tucked into an elegant meal in the Trans-Pecos region, that section of the state collectively called the Big Bend, because it forever changed my view of what has become an epicurean's dream come true—a culinary oasis in the Chihuahuan Desert. Moments into dinner at the sophisticated Maiya's, a hot spot in the art-ridden town of Marfa, I was swooning over a bowl of fresh carrot soup, which bore a swirl of goat cheese and red chile, when an annoying thought sneaked up to sucker-punch me: How would I enjoy another meal out in this part of the world after this one? If this dinner at Maiya's winds up claiming the best bites in my many trips to this forbidding region, my favorite place for escapes, would every morsel henceforth fall short? Perhaps, I thought, and worse—it might have spoiled me for eating anywhere else in Texas.

Fortunately, my anxieties proved needless. Throughout that weeklong adventure amid the provocative scenery generously provided by the Guadalupe, Davis, Chinati, and Chisos mountain ranges, I tasted a shocking number of remarkable dishes, the memories of which have remained strong, a long while afterward.

Musing over this startling good fortune, I realized the symbiosis of the success of this exceptional food in such a remote part of our world: If the pioneers of a century or so past could carve out an existence in these craggy badlands, why couldn't a handful of determined chefs? Just as those who built ranches and forts and mining towns across the Chihuahuan Desert, all it takes for creative genius to thrive in a challenging environment is a well of ingenuity and a storehouse of resolve.

The most notable of the Trans-Pecos culinary pioneers today is Maiya Keck, who opened her namesake bistro in spring 2002. A graduate of the Rhode Island School of Design, she relocated to Marfa 11 years ago for its burgeoning art environment, as did many of the Presidio County transplants. From the start, she won fans for her sophisticated sensibilities and the inventive dishes she showcases on her ever-changing seasonal menu, in a space that would be equally at home in San Francisco or Boston.

"The way we do things is a little different, but it's been well-received. Basically, we're bringing fresh but simple dishes to West Texas," she says. "We keep all our produce seasonal, and we try to get good local and regional ingredients. People are gardening here, and we're using their goods."

Some specialty import items, such as cheeses and some seafood, must be shipped via overnight delivery. As more and more folks came to rely on such delicacies—not just at dinnertime, but when wanting to put together an elegant picnic basket—Maiya opened her own little grocery store in Marfa, the Get Go. Now you can pick up a good bottle of Spanish or French wine, a hunk of imported cheese, specialty teas, and organic produce.

Maiya's in-house baking results in treasures like the free-form tartlet that served as a base for yet another dish that had me rolling my eyes in delight on my last visit. Atop a puff pastry stuffed with caramelized onion, fennel, and leeks was a salad of field greens. House-made pasta that evening was a lasagna noodle blanket that hid a plate of Brussels sprouts lavished with Parmesan, but a signature dish that remains always is the penne in a vodka-tomato cream sauce with Gruyere and Parmigiano reggiano.

Great pizza came to town courtesy of Saarin Keck, Maiya's sister. Transforming an abandoned corner gas station into the Pizza Foundation, she created possibly the busiest place in town. I wondered what the fuss was about until I sank my teeth into the bread salad, made with impossibly juicy red tomato wedges, giant, warm croutons that are browned and crisp just at the edges, big chunks of feta, garlic, and fresh basil and red onion in a balsamic vinaigrette.

The crusty pizza deserves praise, as well. My favorite was one I had topped with spinach, chorizo, ricotta, sliced fresh mozzarella, roasted fresh garlic, sweet roasted red bells, and fresh jalapeño. On a pretty night, the patio is a fine place to savor the slices, as the inside dining area can be loud with local kids shooting pool.

The Food Shark in Marfa is wildly popular at lunchtime.

Such success encouraged more *bon vivants* to give their luck a try. A place of much note now is the restaurant Cochineal, two blocks due west of the Pizza Foundation, a charming cottage-turned-gathering place and gourmand's answered prayer. Owner Tom Rapp and partner-Chef Toshi Sakihari left New York for the West, finding in Marfa a home and a receptive audience for Toshi's homegrown dishes, crafted with ingredients from his organic garden and fertile imagination. Months after a visit, I'm still thinking about his delicate pastas and signature date pudding with rum-caramel sauce.

One of the most famous lunch trucks in Texas is Food Shark, Marfa's favorite midday meal destination. Musician Adam Bork and wife-Chef Krista Steinhauer bring in a sizable crowd for an ever-changing menu of Middle Eastern and Mediterranean plates, the most famous of which is the Marfalafel. It's always a good idea to leave room for Krista's baked goods, especially when she has triple-chocolate espresso brownies on the daily menu. And if I hit Marfa on the right weekend, Jack and Lisa Copeland will be serving one of their sublime breakfast menus in the half of their home they call the Austin Street Café, an art-filled stucco once owned by Marfa's art pioneer, Donald Judd.

Memories of these meals continue to linger, and will for a long time. I'm not surprised; their force, and that of those who created them, mirrors that of the beautiful, haunting Chihuahuan Desert and the people who first tamed it.

1

Dallas–Fort Worth

VISITORS TO WEST TEXAS are likely to get their first taste of the state at Dallas–Fort Worth International Airport, which lies between two cities that once were intense rivals.

Fort Worth Star-Telegram publisher Amon G. Carter drew the line in the sand back in the 1920s and '30s, when he used his newspaper to push Fort Worth into the national spotlight and decry the fact Dallas even existed. Legend has it Carter would take a sack lunch when he traveled to Dallas, so he wouldn't have to spend any money there. About the same time, the flamboyant civic booster declared Fort Worth WHERE THE WEST BEGINS.

The rivalry between the Dallas County and Tarrant County seats continued well into this century. Dallas figured it was bigger and richer, and looked down its nose at Cowtown as a hick village trying to be a city. Fort Worth viewed Dallas as a land of too much makeup, bad traffic, and a pretentious attitude.

But over the past decade or so, the edges have softened considerably. A big fence came down when the deep and intense competition between the two newspapers, *The Dallas Morning News* and the *Star-Telegram* was exchanged for cooperative agreements, as the Internet grew more accessible and readers turned away from the printed page. Today, each city agrees the other has something to offer.

Dallas is, for a fact, bigger (2.4 million compared to about 741,000) and probably richer overall. Even today, the Big D hasn't lived down the big-haired ostentatiously rich reputation that the television series *Dallas* helped

LEFT: Billy Bob's in Fort Worth is billed as the world's largest honky-tonk.

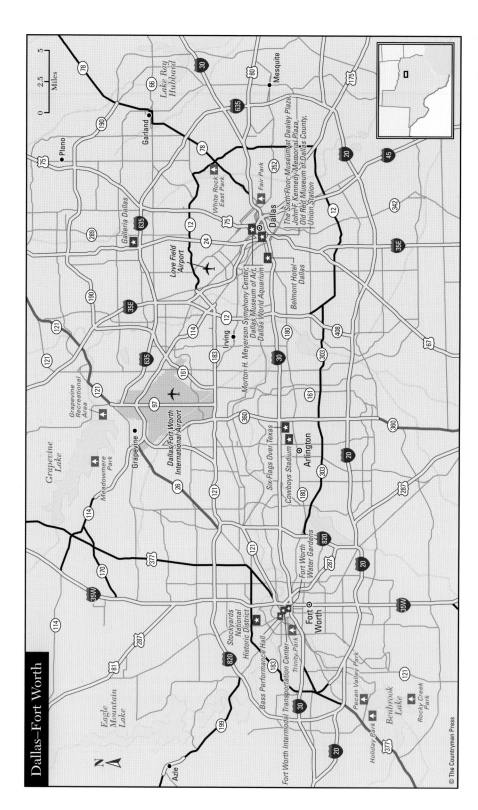

Dallas–Fort Worth

© The Countryman Press

A tour of the Sixth Floor Museum in Dallas includes the book depository from which Lee Harvey Oswald shot President John F. Kennedy.

to foster from the 1970s to 1991. After all, the show's Southfork Ranch outside town still is a tourist stop, and former President George W. Bush chose post-White-House life in tony Preston Hollow. You'll find more glitzy upscale shopping, dining, and lodging in Dallas. But Fort Worth is more walkable and easier on the wallet, harboring nationally respected museums and an increasingly interesting collection of restaurants, both upscale and moderately priced.

They remain as different as an oilman and a cowboy, in many respects. And that's what makes a trip to the Dallas–Fort Worth area so interesting. If you crave world-renowned chefs and over-the-top shopping, spend more time in Dallas. If you're more into cowboy culture and the history of the frontier, lean in the direction of Fort Worth. Or, get the best of both worlds and spend several days in each—they're only 30 miles apart.

Whichever way you choose, you're bound to see something you don't get at home, whether it's a Wolfgang Puck restaurant in a revolving ball atop a tower, or policemen on horseback.

DALLAS

Crisscrossed with freeways full of commuters and residents, Dallas is impossible to explore fully on foot. But you can drive, or take a bus or trolley to sites that you can then explore on foot.

For example, park at the Old Red Courthouse and walk to Dealey Plaza and the Sixth Street Book Depository; or, park at AT&T Performing Arts Center and walk to any of its venues plus the Dallas Museum of Art, the Nasher Sculpture Center, and the Crow Collection.

If you choose to stay downtown, the lodging prices will be considerably higher, but that also buys quick access via trolley or rail to museums and other sights. Otherwise, bring a GPS and make sure you're comfortable with big-city freeway driving.

Despite its reputation, there are plenty of moderate and inexpensive places to eat and stay in Dallas, as in any large city.

And besides, just gazing into the display windows at the Chanel boutique can be fun.

Guidance

Dallas Tourist Information Center (800-232-5527; www.visitdallas.com), 100 S. Houston Street. Open daily. The center is in the Old Red Courthouse, itself a fun site to visit with its Pegasus neon sign and countless more Dallas artifacts. You'll find Internet access, as well as a helpful staff with tons of information, and usually coupons with discounts to some popular attractions.

Media

The *Dallas Morning News* is the daily newspaper (www.dallasnews.com). Other sites to watch for local news and entertainment—and some provocative blogs: *D Magazine* (www.dmagazine.com); and the alternative weekly *Dallas Observer* (www.dallasobserver.com).

Medical Emergencies

There are several major hospitals and many urgent care clinics in Dallas. Dial 911 in an emergency.

The Dallas skyline from the Hotel Belmont.

This neon pegasus in the Old Red Courthouse is a part of Dallas history.

Getting There

Dallas–Fort Worth International Airport (972-973-8888; www.dfwairport
.com) in Grapevine (between Dallas and Fort Worth) is the hub for American Airlines and a stop for 16 more airlines, 10 domestic and 6 foreign.
More than 155,000 passengers move through it daily, the eighth-largest
number in the U.S. Built in 1974, the airport began renovations to four of
the five terminals in 2011. DFW has volunteers stationed throughout the
airport who will guide you to your gate, ticket counter, rental car agency, or
wherever you need to go.

The smaller Dallas Love Field Airport (214-670-6080; www.dallas-love
field.com) in Dallas is home to Southwest Airlines. Continental and Delta
also fly from here.

Getting Around

By car: If you're starting a trip to West Texas from here, you'll probably
rent a car on arrival at Dallas–Fort Worth International Airport. You should
have no trouble getting into Dallas from the airport if you're accustomed to
big-city driving. If you're not, have someone help navigate, because the
exits can come up fast, and unless it's the morning or evening rush (roughly
6–9 AM and 4–7 PM) the traffic on the freeways usually is moving at around
70 mph even though the speed limit is 60. Driving around Dallas can be
confusing, so get a GPS in the rental or bring one along.

By bus or rail: Dallas Area Rapid Transit or DART (214-979-1111; www
.dart.org) operates all the public transportation—both bus and rail are
considerably less expensive than taxis and they'll get you where you need

Free in Dallas

Even on a quick trip it's possible to see some attractions for free in Dallas. Just a few of them:

Dallas Museum of Art, free the first Tuesday of each month.

Crow Collection, always free.

Founders' Plaza, an observation area on DFW International Airport lets you watch takeoffs and landings while listening to ground control. At Texan Trail and North Airfield Drive.

to go in many cases. The bus coverage is extensive and includes express routes, airport shuttles, and buses just for NorthPark Center and Southern Methodist University. A good way to travel in Dallas once you've stashed your bags at your hotel is the DART rail. You can get on in the West End or Union Station downtown and go to—or at least near—a plethora of destinations (the Web site has a detailed list with stops and lines for popular destinations.) Your best bet is to consult the Web site for your destinations and plan it out.

Trinity Railway Express Commuter Rail (817-215-8600; www.trinityrail wayexpress.org). The TRE connects downtown Dallas with Fort Worth and Dallas–Fort Worth International Airport. Service is Monday through Saturday. Single-ride fares start at 75 cents and go up to $5. Definitely designed with commuters in mind, it's best used to and from the airport or to Dallas—the Fort Worth station is not located within walking distance of attractions.

By trolley: The M-Line Trolley (214-855-0006; www.mata.org) is free and takes you to all the major downtown and Uptown attractions. It runs 7–10 Monday through Thursday; 7–midnight Friday; 10–midnight Saturday; 10–10 Sunday and holidays. Wait for a car at the round signs marked M-Line Trolley.

Tours

Dallas Segway Tours (800-880-2336;www.dallassegwaytours.com).

All in One Tour Services (214-698-0332; www.allinonetourservices.com).

Big D Tours (888-828-8834; www.bigdtours.com).

Texas Toast (817-239-1634 or 817-228-5220; www.texastoastculinarytours .com) for culinary tours.

To See and Do

Dallas World Aquarium (214-720-1801; www.dwazoo.com), 1801 N. Griffin Street. Open 10–5 September 1 through February 28; 9–5 March 1 through August 31. Extensive exhibits include the rainforest, with a 40-foot waterfall; the Cenote, with a 40-foot tunnel for viewing marine life; Mundo Maya, including rays and sharks and more. Adults, $20.95; children 3–12, $12.95; 60 and older, $16.95; 2 and under free.

The Dallas arts district has been growing off and on since the Dallas Museum of Art opened in 1984, and exploded into full bloom with opening of the AT&T Performing Arts Center (see Entertainment) in 2009. The other elements in the downtown arts district are H. Meyerson Symphony Center; Crow Collection of Asian Art in the Trammell Crow Center; Nasher Sculpture Center; and Booker T. Washington High School for the Performing and Visual Arts.

Dallas Museum of Art (214-922-1200; www.dallasmuseumof art.org), 1717 N. Harwood Street. Open 11–5 Tuesday, Friday, Saturday, Sunday; and Wednesday, 11–9. Also open until midnight the third Friday of each month. Some 23,000 works in the permanent collection span the globe from ancient times to contemporary pieces. The museum houses collections from Africa, Asia, the Mediterranean, Europe, and more in a building designed by I. M. Pei. Adults, $10; seniors 65 and over, and military, $7; students with Texas ID, $5; under 12, free.

Crow Collection of Asian Art (214-979-6435; www.crowcollection .org), 2010 Flora Street. Open 10–9 Tuesday through Thursday; 10–6 Friday through Sunday. Expect instant serenity as you gaze at exotic Chinese jade, magical

The Dallas Museum of Art is within walking distance of two other museums: Nasher Sculpture Center and the Crow Collection.

Remembering the Kennedy Assassination

President John F. Kennedy's motorcade was passing **Dealey Plaza**, 411 Elm Street, when he was assassinated. Named for former *Dallas Morning News* publisher George B. Dealey, the park lies outside the book depository from which Lee Harvey Oswald fired the fatal shot on November 22, 1963. Just to stand at the curb looking out at the spot where a president was shot is a moving experience.

Inside the **Sixth Floor Museum** (214-747-6660; www.jfk.org), open 10–6 Tuesday through Sunday; noon–6 Monday, a guided audio tour takes you through Kennedy's life and accomplishments while televisions play news coverage of the time. Anyone who remembers where they were when the president was shot will feel eerily transported back in time to relive the moment. Exhibits provide detailed information and photos of everything about Kennedy's term as president and what is known about the assassination. Stand near the spot inside the depository where Oswald is said to have fired.

Architect Philip Johnson created the John F. Kennedy Memorial in Dallas as a place for contemplation.

Adults, $13.50; seniors and youth, $12.50; children 0–5, free.

The **John F. Kennedy Memorial Plaza** (214-653-6666; www.jfk .org) at 646 Main Street is another tribute to the slain president. The simple open-top enclosure was designed by architect Philip Johnson as a place for reflection. Free.

Japanese spheres, and Buddhist sculpture. The works from China, Japan, India, and Southeast Asia range from 3500 B.C. to the early 20th century. Free.

Union Station (214-741-7825; unionstationdallas.com), 400 South Houston Street. The 1916 Beaux-Arts Classic building had a $23 million renovation in 2008. There's a Wolfgang Puck-catered meeting and party space on the upper level, while the lower is an Amtrak station, Dallas

The Crow Collection in Dallas is a contemplative world away from the noisy streets outside.

station for the Trinity Railway Express commuter line, and a DART light-rail station. Free just to look at the beautiful old building.

East Dallas

Fair Park. Besides the State Fair of Texas (see Special Events), the annual Cotton Bowl football game took place here for many years, but has moved to Cowboys Stadium in Arlington. Fair Park is still the scene for many out-door concerts and, of course, the fair. Museums are open year-round. Among them are the African-American Museum (214-565-9026; www .aamdallas.org), 3536 Grand Avenue. Open 11–5 Tuesday through Friday; 10–5 Saturday, includes collections of African, African American, and folk art, free. And Museum of Nature and Science (214-428-5555; www.nature andscience.org), 3535 Grand Avenue and 1318 S. 2nd Avenue. Open 10–5 Monday through Saturday; noon–5 Sunday. Find the IMAX theater here, as well as a planetarium and an animatronics dinosaur exhibit. Admission varies from $10–17 adults; $7–17 ages 2–11; $9–19 seniors 62 and over, and students 12–17; under 2, free.

Dallas Arboretum (214-515-6500; www.dallasarboretum.org), 8525 Garland Road. Open 9–5 daily. Right beside White Rock Lake, see some 36 different gardens or attractions including fountains, a gazebo, sunken gardens, a pecan grove, and a restaurant. Admission, adults $12; seniors 65 and older, $10; children 3–12, $8; under 3, free. Self-parking is $7.

Don't Miss

Nasher Sculpture Center (214-242-5100; www.nashersculpture center.org), 2001 Flora Street. Open 11–5 Tuesday through Sunday. The brilliant permanent collection of sculpture includes huge outdoor works and smaller pieces inside. The artists represented include contemporary sculptors such as Donald Judd; older masters include Matisse, Picasso, Miro, and Giacometti. The café is a calm place to sit and have a sandwich or cup of coffee, enjoying the view of the outdoor sculptures. Adults $10; 65 and older, and military, $7; student with ID, $5; 12 and under, free.

A Nasher Sculpture Center exhibit called "Statuesque" spilled out to the front of the museum with "Big Pink" by Aaron Curry.

Plano

SouthFork Ranch (800-989-7800; southforkranch.com), 3700 Hogge Road. Open daily. Yep, this is it, the filming location for *Dallas*, the 1978–1991 television series that famously posed the question WHO SHOT J. R.? and kept millions glued to their sets every week. Today you can take a tour and see the Ewing Mansion, where longhorns graze and quarter horses are kept. The ranch also has evening chuck wagon dinners with cowboy singing and poetry reading. Adults, $9.50; seniors $8; children 5–12, $7; 4 and under, free.

Golf

Dallas, Fort Worth, and surrounding suburbs have more than 70 golf courses. There's a comprehensive listing with ratings at www.golflink.com.

Walking, Running, Biking

Katy Trail (www.katytrail.org). You can access the popular 3.5-mile trail downtown by parking in the American Airlines Center's north parking lot when no event is taking place. There are three other trailhead accesses in the city, and plans call for more. Check the Web site for current trailheads and parking areas; construction in parks along the way may change your best access point.

SPECTATOR SPORTS

Of course Dallas is the home of the Dallas Cowboys, but they play at Cowboys Stadium in Arlington (call 800-745-3000 for a stadium tour; www .dallascowboys.com) at 900 E. Randol Mill Road. The Dallas Mavericks' basketball games are at American Airlines Center (214-221-8326; www.nba .com/mavericks), 2500 Victory Avenue, as is hockey with the Dallas Stars (214-221-8326; stars.nhl.com). The Texas Rangers (817-273-5222; www .texasrangers.com) play at 1000 Ballpark Way, Arlington.

Pick Your Spot

Best places to stay in and around Dallas

On your way west you'll want to either spend an evening in the lap of luxury or grab an economical place for the night.

Inexpensive hotel and motel chains abound here—you won't have any trouble booking a room in the Dallas area at your favorite, although you might book early if the State Fair or another popular event is on. If you're in the mood for a special experience, here are a few great places at the higher end of the scale.

Downtown

Hyatt Regency (214-651-1234; www.dallasregency.hyatt.com), 300 Reunion Boulevard East. This is the hotel with the big revolving ball on top, which contains the Wolfgang Puck restaurant Five Sixty. An underground pedestrian tunnel reaches from here to Union Station. Expensive.

The Adolphus (800-221-9083; www.hoteladolphus.com), 1321 Commerce Street. Seen as the grande dame of Dallas hotels, the 21-story hotel was built in 1912 by beer tycoon Adolphus Busch. Famous guests include Donald Trump, U2, and Queen Elizabeth II. Expensive.

The Joule (214-748-1300; www .luxurycollection.com), 1530 Main Street. The 1920s Dallas National Bank building reopened after a contemporary makeover in 2008. Now it's a Starwood hotel. Very expensive.

The W Dallas-Victory (214-397-4100; www.starwoodhotels .com), 2440 Victory Park Lane. All done up with cowhides and a Bliss spa, this is a busy hotel right next to American Airlines Center. Very expensive.

Oak Cliff

Hotel Belmont (866-870-8010; www.belmontdallas.com), 901 Fort Worth Avenue. Other hotels in Dallas may be grander or taller but few are cooler than the Belmont, a renovated Charles Dilbeck building perched on a hillside. (Dilbeck was a Dallas mid-century architect whose work is still highly sought-after today.) The saltwater pool has a great view of downtown; the restaurant, Smoke, gets constant praise for its way with meat, poultry, and just about everything else (try the pork jowl appetizer, or the *churros* for dessert); and the Bar Belmont attracts a hip, local crowd. The hotel is also in the same area as the emerging Bishop Arts District, lined with interesting shops and more restaurants. Moderate.

Uptown

Hotel ZaZa (800-597-8399; www .hotelzaza.com/dallas), 2332 Leonard Street. Fun and imaginative,

Smoke, the restaurant at the Belmont Hotel, is famous for its pulled pork.

Bishop Arts District

Located in North Oak Cliff in what used to be a sleepy community of artists, Bishop Arts District now is home to some of Dallas's most original restaurants, and the selection is growing. The **Belmont Hotel** is a short drive from Bishop Avenue, where much of the activity is, as well as on surrounding blocks, all very walkable.

The Bishop Street Market is a great gift-shopping stop.

Shopping ranges from candles and art glass pieces at **Bishop Street Market** (214-941-0907; www.bishop streetmarket.com), 419 N. Bishop Avenue, to a study of the art of flower arranging using repurposed items like Ball jars and even an old piano as a backdrop, at **Dirt** (214-242-9533; www.dirt flowers.com), 417 N. Bishop Avenue.

Stroll around the blocks surrounding Bishop and look for **Café Brazil** (214-946-7927; www.cafebrazil.com), 611 N. Bishop Avenue, late-night eatery and coffee-house; **Espumoso Coffee and Juice Bar** (214-948-2055), 408 N. Bishop Avenue #105; **Hattie's** (214-942-7400; www.hatties.com), 418 N. Bishop Avenue, American bistro; **Tillman's Roadhouse** (214-942-0988; www.tillmansroadhouse.com) 324 W. 7th Street, Texas road-house fare; **Spiral Diner and Bakery** (214-948-4747; www.spiraldiner .com) 1101 N. Beckley Avenue, vegan; **Eno's Pizza Tavern** (214-943-9200; www.enospizza.com), 407 North Bishop Avenue; and several Mexican-food restaurants.

Seriously consider saving room for dessert at **Dude, Sweet Chocolate** (214) 943-5943; www.dudesweetchocolate.com), 408 W. 8th Street.

contemporary meets antique meets Mediterranean. A series of concept suites like the Zen or the Moulin Rouge defy you to put the ZaZa into any particular category. Very expensive.

The Stoneleigh Hotel (800-921-8498; www.stoneleighhotel.com), 2927 Maple Avenue. The Art Deco property built in 1923 has been renovated to preserve the original feel and renewed with contemporary amenities. Very expensive.

The Rosewood Mansion on Turtle Creek (888-767-3966; www.mansiononturtlecreek.com), 3411 Gillespie Street. Originally a private mansion, this is where the area's old money elite tend to gravitate for R&R, with its luxe but comfortable suites and a 2–1 staff-to-guest ratio. Very expensive.

Ritz Carlton Dallas (214-922-0200; www.ritzcarlton.com), 2121 McKinney Avenue. The elegant guest rooms in buttery hues and silk-swathed walls in public areas leave no doubt you're in a high-rise world of luxury. Chill in the spa (try the surround shower followed by the dry sauna, or go for the Vichy treatment); see and be seen in the Rattlesnake Bar, with a rail fashioned as a snake; and dine at Fearing's, one of the city's best. Very expensive.

North Dallas

Hotel Palomar (214-520-7969; www.hotelpalomar-dallas.com), 5300 E. Mockingbird Lane. Should you crave a stylish stay but want to avoid downtown, this is your spot. The Kimpton hotel uses earth tones in contemporary style, emphasizing art—a stash of art supplies comes in the room. You can also get a goldfish to stay with you, if you feel lonely. Very expensive.

Westin at the Galleria (972-934-9494; www.westin.com/galleria dallas) You can shop all day at the adjacent Galleria (Louis Vuitton, Saks Fifth Avenue, Gucci, and a slew of similar or more mainstream retailers) and then fall into bed—this is part of the Galleria complex. Moderate.

Local Flavors

Taste of the town—restaurants, cafés, bars, bistros, etc.

Dallas has more than 8,000 restaurants. These listings barely scratch the surface. If you don't see something you like here, go to www.visit dallas.com for more choices.

DINING OUT

Downtown

Dragonfly at the Hotel ZaZa (800-597-8399; www.hotelzazadallas .com), 2332 Leonard Street. Open daily. The diverse menu incorporating seasonal and local ingredients means everyone will find something to like, from steak to seafood or chicken. The dining rooms are elegantly decorated in a cutting-edge

Stop in at Café Brazil for iced or hot coffee and a bite to eat if you're in the Bishop Arts District in Dallas.

kind of way, the cuisine modern American. Moderate-expensive.

Fearing's (214-922-4848; www.fearingsrestaurant.com), 2121 McKinney Avenue (at the Ritz-Carlton). Open Monday through Saturday for breakfast, lunch, and dinner; Sunday for brunch and dinner. Executive Chef Dean Fearing, the Father of Southwestern Cuisine, started building his name in Dallas with a long tenure at the Mansion at Turtle Creek. He came to the Ritz in 2007, and has developed a highly sophisticated, changing menu with complex flavors and dishes, using regional, seasonal ingredients. His tacos are legendary—one version was charred corn and pheasant-chorizo street tacos with avocado fries, charred tomato salsa, and spicy queso. Expensive.

Five Sixty (741-5560; www.wolfgangpuck.com), 300 Reunion Boulevard East. Open for dinner Monday through Saturday. You can't beat the view from this Wolfgang Puck concern in the rotating sphere at the top of Reunion Tower. The dining inspiration is Asian, and seafood is prominent, but there's also steak and duck and Kobe beef short ribs, all done in ways at least one food critic deems "genius." Expensive.

Arts District

Stephan Pyles (214-580-7000; www.stephanpyles.com), 1807 Ross Avenue. Open Monday through Friday for lunch, Monday through Saturday for dinner. Pyles has both this restaurant and his Samar (214-922-9922), 2100 Ross Avenue at Olive Street, open the same days, in Dallas. Pyles is another celebrity chef who has a fabled touch with Southwestern cuisine, and he labels the fare at his epony-mous restaurant New Millennium Southwestern Cuisine. Flavors from Texas, the Middle East, Spain, and other exotic locales influence everything at Stephan Pyles, from sides with rib eye steak (red chile onion rings) to halibut (wild-caught and pan-seared) with fava-quinoa risotto. Samar serves small-plate dishes, with the menu divided into cuisine inspired by Spain, the Eastern Mediterranean, and India. Both restaurants, expensive.

Uptown

Bolla at the Stoneleigh (800-921-8498; www.stoneleighhotel.com), 2927 Maple Avenue. Open daily for breakfast and lunch; Tuesday through Saturday for dinner. New American cuisine, such as sea scal-lops with smoked cheddar grits, spinach, and red-eye gravy is the fare. There's a prix-fixe menu that serves four courses for $40. Moder-ate to expensive.

Abacus (214-559-3111; www.kentrathbun.com), 4511 McKinney Avenue. Open Monday through Saturday for dinner. This is one of Chef Kent Rathbun's several restaurants in the Dallas area (the others include Jasper's in Plano and Blue Plate in North Dallas). The influence is Asian—sushi is on the menu—though you'll also find steaks and plenty of choices for any

Don't Miss

Bob's Steak & Chop House
(214-528-9446; www.bobs-steakandchop.com), 4300 Lemmon Avenue (at Wycliff). Closed Sunday. Actually just north of Uptown, Bob's Kansas City strip is so good it makes a steak-lover want to cry—it's crisp on the out-side, firm-textured and juicy on the inside. This is a Dallas institution, where the rich and famous come and order dishes off-menu. Bob's is also known for the giant carrot that comes in the middle of each plate. Yes, you're sup-posed to eat it. Expensive.

foodie (scrambled duck eggs, for example). Expensive.

Victory Park

Craft Dallas (214-397-4111; www.craftrestaurant.com), 2440 Victory Park Lane (at the W Hotel). Open daily. Chef Tom Colicchio of New York City Craft restaurant fame has included some of the New York favorites—braised short ribs, for example—on a menu here that also emphasizes dishes pre-pared with fresh, Texas ingredi-ents. Expensive.

North Dallas

Pappas Bros. Steakhouse (214-366-2000; www.pappasbros.com),

Don't Miss

Mia's (214-526-1020; www
.miastexmex.com), 4322 Lemmon Avenue. Open Monday
through Sunday for lunch and
dinner. Patrons come from
miles around to eat the brisket
tacos. You should, too. Tender,
savory beef on a grilled flour
tortilla is served with mouth-
watering beef gravy. Inexpensive to moderate.

Al Biernat's (214-219-2201; www
.albiernats.com), 4217 Oak Lawn
Avenue. Open daily for dinner,
Monday through Friday for
lunch, Sunday for brunch. A big
menu that also includes quail,
osso bucco, and calves liver has
kept regulars coming back for
many years. The dining room gets
so busy it's hard to hear sometimes, but being part of the scene
is part of the fun. Expensive.

EATING OUT

North Dallas

Celebration (214-351-5681; www
.celebrationrestaurant.com), 4503
W. Lovers Lane. Open daily. An
extensive menu offers superlative,
home-cooked comfort food—
meat loaf, fried chicken, grilled
or fried catfish, served family
style for more than 30 years.
The menu is homey, but it's nice
enough for a casual date. Moderate to expensive.

Uptown

Fireside Pies (214-370-3916;
www.firesidepies.com), 2820
N. Henderson Avenue. Locations also in Fort Worth and
Grapevine. Open daily for dinner.
Some of the most innovative (and
delicious) pizza you'll ever run
across is handcrafted and baked
in wood ovens. Try the Triple
'Roni, with pepperoni, creamy
fresh mozzarella, basil, and truffle
oil. Moderate.

10477 Lombardy Lane. Open
daily for dinner. Quiet, dark, and
lush interiors set the stage for
what's generally considered the
absolute top choice in Dallas for
high-end steak. But you should
also sample the upscale comfort
food—the homemade mac and
cheese will make you forget all
about Mom's. The wine and spir-
its menus are extensive; and
Wine Director Barbara Werley is
one of few female master som-
meliers in the world. Expensive.

The Mansion on Turtle
Creek (214-559-2100; www.man
siononturtlecreek.com), 2821
Turtle Creek Boulevard. The
restaurant at the landmark Dallas hotel, long the considered
standard of luxury here, has
changed with the departure of
Chef Dean Fearing to The Ritz-
Carlton, but the famous lobster
tacos still are on the menu.
Expensive.

About Deep Ellum

This was an African and European immigrants' neighborhood in the 1800s, changed from Deep Elm to Deep Ellum because of the way its residents pronounced it. By the 1920s, the area was a hotspot for jazz and blues musicians, with shows by Bessie Smith, Huddie "Leadbelly" Ledbetter, and Blind Lemon Jefferson. The area declined after World War II, when the street car and rail lines were moved to make way for Central Expressway, but saw a resurgence in the 1980s and '90s, when young artists and musicians moved in. The popularity of the warehouse district ebbs and flows but is still home to some cutting-edge art galleries as well as a burgeoning restaurant scene.

Oak Lawn

Cosmic Cafe (214-521-6157; www .cosmiccafedallas.com), 2912 Oak Lawn Avenue. Open daily for lunch and dinner. Dallas's best-known vegetarian restaurant stands out both for its brightly painted exterior and its inventive vegetarian fare like "i hate eggplant"—eggplant, bell pepper, and onions sautéed with garlic and fresh basil, then served on naan with mozzarella cheese. Moderate.

Deep Ellum

Monica Aca y Alla (214-748-7140; www.monicas.com), 2914 Main Street. Open daily for lunch, Tuesday through Sunday for dinner. The Mexico City-style shrimp cocktail, in a tomato sauce with cilantro, lime, onions, and avocado is reason enough to grab a table. The rest of the menu includes the usual Mexican cuisine specialties, some done Tex-Mex style, others a la Mexico City. Moderate.

Multiple Locations

These restaurants are small local or regional chains with outstanding food and mostly moderate prices. I've listed one location for each; call or check Web sites for more.

Campisi's Egyptian Restaurant (214-827-0355; www.campisis.us), 5610 E. Mockingbird Lane. Open daily. Despite the Egyptian name, the Dallas institution is known for thin-crust pizza and also serves up a variety of other Italian fare. This original location also is known for being the spot where Lee Harvey Oswald's killer, Jack Ruby, dined the night before President John F. Kennedy was assassinated. Inexpensive.

La Duñi (214-520-6888; www .laduni.com), 4264 Oak Lawn Avenue; locations also in North Park Mall and on McKinney Avenue. Open daily for breakfast, lunch, and dinner plus weekend brunch. Colombian chef Dunia Borga and her husband have created a EuroLatin dream of flavors with dishes like marinated, grilled-pepper-crusted beef loin served with chimichurri sauce and Manchego cheese. Do not miss the pastries. Borga has a sure and imaginative hand, offering treats that were her favorites growing up. Try the agave-filled, buttery Pastel Gloria. Moderate.

Mi Cocina (214-521-6426; www.mcrowd.com), 77 Highland Park Village. Open daily for lunch and dinner. With 15 locations across the Metroplex, some at higher-end shopping centers, you probably won't have trouble finding one. The contemporary decor complements traditional Mexican dishes done in a modern way. Try the enchiladas Esperanza, and if you like a cheese sauce, substitute Sunset sauce. Chimichanga fans return again and again for the Lucy-changa, which is gigantic. Moderate.

Taco Diner (214-521-3669), 3699 McKinney Avenue. Four other locations, including one in Southlake, one in Irving, and others in North Dallas. Open daily for lunch and dinner. Owned by the same group as Mi Cocina, Taco Diner is more strongly influenced

by Mexico City cuisine. Try the fish tacos or the crispy green enchiladas—it's one of the few places in the area that serves a green sauce, this one made with tomatillos. Moderate.

Twisted Root Burger (741-7668; www.twistedrootburgerco .com), 2615 Commerce Street. Locations in Deep Ellum and at Southern Methodist University, Richardson, Roanoke, and Fairview, with more on the way. Open daily. A chef-owned burger joint with its own pastry chef, Twisted Root does burgers in beef, game meats, turkey, and veggie; buttermilk-battered and fried sweet potato chips, potatoes, green beans, and pickles; deep-fried hot dogs; and milkshakes. Inexpensive.

Urban Taco (214-823-4723; www.urban-taco.com), 5331 E. Mockingbird Lane #125; one more location plus kiosks in Dallas–Fort Worth Airport and Parkland Hospital. Open daily for lunch and dinner. Restaurateur Markus Pineyro got entirely away from the usual Tex-Mex to create a modern menu filled with unusual flavors such as yucca fries and peanut-habañero salsa, in a hip setting. Moderate.

Specialty Foods and Grocers

Dude, Sweet Chocolate (214-943-5943; www.dudesweetchocolate .com), 408 W. 8th Street. Closed Monday. Chef Katherine Clapner creates utterly unexpected and divine flavor combinations at her Oak Cliff store (wild, sweet mushrooms and black garlic in an artisan chocolate called Black Gold, for example) that

Dude, Sweet Chocolate uses unlikely combinations like blue cheese and dark chocolate to delicious effect.

will blow you away. The ever-changing selection includes truffles, chocolate bars, Russian marshmallows, nuts, popcorns, etc.

Scardello Artisan Cheeses (214-219-1300; www.scardellocheese.com), 3511 Oak Lawn. Open daily. Owner/cheesemonger Rich Rogers loves and understands good cheeses and wants to make sure everyone else does, too. The emphasis is on American cheeses with Texas dairies represented. The warm, spacious tasting room is a nice spot to enjoy a glass of wine with cheese (he'll guide you to a pairing).

The Mozzarella Co. (214-741-4072; www.mozzco.com), 2944 Elm Street. Open Monday through Saturday. The tiny factory in Deep Ellum turns out everything from a buttery mascarpone to more complex cheeses, plus fresh award-winning mozzarellas, supplying many restaurants in North Texas. You can also buy some to take with you.

Chocolate Secrets (214-252-9801; www.chocolatesecrets.net), 3926 Oak Lawn Avenue. Closed Monday. Chocolatier Kate Graver dreams up pretty concoctions in her confectionary kitchen—a deep cobalt blue chocolate faceted like a gem, a brilliant sunflower. She also experiments with flavors in confections like burnt butter bonbons, or her chocolate and blue cheese mice.

Eatzi's (214-526-1515; www.eatzis.com), 3403 Oak Lawn Avenue. Open daily, with a second location at 5600 W. Lover's Lane, Suite 136 and another planned in Grapevine. It's hard to go wrong, whether you want bread, wine, cheese, cooked meats, sandwiches, or a complete meal. The European-style market makes up box lunches, or you can just pick up a loaf of Jewish rye or ciabatta, fresh fruit, and put one together yourself.

Whole Foods Landmark Store (214-342-4850; www.wholefoodsmarket .com), 8190 Park Lane, Suite 351. I wouldn't normally recommend a large supermarket, much less a chain, but this store can be life-changing—it caused me, a lifelong meat-eater, to try a raw diet for a while. Try the raw brownies, you might convert, too. There's also a cupcake bar, wine bar, olive bar, kiosks for organic makeup, and a computer menu planner. Plus huge selections of all the organic brands, along with their in-house brands.

Selective Shopping

Shopping in Dallas is an art form, and deep pockets are required to get the full effect; however, you can always try just to look. Assuming your trip to Dallas is a quick one, try these primary malls and shopping centers so you get the most bang for your trip across town; I've also included REI, in case you're planning to camp in the Big Bend and need gear. For more shopping also see Bishop Arts District.

NorthPark Center (214-363-7441; www.northparkcenter.com), 8687 N. Central Expressway. Open 10–9 Monday through Saturday; noon–6 Sunday. This is the big gun of Dallas mall shopping, with designer boutiques from Hugo Boss to Oscar de la Renta, anchored by Neiman Marcus, Barney's New York, Nordstrom, Macy's, and Dillard's.

The owner of Dirt in the Bishop Arts District has a way with repurposing objects together with plants.

Galleria Dallas (972-702-7100; www.galleriadallas.com), 13350 Dallas Parkway. Open 10–9 Monday through Saturday; noon–6 Sunday. The Galleria has its draws, too, like an ice-skating rink, a Thomas Pink store, and the trendy Spanish retailer Zara. Anchors include

Macy's, Nordstrom, and Saks Fifth Avenue—and you can stay at the Westin in the same complex.

Highland Park Village (214-559-2740; hpvillage.com), 47 Highland Park Village. Open 9–5 weekdays. Some 50 stores (Chanel, Christian Louboutin, Kiehl's) are in the pretty, Mediterranean-style National Historic Landmark center built in 1931. The small movie theater was recently renovated.

OPEN-AIR SHOPPING

First Monday Trade Days (903-567-6556; www.firstmondaycanton.com), 800 Flea Market Road, Canton, Texas. Open dawn to dusk. It's an hour east of Dallas in the town of Canton, but if you're a flea market nut, you have to go—it's enormous, with everything from scary knife collections to gorgeous antiques. There are about 28 miles of walkways, so keep in mind it's easy to get lost and never get back to that treasure you found. Takes place the Thursday through Sunday before the first Monday of each month. If you go in the summer, buy or take water. Parking, $4.

Dallas Farmers Market (214-939-2808; www.dallasfarmersmarket.org), 1010 S. Pearl Expressway. Open 8–6 daily. Vendors of everything from fresh produce to prepared foods to shrubs come from as far as 150 miles away to set up shop at this big (four large sheds) outdoor market. Restaurants also are on-site.

OUTDOORS

REI (972-490-5989; www.rei.com), 4515 LBJ Freeway. GPS coordinates: 32° 55.583' N 96° 49.949' W (WGS84). Open 10–9 Monday through Saturday; 11–6 Sunday. The outdoor sports giant has just about every conceivable piece of camping gear you need, along with kayaks, bicycles, and more fun gadgets than you know what to do with.

Entertainment

AT&T Performing Arts Center (214-954-9925; www.attpac.org), 2403 Flora Street, and various locations downtown. The center, opened in 2009, includes an opera house, theater, outdoor performance venue, and a park. Winspear Opera House stages such disparate acts as Jerry Seinfeld and a Horton Foote Festival; Wyly Theatre stages small concerts as well as plays; Annette Strauss Square, the outdoor venue, brings in music like a jazz collective; H. Meyerson Symphony Center is the venue

Retail Beginnings

Neiman Marcus (214-741-6911; www.neimanmarcus.com), 1618 Main Street, Downtown. Open 10–6 Monday through Wednesday and Friday through Saturday; 10–7 Thursday. I can still remember the monthly excitement when my mother—a native West Texan—got an envelope from Neiman's, with its sheaf of glossy sheets bearing photographs of the latest styles; or when the annual Christmas catalog came, with its one-of-a-kind outrageous gifts. Best of all was when one of us opened a Christmas gift to find a creamy, glossy box with Neiman-Marcus (it was hyphenated then) printed in elegant, deep coffee tones in the center of the top. Something extraordinary was bound to be inside.

Dallas has been known as an upscale shopping mecca for years, and Neiman Marcus, known around here as Neiman's for short, started it all in 1907. The first store was founded after the Marcus family decided not to take a chance investing in Coca-Cola. Today, of course, there are dozens of locations in the U.S., including many in Texas (Dallas has another location in NorthPark Center, and there's one in Fort Worth, as well) but at the time it was a Dallas concern—and it sold goods unavailable anywhere else in the state.

for symphonic music. The Meyerson's Need to Eat program lets you add $35–75 to your event ticket and dine at one of some 14 area restaurants. To learn more and check performance schedules, visit www.attpac.org and www.thedallasartsdistrict.org.

Nightlife

Dallas has a diverse collection of nighttime scenes including: Deep Ellum (see sidebar), big with the not-so-mainstream crowd; Oak Lawn, a vibrant, fun GLBT scene; Lower Greenville, a combination of dance clubs, cool beer joints, and sports bars; the West End, provides chains like Dick's Last Resort and the House of Blues; Knox-Henderson, with nightclubs on the Henderson side; West Village, offers patios to sip wine or enjoy a coffee outdoors. Check *D Magazine* (www.dmagazine .com); the *Dallas Observer* (www.dallasobserver.com); and the *Dallas Morning News* (www.dallasnews.com) for what's current. The *Morning News* has a visitor's guide online, too, with local weather and other current information.

Special Events

January

Martin Luther King Birthday Parade (214-670-8438; www.dallas cityhall.com). Starts at 10 AM the Saturday before MLK Day at City Hall and ends at Fair Park.

St. Patrick's Day Parade (www.greenvilleave.org). Traditionally starts on Greenville Avenue at 11 AM the Saturday before St. Patrick's Day. Some 90,000 people attend.

March through April

Dallas International Film Festival (www.dallasfilm.org). The festival, at various locations around town, shows more than 150 films, including some world premiers.

July

Fair Park Fourth (www.fairpark.org), 1200 S. 2nd Avenue. Free fireworks and admission to all museums at Fair Park.

September

State Fair of Texas (www.bigtex.com), Fair Park. General admission $15; $12.95 advance; children and seniors $11; $9.95 advance.

FORT WORTH

Cowtown is a breath of fresh air in a world of congested cities, offering ample parking downtown, a beautiful world-class Cultural District, cowboy culture in the Stockyards, and a growing list of original restaurants.

While there's plenty to experience here, you don't feel the rushed vibe that's prevalent in Dallas. People tend to be more relaxed, informal, and the traffic is easier to navigate—although Fort Worth does have a seriously time-wasting rush hour on the freeways in and out of the city from about 4 to 6 PM weekdays (it can start as early as 3 PM on Fridays).

If you do nothing else here, stop in the Cultural District and take in the museums, maybe grab a bite at the Modern. It will center you for the long drive ahead into West Texas.

Guidance

Fort Worth Visitor and Convention Center (817-336-8791; www.fort worth.com) has three locations: Fort Worth (817-698-3300), 508 Main Street on Sundance Square, open 10–6 Monday through Saturday; Stock- yards National Historic District (817-624-4741), 130 E. Exchange Avenue,

Suburbs: Arlington and Grapevine

There are many suburbs around Dallas and Fort Worth, but these are roughly between the two cities and have some major attractions that should be mentioned. Arlingtonians will argue their city is not a suburb, but in any case, it's where you'll find Cowboys Stadium, the Ballpark at Arlington (home of the Texas Rangers), and **Six Flags Over Texas** (817-640-8900; www.sixflags.com), 2201 Road to Six Flags; closed January through February. You'll be happiest if you go to the huge amusement park with adjoining Hurricane Harbor water park in spring or fall. The lines will be long almost no matter what, but at least you won't be standing in 100 degrees; kids love it, regardless. General admission, $54.99; children under 48 inches, $34.99; 2 and under, free. If you buy online, adults pay kids' prices. In Grapevine, adults who are into hunting, fishing, camping, and boating plan entire weekends around a visit to **Bass Pro Shops** (972-724-2018; www.bassproshops .com) 2501 Bass Pro Drive, Grapevine. GPS coordinates: 32.95707°N, 097.0428°W (WGS84/NAD 83). Open 9–10 Monday through Saturday; 10–7 Sunday. In fact, serious hunters, fishermen, and boaters probably know about this place and have already booked a room at the nearby Embassy Suites. While REI (see Selective Shopping in Dallas) leans in the outdoor recreation direction, this huge store is all about the pursuit of wild game and a good time. Also in Grapevine is a huge kid-favorite hotel, **Great Wolf Lodge** (817-488-6510; www.greatwolf.com/grapevine), 100 Great Wolf Drive, Grapevine. With its own indoor water park exclusively for hotel guests, suites with separate "wolf dens" for the kids (think bunk beds), and lots more kid-friendly features, the younger members of your party will be in hotel heaven.

The sun sets over Lake Grapevine.

open 9–6 Monday through Saturday, 10–4 Sunday; and Fort Worth Cultural District (817-882-8588), 3401 W. Lancaster Avenue, open 9–5 Monday through Saturday.

Media

The *Fort Worth Star-Telegram* (www.star-telegram.com) is the local newspaper. The *Fort Worth Weekly*, (www.fwweekly.com) is the alternative newspaper. The Web site www.dfw.com is also produced by the *Star-Telegram*.

Free in Fort Worth

The following attractions are free to all. Check online for open hours and days.

Amon Carter Museum of American Art

Kimbell Art Museum

Fort Worth Herd

Stockyards Museum

Fort Worth Water Gardens

Medical Emergencies

Like Dallas, the city is a health-care hub with several major hospitals, which serve thousands of people both in the city, adjoining suburbs, and from outlying areas hundreds of miles away. There also are plenty of urgent-care clinics including the CareNow chain. Dial 911 in a true emergency.

Getting Around

By car: One tip here—the best rental prices may not be in and around DFW Airport. It may be worth a few extra calls to the same agencies in different parts of the Metroplex, including Fort Worth, to get better prices. It's not hard to drive here, as the city is logically laid out for the most part, and the attractions tend to be grouped together.

By bus: The T (817-215-8600; www.the-t.com), run by the Fort Worth Transportation Authority, gets you around town and to many area attractions handily, starting at $1.50. Red, white, and blue buses downtown are free.

By trolley: The free Molly the Trolley (817-215-8600; www.mollythetrolley .com) has three routes: one downtown, one to the Stockyards, and one from West Downtown to Sundance Square.

By foot: The city has large walkable areas including Downtown, the Cultural District, and the Stockyards.

Tours

Cowtown Segway Tours (817-255-9540; www.cowtownsegwaytours.com), 1501 Montgomery Street; Epic Helicopter Tours (817-625-1800; www .epichelicopters.com), 4201 N. Main Street; Fort Worth Tours (Call 817-

514-9567; www.fortworthtours.com), driving and walking; Fort Worth Trails and Tours (817-731-3875; www.fwtoursntrails.com), 4048 Ridglea Country Club Drive, #1208, walking and bus; Heritage Trails (817-338-3330; www.fortworthheritagetrails.com), walking tours of Downtown; Stockyards Historic Walking Tours (817-625-9715; www.stockyardsstation .com), 130 E. Exchange Avenue; The GPS Ranger (817-625-9715; www .fortworth.com), 130 E. Exchange Avenue, rent a handheld computer with 24 points of interest at the Stockyards Visitor Center. Also see Texas Toast in Dallas tours.

To See and Do

Downtown

Bass Performance Hall (817-212-4200; www.basshall.com), 525 Commerce Street. The gorgeous building with its trumpeting angels has become a symbol of downtown's revival. The hall is the site of the Cliburn International Piano Competition every four years, and is the venue for Fort Worth Opera, the Fort Worth Symphony, the Fort Worth Ballet, and many other visiting acts, such as singer Lyle Lovett, through the year. The nearby McDavid Hall is a more intimate performance space that's popular with Texas musicians.

Fort Worth Water Gardens (817-392-7111), 1502 Commerce Street. Designed by Philip Johnson in 1974, this is a relaxing spot to sit and eat a takeout lunch if you're walking around downtown.

Don't Miss

Sundance Square (817-255-5700; www.sundancesquare.com) is the result of a huge remake of downtown Fort Worth in the late 1970s and '80s. Once the scene of saloons and other businesses that catered to thirsty cowboys, the area had followed the path of many big-city downtowns in the U.S.—often deserted after business hours. The renovation efforts began when a prominent Fort Worth family, the Basses, began acquiring property downtown in the late 1970s. Today it's one of the most walkable downtowns in Texas, with more than 35 developed blocks. Two free parking lots make it a snap to pull in and spend an evening here. Start with dinner at Reata or GRACE; catch a show at Bass Hall or a movie at the AMC Palace 9; and grab a nightcap later at 8.0 or one of the other nightspots. Or, if you're staying downtown, you can walk to all of the above.

Sid Richardson Museum (817-332-6554; www.sidrmuseum.org), 309 Main Street. Named after the oil-man and philanthropist whose collection of Western paintings and sculpture started it, the exhibits are a must for fans of Frederic Remington and Charles M. Russell. Free.

Cultural District

Amon Carter Museum of American Art (817-738-1933; www.carter museum.org), 3501 Camp Bowie Boulevard. Open 10–5 Tuesday, Wednesday, Friday, Saturday; 10–8 Thursday; noon–5 Sunday. Started by the daughter of newspaper publisher Amon Carter as one of his several legacies to Fort Worth, the permanent collection includes many works by iconic Western artists Charles Russell and Frederic Remington; classic American masters; and a few modern pieces, too. The museum also has more than 30,000 photographic prints, shown in rotating exhibits. Free.

Bass Hall, with its trumpeting angels, in downtown Fort Worth, is a world-class performance hall.

Admission to the Amon Carter Museum of American Art is always free.

Mounted Patrol

The volunteer mounted patrol—the guys in uniform riding horses downtown—started in the Stockyards in the 1970s. Today, the horsemen undergo rigorous training before they're allowed to saddle up and assist with crowd control, searches, or help out anywhere a horse's maneuverability is needed.

Fort Worth Museum of Science and History (817-255-9300; www .fwmuseum.org), 600 Gendy Street. Open 10–5 daily. A new building completed in 2009 is home to the Omni Theatre (an IMAX dome); a planetarium; the hands-on Innovation Studios; the Fort Worth Children's Museum; and the Cattle Raisers Museum. Tickets to the museum exhibits only are $14 adults, $10 children and seniors. Admission to the Omni and planetarium are separate.

Fort Worth Botanic Garden (817-871-7686; www.fwbg.org), 3220 Botanic Garden Boulevard. Grounds are open from dawn to dusk; Garden Center, Conservatory, and Japanese Garden are open daily, all with varying hours, beginning with the Garden Center at 8 Monday through Saturday and 1 on Sunday. The contemplative Japanese Garden, with its brilliant koi, fragrant pines, and visiting heron, is alone worth the price of admission. But different ticket prices also will take you to see roses, perennials, tropicals (in the Conservatory), a fragrance garden, and more. Admission varies according to where you're going, starting

The Fort Worth Museum of Science and History is in the city's Cultural District.

"Vortex," a Richard Serra sculpture, stands outside the Modern Art Museum in Fort Worth.

Don't Miss

Modern Art Museum of Fort Worth (817-738-9215; www.themodern .org), 3200 Darnell Street. Open 10–5 Tuesday through Thursday and Saturday through Sunday; 10–8 Friday. A serene but thought-provoking experience awaits beyond the doors of the Tadao Ando-designed build-ing, itself a work of modern art. The permanent collection of more than 2,000 pieces includes works by Mark Rothko, Jackson Pollock, Robert Motherwell, and Donald Judd. Adults, $10; students with ID and seniors, $4; free for 12 and under.

at $1 adults; 50 cents, seniors and children 4–12; and free, under 4. (The Japanese Garden is $4 adults weekdays, $4.50 weekends; seniors 50 cents off regular admission; $3 children 4–12; under 4, free.)

Fort Worth Zoo (817-759-7555; www.fortworthzoo.org), 1989 Colonial Parkway. Open daily; hours vary from 10–4 to 10–6 according to season. The animals, including penguins, giraffes, elephants, kangaroos, primates, and more, look good; and kids have a great time riding the train and check-ing out the petting corral. Adults, $12; kids 3–12 and seniors, $9; free, under 2.

Beyond the entrance to the Fort Worth Botanic Garden, a soothing Japanese garden and other wonders await.

Kimbell Art Museum (817-332-8451; www.kimbellart.org), 3333 Camp Bowie Boulevard. Open 10–5 Tuesday through Thursday and Saturday; noon–8 Friday; noon–5 Sunday. The nationally respected museum's permanent collection is small—fewer than 350 works—but they are meticulously chosen pieces by the likes of Rembrandt, Goya, Monet, Cézanne, Picasso, Mondrian, and Matisse; antiquities; Asian art; pre-Columbian pieces; and African and Oceanic art. Free.

Log Cabin Village (817-392-5881; www.logcabinvillage.org), 2100 Log Cabin Village Lane. Open 9–4 Tuesday through Friday; 1–5 Saturday and Sunday. The living museum comprises six log cabins, all authentically furnished. Ages 4–17 and 65 and older, $4; 18 and older, $4.50; 3 and under, free.

Best of Fort Worth

Modern Art Museum of
Fort Worth

Bass Hall

Kimbell Art Museum

Stockyards National Historic
District

Sundance Square

National Cowgirl Museum and Hall of Fame (817-336-4475; www.cowgirl.net), 1720 Gendy. Open 10–5 Tuesday through Sunday. Saddles, boots, spurs, photographs, and more, remembering accomplished women from potter Maria Martinez to Patsy Cline. Adults, $10; seniors over 60 and children 3–12, $8; 2 and under free. Included with Museum of Science and History admission.

Stockyards National Historic District

Fort Worth Herd (817-336-4373; www.fortworth.com/the-herd), Stockyards National Historic District. 11 AM and 4 PM. The herd is not the thundering, scary stampede of the movies. The 19 longhorns are fairly domesticated, with names like Snort and Walter. The drovers put them through their paces every day, and you can also visit them in their corral. Watch the cattle drive from the visitor center at 130 E. Exchange Avenue. Free.

Stockyards Museum (817-625-5082; www.stockyardsmuseum.org), 131 E. Exchange Avenue in the Livestock Exchange Building, once known as the Wall Street of the West. Open 10–5 Monday through Saturday. Fort Worth's history as a cattle capital, and as such, a layover for cowboys, is explored here. Free.

Texas Cowboy Hall of Fame (817-626-7131; www.texascowboyhalloffame .org), 128 E. Exchange, Suite 100. Open 10–6 Monday through Thursday; 10–7 Friday through Saturday; 10–7 Sunday. The criteria include contributions to the sport of rodeo and the Western lifestyle, so the honorees have included a variety of folks from actor Tommy Lee Jones to cowboy poet

The Fort Worth Stockyards is a must-see during a visit to Cowtown.

Lakes in Texas

Lacking a nearby seashore, on weekends when they're in the mood for water, North Texans traditionally flock to area lakes formed by dams. The lakes also are good for picnicking and camping (although be warned, summertime camping is a hot enterprise unless you have access to air-conditioning, as in an RV). Here are a couple of popular lakes with swimming beaches in the Fort Worth area:

Benbrook Lake (817-292-2400; www.swf-wc.usace.army.mil/ben brook), 7001 Lakeside Drive. Picnic spots abound, and swimming is allowed everywhere but boat-launch areas. Swimming beaches are at North Holiday Park, Baja Beach, and Mustang Point. Admission for day use is $3 per car. **Lake Grapevine** (www.swf-wc.usace.army.mil/ grapevine). With 196 miles of shoreline, four marinas, grassy parks for camping and picnicking, boat and Jet Ski rentals, and two swimming beaches, it's easy to find a spot to relax. A tip: Meadowmere Park has a fee per car even for day use, but its longish swimming beach is the best one. Other hiking and picnic areas are free. Fees for other uses vary. You can also book a trip into the lake on a WWII amphibious vehicle from Duck Rider tours, www.duckriders.com. It leaves for 75-minute rides from the Gaylord Texan Hotel and Resort; Great Wolf Lodge; and Grapevine Mills mall.

See Possum Kingdom Lake, Chapter 3.

Red Steagall. Adults, $5; students 13–17, $4; ages 5–12, $3; 4 and under and military with ID, free.

Texas Trail of Fame (www.texastrailoffame.org), 140 E. Exchange Avenue. The bronze markers inlaid in the walkways honor people like Lily Langtry and John Chisum, who contributed to the Western way of life. Free.

SPECTATOR SPORTS

Stockyards Championship Rodeo and Pawnee Bill's Wild West Show (817-625-1025; www.cowtowncoliseum.com), 121 E. Exchange Avenue. The rodeo is at 8 PM every Friday and Saturday, year-round. Here's your chance to see bull riding, barrel racing, team roping—the whole shebang. The Wild West Show, which takes place once a month, includes trick roping and riding. Rodeo box and VIP seats, $20; general admission, $15; ages 3–12, $10; seniors, $12.50. Wild West Show box, $15; adults, $12; seniors, $9; children 3–12, $8; under 3, free.

Texas Motor Speedway (817-215-8593; www.texasmotorspeedway.com), 3545 Lone Star Circle. Most races take place from April to November. NASCAR fans camp out for the duration on race weekends for major national events that include the NASCAR Sprint Cup and the Nationwide Series.

OUTDOORS

Fort Worth Nature Center & Refuge (817-392-7410; www.fwnaturecenter .org), 9601 Fossil Ridge Road. Open 8–5 daily October through April; 8–7 Monday through Friday and 7–7 Saturday and Sunday, May through September. The 3,621-acre center has more than 20 miles of hiking trails and is home to deer, raccoons, and other critters. Adults, $5; children 3–12, $2; seniors 65 and older $3; military discount of $1 with ID.

Trinity Trails (www.trinitytrails.org). More than 40 miles of trails along the Trinity River and its tributaries, connect to the Fort Worth Botanic Garden, Fort Worth Zoo, Downtown, and parks. They're used by joggers, cyclists, picnickers, kayakers, and equestrians. More trails and bridges are being built all the time, so check the online map for what's current before you go.

Pick Your Spot

Best places to stay in and around Fort Worth

Ashton Hotel (817-332-0100; www.theashtonhotel.com), 610 Main Street. Fort Worthians in the know come here to the Six 10 Grille for long lunches when they need a quiet spot for dining and conversation. The small (39-room), contemporary boutique hotel in the heart of downtown has bright rooms with large windows, appointed with custom fabrics that make it feel luxe without being over the top. Expensive.

Omni Fort Worth (817-535- 6664; www.omnihotels.com), 1300 Houston Street. Composed of native stone and a soaring glass tower, the Omni is Fort Worth's newest addition to downtown lodging and features an in-house spa, several dining spots, and roof-top bar. The bustling hotel is popular with business travelers and tourists, who can ride Molly the Trolley to Sundance Square for sightseeing. Moderate.

Worthington Renaissance Fort Worth (817-870-1000; www.marriott.com). The 12-story, luxury hotel is within easy walking distance of Sundance Square. It features a Southern-cooking in-house restaurant, piano bar, and fitness center, among other amenities. Expensive.

Local Flavors

Taste of the town—restaurants, cafés, bars, bistros, etc.

DINING OUT

Bailey's Prime Plus (817-870-1100; www.baileysprimeplus.com), 2901 Crockett Street. Open for lunch and dinner Monday through Friday, dinner Saturday and Sunday. The gorgeous contemporary decor makes it a good place for a dinner date. The prix-fixe classic for $39 gives you a choice of salad, entrees like filet mignon or Scottish salmon, plus a seasonal dessert of the day or fresh berries. Expensive.

Blue Mesa Grill (817-332-6372; www.bluemesagrill.com), 1600 S. University Drive #609 in University Park Village. Open daily. A Jewish couple from New York came up with a whole new, tasty twist on Southwestern cuisine, and the rest is history. Blue Mesa also has locations in Dallas, Southlake, and elsewhere in the Metroplex. Try the blue corn enchiladas, or the red chile-crusted salmon. If you're in town in the fall, Blue Mesa serves up seasonal New Mexico green chile, too. Moderate.

Bob's Steak & Chop House (817-350-4100; bobs-steakandchop .com), 1300 Houston Street in the Omni Fort Worth Hotel. *See North Dallas.*

Bonnell's Fine Texas Cuisine (817-231-8827; www.bonnellstexas .com), 4259 Bryant Irvin Road. Open for lunch and dinner Tuesday through Saturday. Wild game (crispy quail legs, elk mini-tacos) mingles with Southwestern and Creole cuisine (the Southwestern filet is topped with poblano pepper and tasso sauce) under Chef Jon Bonnell's sure hand, with mostly locally grown and organic ingredients. Expensive.

Brownstone (817-332-1555; www.brownstonerestaurants.com), 840 Currie Street. Open for dinner Tuesday through Sunday; also lunch Friday and brunch Sunday. Another pretty restaurant in the West 7th development, the emphasis here is on Southern-inspired dishes tweaked into sophistication, like Kobe cheek "pot roast" or an appetizer of squash "casserole" spread. Expensive.

Ellerbe Fine Foods (817-926-3663; www.ellerbefinefoods.com), 1501 W. Magnolia Avenue. Open Tuesday through Friday for lunch and dinner, Saturday for dinner. Expect fresh, local, and seasonal ingredients used in inventive ways—chile-rubbed wild boar with mesquite-bean blinis and house-made pepper jelly, for example, or a dessert of cornmeal pound cake with almond whipped cream. Bon Appetit named Ellerbe, cozily situated in a former gas station, one of the 10 best new restaurants in America in 2010. Expensive.

GRACE (817-877-3388; www .gracefortworth.com), 777 Main Street. Open for dinner Monday through Saturday. Clean, modern

The Dining Scene

There's a constantly expanding and increasingly sophisticated array of options. Of course, this is Cowtown, long known for beef in all its incarnations from barbecue to filet mignon, and you can definitely sink your teeth into that during your stay. Chefs such as cowboy cook Grady Spears, urban Western-cuisine creator Tim Love, and imaginative ranch-style Chef Lou Lambert keep those offerings fresh, while the tried-and-true institutions like Del Frisco's still dish up ele-

Tillman's Roadhouse serves Texas roadhouse fare.

gant, traditional steaks in formal settings. Tex-Mex is ubiquitous, but a few family-run holes-in-the-wall keep it authentic. Likewise, the best Asian cuisine is at smaller spots, and a wave of new sushi restaurants is wowing diners with creations that are both beautiful and delicious. New developments along West 7th Avenue just west of downtown have attracted upscale offerings like Brownstone's Southern-inspired cuisine, the steakhouse Bailey's Prime Plus, and a Fort Worth version of Dallas's lively Tillman's Roadhouse. Finally, a small but eclectic strip of selections along Magnolia Avenue is emerging as one of the top spots for seasonal, locally sourced cuisine, inventive homestyle Italian, and more.

decor matches the Modern American Classic fare, like cuts of beef that can be paired with toppings like black truffle butter, Hudson Valley foie gras, or an organic egg; or buttermilk-fried chicken with three-cheese mac and cheese. Expensive.

Grady's (817-922-9980; www

.gradysrestaurant.com), 2443 Forest Park Boulevard. Open for dinner Tuesday through Saturday. Chef Grady Spears has taken meat-and-potatoes cowboy fare and kicked it up into Cowboy Cuisine. Fresh Texas ingredients go into dishes like Rahr beer-battered chicken-fried steak with green onion mashed potatoes, or cornmeal-crusted Gulf oysters with horseradish crema. Expensive.

Lambert's Steaks, Seafood and Whiskey (817-882-1161; www .lambertsfortworth.com), 2731 White Settlement Road. Open for dinner Tuesday through Saturday; brunch Sunday. Chef Lou Lambert creates ranch cuisine with a grill and smoker responsible for flavors of many of the beef and seafood dishes. The sides are brasserie-simple, like Parmesan house fries or sautéed mushrooms. Expensive.

Reata Restaurant (817-336-1009; www.reata.net), 310 Houston Street, Sundance Square. Open daily for lunch and dinner. The atmosphere and definitely Western menu make this the place Fort Worthians tend to take visitors. A huge favorite for years has been the tenderloin tamales with pecan mash appetizer. Expensive. *Also see Reata in Alpine, Chapter 4.*

Tillman's Roadhouse Fort Worth (817-850-9255; www .tillmansroadhouse.com), 2933 Crockett Street. Open for lunch and dinner Tuesday through Saturday; brunch and dinner Sunday. The fascinating interior design (check out the peacock and wood fixture in the side dining room) and upscale Texas-centric menu (chicken-fried hanger steak, wildflower honey lavender-glazed salmon) make for a lively experience. Expensive.

Sundance West, Fort Worth's first downtown apartment building, looms over Reata, which has a rooftop patio.

Lonesome Dove Western Bistro (817-740-8810; www.lonesomedovebistro.com), 2406 N. Main Street. Open Tuesday through Saturday for lunch; Monday through Saturday for dinner. Iron Chef Tim Love's fine-dining restaurant in the Stockyards has a wide-ranging menu filled with everything from Wagyu beef and grilled Maine lobster to flounder *en papillote* to seared Texas quail with fried pepita (pumpkin seed) biscuit and juniper pan gravy. Expensive.

EATING OUT

Bailey's Barbeque (817-335-7469), 826 Taylor Street. Open Monday through Friday mid-morning to late afternoon. Downtown lunch crowds know a good barbecue sandwich when they see one, and flock to this hole-in-the-wall in lieu of the sandwich chains. There usually is a line, but it moves quickly. Inexpensive.

Blue Bonnet Bakery (817-731-4233; www.bluebonnetbakery.com), 4705 Camp Bowie Boulevard. Open Monday through Saturday. There's something ironic about a bakery full of sinful sweets in a renovated church. Forget about the diet and the sins and get the monkey bread. Or the Italian cream cake. Or, just about anything, really, it's all good, and made from recipes passed down for more than 75 years. Sandwiches served, too. Inexpensive to moderate.

Buffet Restaurant at the Kimbell Art Museum (817-332-8451; www.kimbellart.org), 3333 Camp Bowie Boulevard. Open for lunch Tuesday through Sunday; beverages and desserts served after 2 PM; buffet Friday evening. The Friday buffet with live music is the way to go—dine on homemade soups, quiches, desserts, and then walk through the galleries. Moderate.

Cafe Modern (817-840-2175; www.thecafemodern.com), 3200 Darnell Street. Open for lunch Tuesday through Friday; dinner Friday; brunch Saturday and Sunday. The café looks out on The Modern's reflecting pond, making it a lovely spot to try scrumptious global cuisine crafted from local ingredients. Moderate to expensive.

Central Market & Café On The Run (817-377-9307; www.centralmarket.com), 4651 West Freeway, #100. Open daily for breakfast, lunch, and dinner. Foodies flock to the amazing supermarket and then stay for ample, tasty salads and sandwiches for lunch, or specials like Mexican barbecued chicken in the evenings on the patio, sometimes with live music. Moderate.

Costa Azul (817-624-3199), 1521 N. Main Street. Open daily for lunch and dinner. The shrimp cocktail is good, but the fish tacos are divine. Inexpensive.

Daddy Jack's New England Lobster & Chowder House (817-332-2477; www.daddyjacks.org), 353 Throckmorton Street, on Sundance Square. Open for lunch Monday through Saturday; dinner daily. This eatery dedicated to seafood has locations in Fort Worth and Dallas's Lower Greenville. The blackened-tuna sandwich served with Italian potato salad is a good choice for lunch. Moderate.

Esperanza's Restaurant and Bakery (www.joets.com), locations at 1601 Park Place (817-923-1992) and 2122 N. Main Street (817-626-5770). Open daily for breakfast, lunch, and dinner. Plenty of locals prefer the food here to that of the venerable and atmospheric Joe T. Garcia's, owned by the same family. Try the chilaquiles (tortilla pieces fried with scrambled eggs, cheese, and optional chorizo) and get some pan dulce for later. Inexpensive.

Fireside Pies (817-769-3590; www.firesidepies.com), 2949 Crockett Street. Open daily for dinner. *See Dallas, Eating Out.*

Flying Fish (817-989-2277; www.flyingfishinthe.net), 2913 Montgomery Street. Open daily for lunch and dinner. Order at the register from the lengthy menus, from catfish and crawfish to grilled salads. Try the grilled tilapia tacos, served with pico de gallo (a fresh salsa of chopped tomatoes, onions, jalapeño, and cilantro), slaw, rice, and beans. The small chain also has five more locations: in Dallas (6126 Luther Lane, 214-696-3474), Addison, and Garland; Arkansas, and Tennessee. Moderate.

Fred's Texas Cafe (817-332-0083; www.fredstexascafe), 915 Currie Street. Open for lunch and dinner Tuesday through Sunday; brunch Sunday. Bite into a Diablo burger dripping with cheese and you won't mind that you feel like the only person in the little room who isn't a local. Sunday brunch includes mimosas in a schooner, should you feel like taking it easy for the day. Moderate.

Fuzzy's Taco Shop (817-924-7943; www.fuzzystacoshop.com), 2917 W. Berry Street. Closed Thursday; open Friday through Wednesday for breakfast, lunch, and dinner. A longtime Texas Christian University tradition is eating the Tempura Baja Taco, which means the entire taco is battered and fried. There's been some complaining, though, that Fuzzy's isn't as good since it turned into a real chain, with locations all over Texas, New Mexico, and Oklahoma, plus one in Wisconsin and more to come. You'll have to be the judge. Inexpensive.

Gloria's Restaurant (817-332-8800; www.gloriasrestaurants.com), 2600 W. 7th Street, #175 in Montgomery Plaza. Open daily for lunch and dinner. The menu of both Tex-Mex and Salvadoran dishes makes it fun to order both and share. Gloria's started out in Dallas and now has 13 locations, including this one. People swoon over the *carne flameada*—beef ensconced in a blanket of melted cheese and mushrooms. The margarita bar might make you swoon, too. Moderate.

Hui Chuan Sushi, Sake and Tapas (817-989-8886; www.hui chuansushi.com), 6100 Camp

Bowie Boulevard in Ridglea Village Shopping Center. Open for lunch Monday through Saturday, dinner daily. Although the owner for whom the restaurant was named has moved on, the Burmese brothers who bought it are carrying on a tradition of beautifully prepared sushi dishes, both traditional and unconventional—like the tsunami roll: yellowtail with cream cheese, jalapeños, and avocado, lightly fried. Expensive.

Joe T. Garcia's Mexican Restaurant (817-626-4356; www .joets.com), 2201 N. Commerce Street. Open Monday through Thursday for lunch, daily for dinner. People line up around the block for a chance to sit on the gigantic patio (that winds through many different areas) and sip margaritas. The food is standard Tex-Mex—the atmosphere is what pulls in the crowds. Cash or check only. Moderate.

Kincaid's Burgers/Market (817-732-2881; www.kincaidsham burgers.com), 4901 Camp Bowie Boulevard. Open daily for lunch and dinner. Old-school burgers patted out by hand and served in a plastic basket have kept diners coming back since 1946. Two more locations in Fort Worth, as well as in Southlake, Arlington, and Weatherford. Inexpensive.

La Familia (817-870-2002; www.lafamilia-fw.com), 841 Foch Street. Open Monday through Saturday for lunch and dinner. Flautas (corn tortillas rolled up with cheese and chicken or beef and fried crisp) are something of a rarity in these parts, but you'll find them here. Vegetarians can have Tex-Mex, too, in the form of veggie tacos and enchiladas. Inexpensive.

Lili's Bistro on Magnolia (817-877-0700; www.lilisbistro.com), 1310 W. Magnolia Avenue. Open for lunch Monday through Thursday, dinner Tuesday through Saturday. A continually surprising menu of inventive dishes like skewered bacon-wrapped tenderloin fillets, grilled and glazed in Coke and molasses and served with goat-cheese potatoes keeps Fort Worth foodies happy, at one of the stops along a growing stretch of Magnolia Avenue. Moderate to expensive.

Lanny's Alta Cocina Mexicana (817-850-9996; www.lannyskitchen .com), 3405 W. 7th Street. Open for lunch Tuesday through Friday, dinner Tuesday through Saturday. The great-grandson of Joe T. Garcia (see above) grew up in the restaurant business, traveled Mexico, went to the Culinary Institute of America, came home, and opened his own restaurant. The result is a melding of cuisines and techniques, like agave nectar-glazed duck breast with nopal and mushroom risotto. Moderate lunch, expensive dinner.

Love Shack (817-740-8812; www.loveburgershack.com), 110 E. Exchange Avenue and 817 Matisse Drive. Open daily for lunch and dinner. The gourmet burgers, sandwiches, and hot dogs by Iron Chef

Tim Love are simple, but done well. Inexpensive.

Lucile's Stateside Bistro (817-738-4761; www.lucilesstateside bistro.com), 4700 Camp Bowie Boulevard. Open daily for lunch and dinner, Saturday and Sunday for breakfast. Classic American food (fish, pizza, pasta, burgers) that appeals to a wide variety of diners makes Lucile's a popular lunch stop for the business crowd. Moderate.

Mi Cocina (817-877-3600; www.mcrowd.com), 509 Main Street, Sundance Square. Traditional Mexican dishes done in a modern way. For more details, see Dallas Eating Out.

Nonna Tata (817-332-0250), 1400 W. Magnolia Avenue. Open Tuesday through Friday for lunch and dinner. The tiny space is like eating at your mom's, if your mom were a fabulous Northern Italian cook. The pasta is hand-made and it tastes like it. Cash only. Moderate.

Paris Coffee Shop (817-335-2041; www.pariscoffeeshop.net), 704 W. Magnolia Avenue. Open Monday through Friday for breakfast and lunch; breakfast only on Saturday. Hefty breakfasts and seriously good biscuits keep the place packed in the morning. Inexpensive.

Piranha Killer Sushi (817-348-0200; www.piranhakillersushi.com), 335 W. 3rd Street in Sundance Square. Open daily for lunch and dinner and just the thing to sate a sushi craving when you're walking around Downtown—you'll find every kind of roll plus teriyaki and tempura. Locations also in Arlington. Moderate.

Railhead Smokehouse (817-738-9808; www.railheadonline .com), 2900 Montgomery Avenue. Open Monday through Saturday for lunch and dinner. Especially in Texas, barbecue is a personal matter. Railhead is my favorite because I like a non-sweet, smoky sauce on brisket or pork. The beer is icy cold. Moderate.

Revolver Taco Lounge (817-820-1022; www.revolvertacolounge .com), 2822 W. 7th St. Open Monday–Saturday. This new addition to Fort Worth has brought small-town Mexico to the city, with choices like huitlacoche, a corn truffle, and Michoacan-style oven-roasted baby goat. Moderate.

Sardines Ristorante Italiano (817-332-9937; www.sardinesft worth.com), 509 University Avenue. Open Sunday through Saturday for dinner; Sunday brunch. Classic Italian dishes loaded with garlic and creamy sauces will fill you up, and the nightly entertainment is jazz pianist Johnny Case, who's been playing here for a quarter-century. Moderate.

Spiral Diner & Bakery (817-332-8834; www.spiraldiner.com), 1314 W. Magnolia Avenue. Open Tuesday through Sunday for lunch and dinner. All vegan, largely organic fare ranges from pasta dishes to tacos and wraps. Inexpensive.

Thai Tina's (817-332-0088; www.thaitinas.com), 600 Commerce Street in the Embassy Suites Hotel. Open daily for lunch and dinner. If you're worried about the location in the Embassy Suites, fear not: Great Thai food with a devoted following includes an amazing steak salad with chili-cilantro-lime sauce. Inexpensive.

Tokyo Cafe (817-560-3664; www.thetokyocafe.com), 8742 Camp Bowie West. Open Monday through Saturday for lunch and dinner. Enjoy sushi, sashimi, bowls, noodles, salads of seaweed, squid, or octopus, or seasonal dishes like a veggie tempura. Inexpensive to moderate.

Wineries

Times 10 Cellars (817-336-9463; www.timestencellars.org), 100 Foch Street. Open daily. The selection includes wines bottled from vineyards in California as well as made from Times 10's own grapes grown in Alpine, Texas. Order chutney and cheeses from the small plates menus, or several Fort Worth restaurants will deliver.

Lightcatcher Winery (817-237-2626; www.lightcatcher.com), 6925 Confederate Park Road/Farm-to-Market (FM) 1886. Opens at noon Friday through Wednesday. The boutique winery makes chardonnay, cabernet sauvignon, Muscat, and others and serves casual bistro fare at its vineyard restaurant.

Selective Shopping

Byrd & Bleecker (817-989-1500; www.byrdandbleecker.com), 4725 Camp Bowie Boulevard. Open Monday through Saturday. The art of writing on beautiful paper printed with letterpress designs lives on here, but stationery is only part of the picture: You'll also find home accessories and "groovy miscellany."

Chiffoniers (817-731-8545), 3811 Camp Bowie Boulevard. Open Monday through Saturday. A happy selection of home accessories, from high-end candles to fun tea towels, will inspire a long browse.

Domain (817-336-1994; www.domainsciv.com), 3100 W. 7th Street. Open 10–6 Monday through Saturday. High-end furniture and home accessories mingle with the best European tableware.

The Greener Good (817-732-1500; www.thegreenergood.com), 925 Foch Street. Open Monday through Saturday. The selection is all eco-friendly but

Leddy's Ranch in Fort Worth's Sundance Square is the place for upscale cowboys and cowgirls to shop.

not at all stodgy and granola-ish. The soft, bamboo baby clothes are especially nice, but the recycled glassware is pretty, too.

Leddy's Ranch at Sundance (817-336-0800; www.leddys.com), 410 Houston Street. Open daily. This Downtown branch of the Stockyards store is where you get your cowboy on, if you're a high-dollar kind of weekend cowboy. They stock beautiful Southwestern and Western clothing, and the jewelry to go with it.

Megan Thorne Fine Jewels (817-731-4374; www.meganthorne.com), 1517 W. Magnolia Avenue. Call for hours. Talented jeweler Megan Thorne creates stunning pieces that look at once Old World and contemporary.

Maverick Fine Western Wear (800-282-1315; www.maverickwesternwear .com), 100 Exchange Avenue. Open daily. Here are your Western dog accessories, home goods, boots, clothes, and books.

M. L. Leddy's (817-624-3149; www.leddys.com), 2455 N. Main Street. Open Monday through Saturday. The original outpost of Leddy's first opened in 1941. Look for Western hats, boots, and if you're really a cowboy, take a gander at the saddles, stirrups, and chaps.

Neiman Marcus (817-738-3581; www.neimanmarcus.com), Ridgmar Mall, 2100 Green Oaks Road. *See Neiman Marcus in Dallas.*

Prim & Proper (817-377-3500), 4823 Camp Bowie Boulevard. Open Monday through Saturday. Just about anyone will love a gift from the well-chosen wares, which include pet accessories, stationery, mugs, and women's accessories.

P.S. The Letter (817-731-2032; www.pstheletter.com), 5136 Camp Bowie Boulevard. Open Monday through Saturday. Eclectic and elegant china (there's a bridal registry) mingles with stationery, soaps and lotions, and more.

Western home accessories as well as clothing are found at Maverick in the Fort Worth Stockyards.

SiNaCa (817-899-0024; www.sinacastudios.org), 1013 W. Magnolia. Call for hours. A glass studio whose mission is educating the community about the art of glassblowing, SiNaCa has a small gallery of gorgeous hand-blown pieces.

Entertainment

NIGHTLIFE

Fort Worth has a fun selection of Western bars, Irish pubs, and 20-something hangouts. Check www.dfw.com and www.fwweekly.com for complete and current club listings. Sundance Square also offers plenty of spots to eat and drink, all within walking distance. Here are a few spots to check out.

Don't Miss

Billy Bob's Texas (817-724-7117; www.billybobstexas.com), 2520 Rodeo Plaza. Billed as the world's largest honky-tonk, Billy Bob's has live bull riding on Friday and Saturday nights. Some of Texas's favorite artists give concerts here, too; Willie Nelson plays here from time to time, and George Strait once was the house band. Check the Web site for the current concert and bull-riding schedule.

8.0 Restaurant and Bar (817-336-0880; www.eightobar.com), 111 E. Third Street on Sundance Square. You're guaranteed either live music (including some very good local bands) or a DJ on the patio on weekends, when the place usually is packed. The bar food's decent, and there's a dining room, too.

Flying Saucer (816-336-7470; www.beerknurd.com/stores/fort worth), 111 E. 4th Street on Sundance Square. Beer gardens on two levels are usually packed, with live music on the bottom, but the upstairs bar inside can be quiet enough for conversation. It's all about the beer with more than 100 on tap. Bar food and sandwiches are served.

Lone Star Night Clubs (817-335-5400; www.lonestarsundance.com), 425 Commerce Street. Six venues under one roof provide something for everyone—dance club, dueling pianos, live music, karaoke, etc.

Bar 9 (817-348-9991; www.bar 9fw.com), 900 Houston. DJs play six days a week at street level, and Thursday through Saturday in the basement. The second level is more low-key, with a volume that permits conversation.

White Elephant Saloon (817-624-8273; www.whiteelephant saloon.com), 102 E. Exchange Avenue in the Stockyards. A bar with a history—there was a gunfight here in 1887. Locals come to grab a beer and catch a little live music.

The original location of Leddy's is in the Fort Worth Stockyards.

Special Events

The White Elephant Saloon was once the scene of a shootout.

January through February

Southwestern Exposition and Livestock Show & Rodeo (817-877-2400; www.fwssr.com), Will Rogers Coliseum, 3400 Burnett Tandy Drive. Livestock barns, rodeo, and the best cinnamon rolls ever.

April

Main Street Fort Worth Arts Festival (817-336-2787; www.main streetartsfest.org). Nine blocks of Main Street are blocked off for live music, food, arts, and crafts.

May

Frontier Forts Days (817-625-9715; www.stockyardsstation.com). Military parades, encampments, and other reenactments of pioneer military life take place in the Stockyards.

Mayfest (817-332-1055; www.mayfest.org). On the banks of the Trinity River. A family-oriented festival with food, live music, arts, and crafts.

Crowne Plaza Invitational at Colonial (817-927-4201; www.crowneplaza colonial.com), Colonial Country Club, 3735 Country Club Circle. A stop on the PGA tour.

May through June

Van Cliburn International Piano Competition (817-738-6536; www.cliburn .org). Once every four years, Fort Worth is transfixed by some of the best young pianists in the world who come to compete in Bass Hall.

June

Juneteenth Celebration at Sundance Square celebrates the day the last remaining slaves in the U.S., who lived in Galveston, Texas, learned that they had been freed.

Fort Worth Symphony Orchestra's Concerts in the Garden (817-665-6000; www.fwsymphony.org), Fort Worth Botanic Garden, 3220 Botanic Garden Boulevard. Evening performances on an expansive lawn, with fireworks.

October

Fort Worth Alliance Airshow (www.allianceairshow.com), Fort Worth Alliance Airport, 2221 Alliance Boulevard. The U.S. Air Force Thunderbirds, aerobatics, static displays.

November

Chesapeake Energy Parade of Lights (817-336-2787; www.fortworthparadeoflights.org). Night-time parade kicks off the holiday season, and ends with lighting of the downtown Christmas tree.

December

Christmas in the Stockyards (817-624-4741; www.fortworthstockyards.org). Events include a petting zoo, ride for toys, CowKid roundup, Christmas tree lighting, appearances by Santa Claus.

2

Prairies to Plains

THE LAND BEGINS TO CHANGE after you leave Fort Worth, out past Weatherford. It's not so noticeable on the interstate—except as more space where the cities wane—but the smaller highways to the north and south are rich with pleasures both simple and luxurious: tree-covered rolling hills, chalky cliffs, great local café fare, at least two upscale resorts, and slices of real, Wild West history.

The North Texas Hill Country, as it's sometimes called, is about two hours west of Fort Worth. The trade-off for taking smaller roads, having more fun, and seeing more of the country is (as usual) time, because in many cases the smaller highways run right through the middle of towns. So if you're in a hurry to get to San Angelo or Abilene, by all means take I-20.

Even from there, the country changes about three hours out, after the hills flatten out to the plains around Abilene. You start to see what West Texas is really about. The beauty is in the space—the sky is enormous. Gaze into the distance—the running joke is that it's so flat you can see the curvature of the earth. Breathe in the freedom, stay the night, and spend some quality time with the stars—enjoy the nightly show.

Travelers who are accustomed to greenery and varied terrain have been known to turn up their noses at what Texans call the Big Empty. Some of the early settlers from the East felt that way. One abandoned his shack and left a note that read:

LEFT: Spots like this earned Young and Palo Pinto counties the nickname North Texas Hill Country.

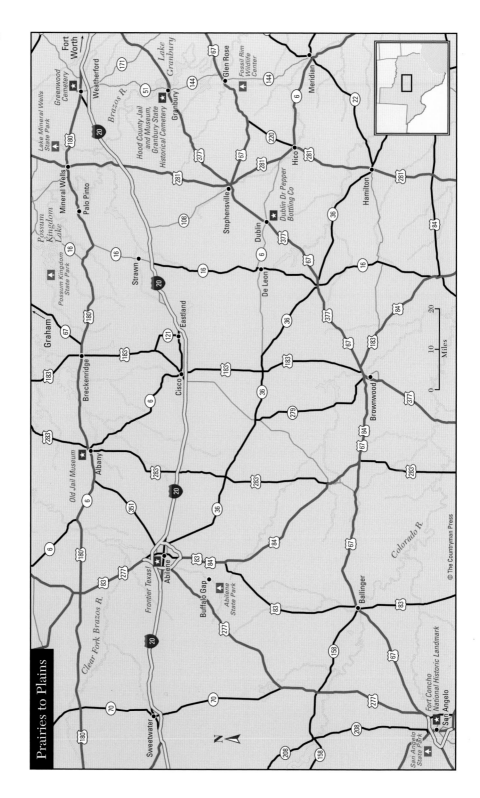

Prairies to Plains

Fort Worth

Weatherford

Greenwood Cemetery

Lake Mineral Wells State Park

171

51

Brazos R.

Lake Granbury

Granbury

Hood County Jail and Museum, Granbury State Historical Cemetery

144

67

Glen Rose

Fossil Rim Wildlife Center

144

Meridian

6

22

20

180

Mineral Wells

Palo Pinto

281

377

67

220

281

Hico

281

Hamilton

281

Possum Kingdom Lake

Possum Kingdom State Park

16

16

Strawn

108

Stephensville

Dublin

Dublin Dr. Pepper Bottling Co

377

36

84

20

16

De Leon

6

67

16

Graham

180

67

Breckenridge

183

121

Eastland

Cisco

6

183

183

36

377

84

20

Miles

10

0

Brownwood

377

283

Albany

Old Jail Museum

6

183

283

20

6

351

36

279

36

283

84

67

84

67

283

Colorado R.

Abilene

Frontier Texas!

83

84

Buffalo Gap

Abilene State Park

277

Ballinger

183

83

Clear Fork Brazos R.

283

277

83

20

Sweetwater

70

70

277

158

67

San Angelo State Park

Fort Concho National Historic Landmark

San Angelo

180

208

208

158

© The Countryman Press

N

20 MILES TO WATER
10 MILES TO WOOD
6 INCHES TO HELL
MAKE YOURSELF AT HOME

It's true the plains are brown—really brown in a drought—and the towns and cities are few and far between.

While not everyone will love the plains and prairie, anyone can enjoy the history that was made here, and marvel that the place was ever settled at all.

Try to envision Native American life here—on foot, sustained by the buffalo and a few pecan trees, water in short supply. The Spanish were first in a procession of outsiders who would come to the plains, run off the native peoples, or herd them onto reservations and take their land. Once the newcomers had also killed off most of the buffalo, they found themselves in the position of the pioneer who returned back East to his wife's family: hot, dusty, and broke. Unless, of course, they'd learned the cattle business.

The only thing that did more than the longhorn steer to change West Texas forever was the railroad. Many of the cities and towns along this part of the Big Empty are here because of either trains or cattle, or both.

In some of them, time seems to have stopped. Others have grabbed onto the colorful history and put it to good use, or created hospitable, beautiful lodging and dining on open ranchland.

This country is also producing clean power—gigantic wind generators, their three blades turning lazily, are visible for as far as the eye can see in places.

Signs of wealth from cattle ranching and oil money are evident in Albany, which has made a museum of its old jail and hung works by Picasso, Miro, and Giacometti, to name a few. Buffalo Gap, on the other side of Abilene, has an historic village and a nationally acclaimed steakhouse, Perini Ranch, which also offers peaceful guesthouses. Abilene itself has a marvelous, multimillion-dollar attraction called Frontier Texas! that brings pioneer history to life. All along the way, old U.S. Army forts have been restored and opened, giving visitors an intimate glimpse into the lives of frontier soldiers. These are by no means all the dining and lodging options in and around these cities and towns. They are the places I checked out because of enthusiasm from people who live here, or because of their wide popularity in Texas, or because I was lucky enough to come upon them.

All the cities here except Weatherford are within the region called the Panhandle Plains by the state Economic Development and Tourism office.

The guest cabins at Perini Ranch are comfy with all the amenities.

Weatherford is right at the edge of the Prairies and Lakes Region that includes the Dallas–Fort Worth area. I've included it here because it's the first city you'll hit heading west from the Metroplex. The Panhandle is in a separate chapter because, as you'll see, it's really a place apart.

Area Codes

All the cities and towns north of I-20 are in the 325 area code except Weatherford, which is 817 or 940. Cities and towns south of I-20 are 254.

Guidance

Convention and visitors bureaus, chambers of commerce or, in some cases, city Web sites are your best bet for information, as well as the Texas Economic Development and Tourism department. Call or browse:

Abilene Convention and Visitors Bureau (325-727-7704; www.abilene visitors.com).

Albany Chamber of Commerce (325-762-2525; www.albanytexas.com).

Buffalo Gap Historic Village (325-572-3365; www.buffalogap.com).

Graham Convention and Visitors Bureau (866-549-0401; www.visit grahamtexas.com).

Granbury Convention and Visitors Bureau (877-936-1201; www.granbury tx.com).

Glen Rose Convention and Visitors Bureau (888-346-6282; www.glenrose texas.net).

Hico Chamber of Commerce (1-800-361-HICO; www.hico-tx.com).

San Angelo Chamber of Commerce (325-655-4136; www.sanangelo.org).

Texas Economic Development and Tourism (800-452-9292; www.travel tex.com).

City of Weatherford (817-598-4000; www.ci.weatherford.tx.us, click For Visitors).

Getting There

Fly into Dallas–Fort Worth International Airport and then drive to your destination. If you need to get to Abilene quickly, American Eagle, a division of American Airlines, flies there, and also into and out of San Angelo Regional Airport.

The shortest way to get from Fort Worth to Abilene and back is to take Interstate-20. The first part of this chapter is arranged in the order you'll find places along TX 180; the second takes you down several small highways through a more southerly route. Both take you through pretty,

The Abilene Convention and Visitors Bureau is in an old train depot.

hilly country and charming small towns leading to the wide, flat prairie as you near Abilene.

Regarding rental cars: Any car will be fine on the roads suggested in this chapter. But if you're planning on staying at a ranch and aren't accustomed to cattle guards and dirt roads, you might be most comfortable in a vehicle that's higher off the ground, such as an SUV.

Medical Emergencies

Dial 911. Otherwise, in Weatherford, Weatherford Regional Medical Center (817-341-2273; www.weatherfordregional.com), 713 E. Anderson Street, Weatherford; small towns outside Weatherford also go to Texas Health Harris Methodist Hospital Stephenville (254-965-1500; www.texas health.org), 411 N. Belknap, Stephenville.

In Abilene, Hendrick Health System (325-670-3251; www.hendrick health.org), 1900 Pine Street; Abilene Regional Medical Center (325-428-1000; www.abileneregional.com), 6399 Directors Parkway.

In San Angelo, Shannon Medical Center (325-653-6741; www.shannon health.com), 120 E. Harris Avenue; San Angelo Community Medical Center (325-949-9511; www.sacmc.com), 3501 Knickerbocker Road.

WEATHERFORD TO SAN ANGELO AND POINTS BETWEEN VIA TX 180

This way takes you through rolling hills, untouristy small towns, and one remarkable former jail that now is a fine art museum.

Weatherford

This county seat of 26,650 people about 45 minutes west of Fort Worth is the last city until Abilene. It's the official Peach Capital of Texas, so if you're here in the summertime and you see peaches for sale at a roadside stand, don't hesitate to stop and try some. Weatherford also calls itself the Cutting Horse Capital of the World, and many Parker County residents are here because they can have horse property and a rural lifestyle—but still commute to Fort Worth and Dallas to work.

To See and Do

Chandor Gardens (817-613-1700; www.chandorgardens.com), 711 W. Lee Avenue. Open weekends March through November or by appointment. A 3.5-acre estate in Weatherford's historic district, Chandor

Gardens couples Chinese architecture with formal English gardens. It was built by English portrait artist Douglas Chandor, who painted British royalty and considered the property a work of art as well. The 5,600-square-foot mansion and gardens are both popular for special events. Adults, $5; 12 and under free.

Old Greenwood Cemetery, 400 Front Street. Men who were the inspiration for characters in Larry McMurtry's *Lonesome Dove* are buried here: Cattle drover Oliver Loving's dying wish in 1867 was to be buried at home in Parker County, and his friend Charles Goodnight brought his body back here, a 600-mile trip in a wagon. Fans of the book will remember that the main character, Woodrow Call, brought his friend Gus home the same way. The grave of Boze Ikard, on whom the Deets character in the novel was modeled, also is here. Free.

Parker County Courthouse, One Courthouse Square. A working courthouse for the county seat, the Second French Empire–style limestone courthouse is quite a sight, even in a state full of cool old courthouses. It was built in 1885, and recently restored. Free.

OUTDOORS

Possum Kingdom Lake (940-549-1803; www.tpwd.state.tx.us/spdest/findadest/parks/possum_kingdom and www.possumkingdomlake.com). Note: This area was subject to scorching wildfires in the spring of 2011. While the attractions and lodging listed here survived, you'll see the burned areas, and should call ahead in case of temporary closures for renovations.

This enormous lake—some 15,000–18,000 acres, depending on water levels—is a result of the dammed-up Brazos River, and it stretches through the Palo Pinto hills, with cliffs rising on either side in places. The lake is a playground for everyone for miles around. Boaters, water skiers, fishers, even scuba divers use the clear water and camp on the banks on weekends, usually between March and October. Boaters like to zip out to the coves, tie up and party, or picnic for the day. If that's what you're in the mood for, bear in mind that driving a boat while intoxicated is against the law, park rangers cruise the entire lake regularly, and you can wind up in jail in a heartbeat. Possum Kingdom State Park has six cabins and campsites that range from primitive to others with water and electricity. If you decide to go the primitive route, do it in March or October. The rest of those months—even April and September most years—are really hot for camping. Beyond that, all kinds of lodging, from condos to cabins to mobile homes, are available, as are water-sports crafts and boat rentals.

Pick Your Spot

Best places to stay in and
around Weatherford

The Cliffs Resort (940-779-4040 or
888-335-8882; www.thecliffsresort
.com), 160 Cliffs Drive, Graford.
A golf resort on Possum Kingdom
Lake, the Cliffs offers golf packages
and rates for its rooms and suites.
The restaurant serves up fare like grilled rib eye and ahi tuna. Restaurant
and rooms, expensive.

Local Flavors

Taste of the town—restaurants,
cafés, bars, bistros, etc.

DINING OUT

The Wild Mushroom Steak House
and Lounge (817-599-4935; www
.thewildmushroomrestaurant.com),
1917 Martin Drive. Open 5–9
Monday; 5–2 Tuesday–Friday;
5–10:30 Saturday; 11–2 Sunday.
Here it's all about steak and seafood
done well—check out the roast
prime rib, or come for Sunday
brunch. Moderate to expensive.

Clear Fork Station (817- 441-
1551; www.clearfordstation.com),
4971 East I-20 Service Road N.,

Willow Park. Open Tuesday
through Sunday for lunch and dinner. Well-known Texas Chef Grady
Spears opened this restaurant and
then left it, but his trademark
chicken-fried steak stayed behind,
as did a touch of candied bacon in
many of the dishes. Moderate.

Fire Oak Grill (817-598-0400;
www.fireoakgrilll.com), 114 Austin
Avenue. Open Monday through
Saturday for dinner. Texas ingredients like Dr Pepper and Parker
County peaches in season are on
the menu in an historic building
on the square. Entrees include
an espresso-crusted tenderloin
served with bacon-blue cheese
Yukon potatoes gratin. Moderate
to expensive.

Selective Shopping

Teskey's Saddle Shop (888-955-
2955; www.teskeys.com), 3001 West
I-20. This is not a tourist attraction,
but a real tack and saddle shop—a
70,000-square-foot one—for horse owners and riders, stocked with farrier
supplies, feed, fencing, and real ranching equipment. The shopping for
non-horsepeople is in the clothing boutique, where co-owner Anissa Teskey
stocks 7 for All Mankind jeans, silver jewelry, exquisite custom boots, and
fluttery pieces from Johnny Was, along with traditional Western classic lines
like Cinch for men. There's also a hat bar staffed by trained experts, along

with a small home goods section. Teskey also picks up older Navajo silver
jewelry for the store, as well as for their new location in Fort Worth. And
strangely—in a nod to the many boaters and water-sports enthusiasts who
spend weekends at Possum Kingdom Lake and Lake Weatherford nearby—
Teskey's also has a surf shop with board shorts and other swimming gear.

Special Events

July

Parker County Peach Festival
(888-594-3801; www.peachfestival
tx.com). Some 30,000 people attend
this one-day event in downtown Weatherford to sample everything from
peach pies to peach juleps as they browse more than 200 vendor booths and
listen to entertainment on three stages, one a children's stage. You'll also get
to see the winners of the Peach Pageant, and participate in activities like the
Peach Pedal. Adults $5, children 12 and under, free.

Mineral Wells

Back in the 1800s, the water here in Mineral Wells was said to cure everything from arthritis to insanity. Called Crazy Water, it was bottled and sold
all over the country.

Resort spas and hotels attracted thousands, including celebrities such
as Will Rogers, Marlene Dietrich, Tom Mix, General John J. "Blackjack"
Pershing, Jean Harlow, Clark Gable, Judy Garland, Helen Keller, and the
Three Stooges.

Things have calmed down considerably since then. Mineral Wells,
home to about 17,000 people in both Parker and Palo Pinto counties, is a
good stop for rock climbers because of the state park.

To See and Do

Lake Mineral Wells State Park
and Trailways (940-328-1171;
www.tpwd.state.tx.us/spdest/find
adest/parks/lake_mineral_wells),
100 Park Road 71. The 3,000-acre park has trails for hiking, horseback
riding, backpacking, and bicycling, and allows climbing and rappelling on
several sheer rock formations. Climbers and rappellers must check in
before scaling the heights, and no one is permitted on the rocks in wet
weather. Adults, $5; 12 and under, free.

Clark Gardens Botanical Park (940-682-4856; www.clarkgardens.org),
567 Maddux Road. Open daily year-round. A 35-acre property between

North Texas Hill Country

Sometimes called the North Texas Hill Country, the area north and south of Interstate-20 and about two hours west of Fort Worth isn't famous or as large as its cousin down around Austin, but it's blessed with a rugged beauty of its own.

The hills are deep green in a wet year, often vine-covered and thick with trees. In the valleys, spring wildflowers sweep color across grassy meadows. Horses and cattle graze and take refuge from the sun under lone oaks. Cream cliffs hold caves where outlaws may have hidden.

To the north of I-20, along TX 180, is where the Goodnight-Loving cattle trail began, where the herds began a long trip to New Mexico, Colorado, and Wyoming. The land really does call to mind the old West of the movies, with its rough cliffs and hills above the Brazos River.

The land is similar to the south of I-20, down US 377 to Granbury and south to Glen Rose and Hico.

A brilliant display of wildflowers is common in spring in the North Texas Hill Country.

Weatherford and Mineral Wells that began as a private garden in 1972 is a model of sustainable, drought-tolerant landscaping now; historic trees were preserved, also. A G-scale model railroad runs on 1,200 feet of track through the gardens. Adults $7; seniors 65 and older and children 5–12, $5; 4 and under, free.

Palo Pinto

Palo Pinto is a tiny town that's the county seat of Palo Pinto County. What you want to see here is the Old Jail Museum (940-659-2555; www.palo pintohistory.com), on Fifth and Elm Streets; open 9–3 Wednesday through Saturday. (The museum made it through the 2011 wildfires unscathed.) It's made up of eight historical buildings, all of them except the jail moved from other sites in the area and reconstructed. The little museum is a taste of the history that West Texans like to keep alive through preservation of buildings and contributions of everyday items. The buildings include four cabins, one of them a typically furnished one-room log cabin that starkly shows the hardships of pioneer life here: a rope bed for the whole family, stove for both cooking and heat, logs chinked with mud against the elements. The old jail's first floor holds artifacts from daily life of the time—pieces of handmade lace; a women's basketball uniform that consists of long black bloomers and a long-sleeved top; the old flatbed printing press for the *Palo Pinto County Star;* a telephone switchboard complete with cables and plugs. Upstairs is a collection of old saddles.

The old Graham City Hall's first floor is a pizza parlor.

Graham

Graham is a pretty small town with restaurants and a bit of shopping. Stop downtown and see what small town life, sans tourist attractions, is like. You might come upon a huge crowd of people lining outdoor buffet tables in front of the courthouse for the hospital ladies' auxiliary fundraiser. Lacking that, if you're hungry when you're here, try Neri's Gild and Nosh (940-549-8000),

Sewing notions are on display outside a store in downtown Graham.

Old signs on buildings in Graham have been spiffed up.

523 Fourth Street. Open daily for lunch; Thursday through Saturday for dinner. The chilled avocado soup is delicious, and Neri's offers specials that range from meatloaf to mahi-mahi. Inexpensive to moderate. If you're in the mood for Mexican food, the place to stop in Graham is Mi Familia (940-521-0553), 1917 TX 16 South, open Monday through Saturday for lunch and dinner, serving reliably good tacos, enchiladas, etc. Inexpensive.

Strawn

If you make many stops between Dallas–Fort Worth Airport and Graham, you'll probably hear more than one recommendation, while you're in the area, to try the chicken-fried steaks at Mary's Café (254-672-5741), 119 Grant Avenue, in Strawn. Open daily for lunch and dinner, Mary's is packed for lunch because everyone for miles around wants homestyle chicken-fried steak drenched in peppery cream gravy, in huge portions at inexpensive prices.

It's not fancy, but Mary's chicken-fried steak in Strawn is legendary.

Also check out An Ancient Art Soap Co. (254-672-5421; www.strawn soap.com), 108 North Central, open 9:30–5 PM Monday through Saturday;

See Young County History for Yourself

It's interesting to stop and imagine what happened at historic markers around Young County.

Young County is peppered with 50 historical markers where various battles, raids, and massacres took place. The best way to get a feel for what happened here is to take a CD-led driving tour, which you can find at the Graham Convention and Visitors Bureau, just off the square at 458 Oak Street. Plan to devote the better part of a day to the tour if you want to stop and spend time at sites like Fort Belknap, established in the 1850s, or pull over and imagine the days of the Marlow Brothers ambush.

You can pick up handmade soap in bulk or by the bar in Strawn.

1–3 PM Sunday. You can buy a wide range of superfatted, olive oil-based handcrafted soaps in bulk, and have bars cut and wrapped for you. Or, just get one bar at a time.

Pick Your Spot
Best places to stay in and around Graham

Wildcatter Ranch Resort & Spa (888-462-9277; www.wildcatter ranch.com), 6062 Texas 16 South, Graham. This is one of the most scenic and peaceful resorts you'll ever encounter, set on a plateau that looks down on the Brazos River Valley. Guests can stay in rooms in the hotel or in cabins, several to a building, that back up to beautiful views stretching across green hills to the horizon. An exquisite infinity-edge pool seems to drop off the edge of a cliff down to the Brazos, and a fleet of bicycles for kids is parked and ready for action. Horseback riding, hiking, fishing, and skeet shooting are among the activities. Moderate weekdays, expensive weekends.

And who says Texas isn't green? This is the view from Wildcatter Ranch in Young County.

Albany has been on the insiders' list of places to check out in Texas for years, primarily because of its Old Jail Art Center, an amazing treasure that houses several Picassos and a wide range of sophisticated and eclectic works completely unexpected out here on the plains. Oil money is one of the reasons for this happy surprise.

Just after it was settled, though, the area was known more for wildness than for either art or money. Wyatt Earp and Doc Holliday met at Fort Griffin, where the town originally began. Women with names like Big Nose Kate

Take a Drive

For a scenic drive through the North Texas Hill Country, take FM 4 through the Palo Pinto Mountains to Granbury (see pages 109–11), just over an hour from Palo Pinto.

The small city built around Lake Granbury has a busier shopping and tourist scene than the smaller towns up north. You'll find antiques stores, gift shops, restaurants, and more all around the historic courthouse.

Forts Trail

You'll continually see signs in Central West Texas noting you're on part of the Texas Forts Trail. But before you jump in the car for a fort tour, remember you're in a place where distances are long: The forts trail covers about 650 miles in 29 counties, so it's best to see the eight forts as you travel the region rather than trying to see them all at once.

The U.S. Army built 44 posts in Texas from 1848 to 1900 to establish a permanent U.S. physical presence on the frontier, where the Comanches already had both power and presence. Towns often started around forts, as merchants set up shop to provide food, goods, and saloons for the soldiers. At the same time, hospitals at the forts often provided the only medical care available in the vicinity.

The forts all were eventually abandoned, mostly during the Civil War. Some had houses built of wood pickets (with sides like a picket fence and intended to be temporary) that disintegrated over time in the hot sun and wind. But others had rock buildings that still stand.

Generally, the forts are built in a rectangle around large parade grounds: enlisted men's barracks on one long side; officers' quarters on the other; and headquarters, hospital, and other public buildings at the short end or near it.

Wind Power

Travelers unaccustomed to miles and miles of windy, empty space may not be familiar with wind turbines, a source of clean power. Those are the big towers topped with three blades that you'll see for miles and miles in the Albany/Abilene/San Angelo area, and in other parts of West Texas as well. (In Lubbock, the **Wind Power Center** lets you walk right up to one.) The big, three-bladed turbines dotting the landscape in a grid pattern generate electricity for power companies, which sell it.

Huge windfarms produce electricity outside Abilene and elsehwere in West Texas.

frequented the saloons, and so did soldiers, buffalo hunters, cowboys, ranchers, and vigilantes. The town grew slowly until the railroad came in 1881, and then it began to prosper. But its real heyday came after oil was discovered in the early 1900s. The Cook Oil Field northwest of town produced 1,000 barrels a day (current crude oil prices per barrel fluctuate around $75–80 today, to give you an idea of the profitability).

The town of about 2,000 people (down from 6,000 in 1930) and nearby Fort Griffin, now a state park, are a long afternoon's worth of exploring, and are just under an hour from Abilene.

To See and Do

Old Jail Art Center (325-762-2269; www.theoldjailartcenter.com), 201 S. 2nd. Open 10–5 Tuesday through Saturday, 2–5 Sunday; closed Monday. The big, square limestone building cost $9,000 in 1877, outraging the taxpayers. Its simple front belies what's inside now. More than 2,100 works are in the museum's permanent collection, which includes prints, drawings, and paintings by Renoir, Klee, Modigliani, Picasso, and Miro. With additions over the years, the museum has grown to about 15,000 square feet. Free.

Fort Griffin State Historic Site (325-762-3592; www.visitfortgriffin.com), 1701 North US 283, 14 miles north of Albany. Open 8–5 daily except holidays; extended hours Memorial Day to Labor Day are 8–8 Thursday through Saturday. One of a line of forts that today make up the Texas Forts Trail, what remains of Fort Griffith today is ruins on property that is home to part of the Texas Longhorn herd. Few buildings were constructed of long-lasting stone, so a visit is outdoors-oriented, with campsites, shade trees, catfishing in the Clear Fork of the Brazos, and nature trails. Fort Griffin is also the site of one of the region's biggest annual events, the Fandangle.

Local Flavors

Taste of the town—restaurants, cafés, bars, bistros, etc.

EATING OUT

Los Cazadores (325-762-3362), 233 N. Main Street, Albany. Open 6 AM–9 PM Monday through Saturday. The fare here is less Tex-Mex and more a blend of Mexican and New Mexican. That means you're more likely to get fiery salsa with green chiles, and find chiles rellenos on the menu. The atmosphere is simple, but my cheese enchiladas were rich and spicy with chile and the tortilla chips were freshly fried, hot and crispy. Inexpensive.

Pick Your Spot

Best places to stay in and around Albany

Stasney's Cook Ranch (888-762-2999; www.stasneyscookranch.com), Ranch office, 441 S. 2nd Street, Albany, office open 8 AM–5 PM. Here is an authentic Texas ranch experience—room enough for a family or a crowd, nothing fancy, and nothing fancy needed to enjoy miles and miles of peaceful prairie and infinite starry skies. The working cattle ranch with accommodations for a family or a crowd is popular for weddings and reunions, or people who just want to get away, says ranch manager Lance Thomas. Things to do besides just being here include canoeing, fishing, hunting, and touring the wind turbine farm, a large chunk of which is located on ranch property. The original ranch house sleeps 15 to 18. Smaller cabins made to resemble officers' quarters and named after forts in the area have front porches and spare, simple rooms with bits of military memorabilia. They're equipped with refrigerators, microwaves, and coffee pots. Pets can stay, but must be kept on a leash or in an outside kennel. Moderate.

Selective Shopping

Lynch Line (325-762-2212), 328 South 2nd, Albany. This bookstore across the street from the Shackelford County Courthouse is a treasure chest of Texas books and maps not found in the big chain bookstores. And because of its location near the courthouse, the employees have gotten used to being a source for directions around town, if you need them. Stopping here is a must for history buffs.

Special Events

June

Fort Griffin Fandangle (325-762-3838; www.fortgriffinfandangle .com), Office, #2 Railroad Street, Albany. It's hard to talk to somebody in Albany for longer than five minutes without being invited to come back in June for the Fandangle, billed as Texas's largest outdoor musical. Written and directed first by an Albany native in 1938, it's a town project with 400 cast and crew members. The show, which commemorates the role Fort Griffin played in Texas history, draws some 10,000 people each year. The Fandangle performances are the last two weekends in June. Tickets are $7–20.

Fort Worth to Abilene via Granbury, Glen Rose, Hico, and Dublin

These towns are more used to tourists, so the dining and shopping choices are wider. The tradeoffs are that the route is more complicated, and the scenery in places is less interesting. Hico and Glen Rose are popular areas with weekending Dallas–Fort Worth residents, who bring the family to see Fossil Rim wildlife park.

You'll need to travel from Fort Worth down US 377 to Granbury; take TX 144 to Glen Rose; US 67 and then TX 220 to Hico; TX 6 to Dublin; then continue up TX 6 to I-20 and on to Abilene.

Wineries

The general area covered in this chapter is sprinkled with tiny wineries that are open for tastings and that plan regular gatherings. The folks at **www .wayoutwineries.org** have it all mapped out for you with addresses and contact information. They also plan road trips.

Granbury

A pretty, small city on a lake, Granbury's historic town square has a good selection of shops and restaurants. It makes a fine day trip from the DFW area, and should be a stop on a trip through the area.

To See and Do

Granbury Ghosts and Legends Tour (817-559-0849), 7 and 9:15 PM Friday and Saturday. Ghosts, including a lady in red and John Wilkes Booth (legend and conspiracy theorists have it that he was in a sort of witness protection program in Granbury), are part of the scary evening. Adults, $10; children, $7.

Granbury State Historical Cemetery (800-950-2212), 801 North Houston Street. The outlaw Jesse James is buried here. Free.

Granbury Opera House (800-547-4697; www.granburyoperahouse.net), 133 East Pearl Street. Musicals, plays, and melodramas are staged year-round at the restored 1886 building. Tickets from $25 (minus $1 for seniors and students, ½ price for children under 12).

Hood County Jail and Museum (817-573-5135), 208 North Crockett. Usually open 1–4 Saturday and Sunday. Old Western jail built in 1885 with a cellblock and a hanging tower. Adults, $2; children under 10, $1; under 10, free.

Brazos Drive-In Theater (817-573-1311; www.thebrazos.com), 1800 West Pearl Street. Open Friday and Saturday only. Only about 10 drive-ins remain in Texas, this one shows mostly family fare. Call for what's showing. Tickets $18/carload.

Don't Miss

Granbury State Historical Cemetery

Lake Granbury

The historic town square and courthouse

OUTDOORS

Boating, Fishing, Swimming, Water Sports

Lake Granbury (888-922-6272; www.brazos.org). There are five public access areas with boat ramps for fishing and picnics, plus primitive camping at four parks. One of Granbury's nicest features is its City Beach (817-573-5548; www.granburytx.com) right in town at 623 E. Pearl Street—many

Texas lakes require a long drive over a park road to get to a swimming beach, if there is one. Here, they've built tiki huts for shade, plus a pavilion and children's water features.

Golf

An increasingly popular retirement destination, Granbury had, at last count, seven golf courses. Details, www.granburytx.com.

Pick Your Spot

Best places to stay in and around Granbury

Inn on Lake Granbury (877-573-0046; www.innonlakegranbury .com), 205 West Doyle Street. This lakeside bed and breakfast inn combines fine dining options with Texas traditional rooms or more modern suites. Amenities in some rooms include heated floors and body jets in the shower. Expensive.

Nutt Hotel (817-279-1206; www.nutt-hotel.com), 119 E. Bridge Street. A cute historic (1893) hotel on the square, with its rooms the Nutt offers free WiFi and breakfast at the fine-dining Nutt Shell Eatery. Inexpensive.

Local Flavors

Taste of the town—restaurants, cafés, bars, bistros, etc.

EATING OUT

Babe's Chicken Dinner House (817-573-9777; www.babeschicken .com), 114 West Pearl Street. Open 11–2 and 5–9 for lunch and dinner Monday through Friday and 11–9 Saturday and Sunday. Diners here and at the other locations of this regional chain line up outside regularly to wait for tables groaning with crispy fried chicken served family-style. The line usually moves pretty quickly, so if you're a fried chicken aficionado it's worth the wait. Meals include a full dinner including sides and dessert. Moderate.

Nutshell Eatery & Bakery (817-279-8989), 137 E. Pearl Street. Open Sunday through Thursday 7–5, Friday and Saturday 7–8:30. Fans of this little spot enjoy the breakfasts and the burgers. A simple salad also is well done here. Moderate to expensive.

Stringfellow's Casual Dining (817-573-6262; www.granburyrest aurants.com), 101 E. Pearl Street. Open 11–9 Thursday through Sunday. A convenient pit stop on the square. Stringfellows serves casual sandwiches and salads at lunchtime, and brings out a fine-dining menu with steak and chops at night. Moderate to expensive.

Selective Shopping

A leisurely stroll around the square will net you plenty of country cute, a souvenir or two, and ice cream or lemonade. Here are some more possibilities.

Books On The Square (817-573-9672), 119 East Bridge Street. Call for hours. An independent bookseller, they stock a good selection of Texas history and literature here, as well as the usual mainstream fare and children's books.

Brazos Moon Antiques and Uniques (817-579-8202; www.brazosmoon .com), 124 N. Houston. Call for hours. This is an antiques-mall-style store, with more than a dozen dealers' wares on display, and everything from lamps to firearms. Shoppers with an eye for style and patience will enjoy it.

Glen Rose

It's all about the dinosaurs and the zebras and the giraffes in this town where the Paluxy River converges with the Brazos. Nearby is Dinosaur Valley State Park (254-897-4588; www.tpwd.state.tx.us/spdest/findadest/ parks/dinosaur_valley). Follow signs off US 67 for 4 miles west of Glen Rose to see some of the best-preserved dinosaur tracks in the world, as well as two gigantic fiberglass model dinos. The tracks are in the riverbed, so call ahead to check conditions. Adults, $5, 12 and under free.

The exotic and not-extinct critters are at Fossil Rim Wildlife Center (254-897-2960; www.fossilrim.org). Open 8:30–5:30 March 13 through September 30 and 8:30–4:30 October 1–October 31. Purchase feed and drive slowly through this park without fences. You can expect surprises, such as a giraffe sticking his head in your car, if you're lucky. The non-profit park also has free-ranging zebra, oryx, and more. An important note for those with pets: They are not permitted anywhere on the premises, even in your car. There are veterinarians in Glen Rose who will board them. The pricing fluctuates depending on season and day of the week, but basically you're looking at around $20 adults, $17 seniors, $14 ages 3–11, and free for 2 and under during peak season, less from November to February. After a full day at the park, you can stay in rustic cabins and get up the next day to float, canoe, or fish the Paluxy. A wide variety of cabins is listed at www.glenrose texas.net.

For an upscale experience, head to Rough Creek Lodge (800-864-4705; www.roughcreek.com), a beautiful resort well off the beaten path at 5165 FM 2013. Often a destination for high-end Dallas business retreats, the lodge offers hunting, fishing, kayaking, tennis, disc golf, horseback riding, and more. The fine-dining restaurant is consistently rated one of the best in the state, with offerings such as pheasant ravioli and grilled Texas quail. Rates include a three-course dinner and breakfast. Very expensive.

Hico

For years the first thing anyone said when they heard Hico was, "Isn't that where that Billy the Kid guy is?" A fellow in town named Brushy Bill Roberts claimed he really was the kid. You can decide for yourself after taking a look at the Billy the Kid Museum (800-361-4426; billythekid museum.com), 114 N. Pecan Street. Open 10–4 Monday through Saturday and 1–4 Sunday.

An influx of Austin store owners made Hico something of a small-town shopping mecca for a few years, and while some of those closed, others are here for the long haul. One is the Western Otter (254-796-4775; www .westernotter.com), so named because it's in the former Western Auto store at 118 N. Pecan Street. The fun store carries vintage cowboy boots, retro toys, Texana, and more.

It's worth saving your appetite for eating in Hico at the Koffee Kup (254-796-4839; www.koffeekupfamilyrestaurant.com), 300 W. 2nd, known all over Texas for its amazing, sky-high cream pies and giant, crispy onion rings. The burgers are good, too, and you'll be rubbing shoulders with the townspeople in the café, open daily 6:30 AM–9:30 PM. Inexpensive. If you'd rather have Tex-Mex, Jersey Lilly's (254-796-0999), 128 North Pecan Street, has been serving it up here for a long time; moderate.

Should you have a sweet tooth, stop in at Wiseman House (254-796-2828; www.wisemanhousechocolates.com), 106 South Pecan Street, for fancy, handmade truffles in such flavors as apricot and dark chocolate coconut, or peanut-butter meltaways.

Dublin

There's really only one reason to stop in Dublin, but it's a good one: The Dublin Dr Pepper Museum (254-445-3939; www.dublindrpepper.com), 105 East Elm Street. The town is about 70 miles southwest of Fort Worth, at the intersection of TX 377/67 and TX 6. It's impossible to miss the plant and museum—park on the brick street.

Larger high-end groceries like Central Market in the cities have started to carry Dublin Dr Pepper, but for a long time this was one of the only sources. Before online ordering, Texans would make the drive to pick up a supply. What's so special about it? The plant—built in 1891 and the oldest in the world—still uses cane sugar instead of corn sweeteners.

The Dublin Dr Pepper Factory Museum is a fun way to spend a couple of hours.

Dr Pepper was invented in 1885 by a pharmacist up the road in Waco who wanted to duplicate the blend of smells at the soda fountain in just one drink. His concoction—named after the father of a girl he once loved—proved popular in Texas, but really took off nationwide after exposure at the 1904 World's Fair in St. Louis.

Much later, in the 1990s, other plants began to use corn sweeteners because of cost, but the Dublin plant owner refused to make the change and still sticks with Imperial Pure Cane Sugar.

Personally, I can tell the difference—less aftertaste, for one thing. But you can judge for yourself. The small bottling plant still is in operation, and tours go on eight times a day whether it's running or not. You see how the sweet elixir is bottled, and take a look at quality control samples while you drink a bottle. The tour also includes the museum, where the story of Sweet Peggy Pepper is explained, along with a detailed account of the history.

At the small gift shop, you can buy everything Dr Pepper and then eat sandwiches and sample soda, shakes, malts, sundaes, etc. at the soda fountain. Adults, $2.50; seniors and kids older than 6, $2; under 6 free.

A Note about Stephenville

Both the routes to Abilene outlined here miss Stephenville, at about 18,000 people, the largest city in the area—not because there's anything particularly wrong with it, but because the other drives take you straight through the scenic parts of the region that have the most unusual and engaging attractions.

Should you need serious medical attention, a national chain pharmacy, a big-box discount store, auto parts, etc., Stephenville is the place to go on the southern route between Fort Worth and Abilene.

The heart of Stephenville is Tarleton State University, founded in 1899, with an enrollment of about 10,000 students. A safe small city, it's been called the Cowboy Capital of Texas (famed rodeo champion Ty Murray lives here) and named one of the best small cities in Texas to live in.

Special Events

May

Wine and Food Festival (www .hico-tx.com). A chance to try ranch-fed beef and other local foods.

The Texas Steak Cook-off (www.texassteakcookoff.com). Chefs cook for charity.

FORT WORTH TO ABILENE AND SAN ANGELO

Abilene

The freight train and its lonesome whistle blow right through the middle of Abilene, county seat of Taylor County, a reminder that the railroad is as much a part of this small city's roots as the cattle. And roots are important to people here in Taylor County. A visit to this city of about 117,063 feels a little like a trip back in time, with the general emphasis on history at the attractions, and a downtown that still has locally owned office-supply stores.

Frontier Texas! in Abilene is a must-see attraction for learning about the area's history and peoples.

Whether you're a history buff or not, it's worth stopping in Abilene to

Driving Tour

If you're a history fan, it's well worth contacting the Abilene Chamber of Commerce ahead of time to purchase their Windshield Tour CDs. The narratives give you historical stops and details along the way from Fort Worth to Abilene and back.

see Frontier Texas!, with its holographic images of period actors narrating true stories about the early years. The 45-minute experience is a good foundation for what you'll see in the area, and gives you a healthy appreciation for what it took to live here.

Cattlemen and business leaders created Abilene out of thin air when the railroad came in the 1880s. The logical choice for the tracks was Buffalo Gap, then the county seat. But the group of ranchers and others successfully argued to have the tracks laid farther north, on their property. They promised a new city, and named it Abilene after the cattle town in Kansas. The Texas and Pacific, faced with promoting a route through a town that didn't quite exist yet, called it the Future Great City of West Texas. The population in 1890 was 3,194. Abilene was a wild frontier town, but the conservative, churchgoing ethos that prevails today developed early on. The city successfully sought colleges run by churches—what is now Hardin-Simmons University was established by the Baptist church in 1891; what is now Abilene Christian University was established by members of the Churches of Christ in 1906; and the Methodist McMurry University opened in 1923. Saloons were abolished in 1903, and the city remained dry until 1978.

You'll overhear a good deal of conservative political talk, see a fair amount of big hair, find plenty of churches, and run across few saloons. As far as outdoor recreation, remember it's still dry here, climate-wise— the annual rainfall in a good year is just a little over 23 inches—so the sun is out most of the time. Water recreation is on lakes—four were excavated when the city began to provide municipal water. Fort Phantom Hill Reservoir and Lake Abilene at Abilene State Park are popular with birders.

Guidance

The Visitors Center in the old train depot, at 1101 N. 1st Street (325-727-7704; www.abilenevisitors.com), is a good starting point for a walk downtown.

Medical Emergencies

Hendrick Health System (325-670-2000; www.hendrickhealth.org), 1900 Pine Street, and Abilene Regional Medical Center (325-695-9900; www.abileneregional.com) on US 83. Of course, in an emergency, dial 911.

To See and Do

Frontier Texas! (325-437-2800; www.frontiertexas.com), 625 N. 1st. Open 9 AM–6 PM Monday through Saturday, 1–5 PM Sunday. Holographic images of cowboys, Indians, buffalo hunters, pioneer women, and other historic characters pop up as you walk, guiding visitors through a history of West Texas, past exhibits of buffalo, wagons, and other historically accurate parts of daily life in those hardscrabble times. The grand finale is a short theater-in-the-round production complete with thunder, lightning, and fireflies. Small children who are afraid of the dark may not fare well here—

much of the program is under muted light or in the dark, and the characters can be a little surprising. It's an information-packed technological marvel, though, and really does bring history to life in an engaging way. In the visitors' center/gift shop, Texas books and Texana are on sale. Adults, $8; 60 and older and military, $6; students and teachers with ID, $5; ages 3–12 $4; free for children under 3.

The Grace Museum (325-673-4587; www.thegracemuseum.org), 102 Cypress Street. Open 10 AM–5 PM Tuesday through Saturday, and until 8 PM Thursdays. The Grace began life as a hotel for train travelers right across the street from the depot. Parts of life from those days are re-created in the history museum, one of three housed in the landmark building. Mallouf's Boot Shop is a comprehensive re-creation of a 1940s bootmaker's

Visitors to Frontier Texas! in Abilene can relax here before or after seeing the attraction.

workspace, with everything you could possibly want to know about bootmaking. Furnished period rooms show the evolution of living rooms and kitchens in four scenes from 1910 to 1948. A total of five galleries hold rotating exhibits and collections of contemporary works, as well as a small but varied permanent collection. The children's museum has interactive exhibits and a toddler room. Adults $6; seniors, students, military, $5; ages

See how West Texans lived in the early days at the Grace Museum.

4–12, $3; free for ages 3 and younger. Admission is free 5 PM–8 PM Thursdays.

National Center for Children's Illustrated Literature (325-673-4586; www.nccil.org), 102 Cedar Street. Open 10 AM–4 PM Tuesday through Saturday. Both parents and children will have fun and learn about books here. The center collaborates with award-winning illustrators of children's books to line the walls of its huge space with framed works, explanations by the artists of how they developed the books, and copies of the books themselves. For example, when I was there, an exhibition of Chris Raschka's works explained how he was inspired to create lovely kids' books based on works by jazz composers such as Charlie Parker and John Coltrane. Free.

Abilene Zoo (325-676-6085; www.abilenetx.com/zoo), 2070 Zoo Lane, Nelson Park, TX 36 and Loop 322. Open 9–5 daily most of the year; summer hours on Thursdays, Memorial Day through Labor Day, are 9–9. A small zoo, the big attraction here is being able to feed giraffes. Adults, $4; seniors and ages 3–12, $3; under 3 free.

The Center for Contemporary Arts (325-677-8389; www.center-arts.com), 220 Cypress. Open 11–5 Tuesday through Saturday. Walk through four galleries full of contemporary paintings and sculpture, many for sale at accessible prices. The nonprofit center also houses 10 working artists' studios, and coordinates Abilene's ArtWalk, the second Thursday of each month. The event includes street performances and live entertainment as well as exhibits. Free.

12th Armored Division Memorial Museum (325-677-6515; www.12th armoredmuseum.com), 1289 N. 2nd Street. Open 10–5 Tuesday through Saturday. The 12th Armored Division was based at Camp Barkeley near Abilene. World War II buffs will want to look over the memorabilia and equipment. The teaching museum provides academic access to historical items. Adults, $3; ages 7–12, $1; 6 and under, free.

The National WASP WWII Museum

(325-235-0099; www.wasp museum.org), off Loop 170 in Sweetwater, an hour east of Abilene. Open 1–5 Wednesday through Saturday, the museum pays tribute to Women's Airforce Service Pilots, who served in World War II. More than 25,000 women applied to become a WASP in 1942, but only 1,830 were accepted, and 1,074 graduated. During the program's two short years, 38 died in training or while flying in service.

Test-pilot Nancy Harkness Love was instrumental in starting the WASP.

OUTDOORS

Abilene State Park (325-572-3204; www.tpwd.state.tx.us/spdest/findadest/parks/abilene), 150 Park Road 32, Tuscola, TX. Originally built by the Civilian Conservation Corps in the 1930s, this 529-acre park that includes Lake Abilene is popular with birders now. Part of the official state Longhorn herd lives here, as does one buffalo. But the biggest draw may be the shade—picnic areas, campsites, and RV sites are situated beneath tall pecan and oak trees. The original CCC swimming pool is open in the summers, and yurts—one ADA-compliant and all equipped with beds and microwaves—are available for rental. Kids can also fish and wade in the pond. Adults, $4; 12 and under free.

Pick Your Spot

Best places to stay in and around Abilene

Sayles Ranch Guesthouses (325-669-6856, www.saylesranch.com), 1001 Sayles Boulevard. Not a ranch but guesthouses in one of Abilene's finest old neighborhoods, these are on a busy thoroughfare highly

Sayles Ranch is a series of guesthouses in Abilene. This one has a Ralph Lauren feel.

accessible to both downtown and the universities. The largest, Sayles Ranch, has three bedrooms, two baths; Falling Star is a three-bedroom, two-bath Craftsman-style cottage; The Hideout sleeps two; Cabin Fever is a two-bedroom one-bath carriage house behind Browder's private home. Expensive to very expensive for the larger cottages, but they all hold more than two people.

Local Flavors

Taste of the town—restaurants, cafés, bars, bistros, etc.

EATING OUT

Cypress Street Station (325-676-DINE [3463]; www.cypress-street .com), 158 Cypress Street, Abilene. Open 11 AM–2 PM weekdays, and 4 PM UNTIL EVERYONE GOES HOME; 11 AM Saturday UNTIL EVERYONE GOES HOME. A fairly new addition to downtown and the only brew pub in Abilene, Cypress Street has the most comprehensive menu you'll find downtown—soups, salads, pasta, pizza, sandwiches, steaks. The tortilla soup and a house salad were simple and fresh and the service attentive. This is the go-to restaurant for the downtown lunch crowd. The beer selection ranges from Texas ales and beers to foreign wheaten ales and beers. Beer connoisseurs can try the brews in flights. Inexpensive to moderate.

La Popular Bakery and Café (325-672-2670), main location at 1533 Pine Street, Abilene. Besides the main location on Pine, La Popular has a Quick Stop at 3102 S. 14th Street, and its Burrito Stop at 3001 S. Treadway Boulevard. Think soft and flaky homemade flour tortillas wrapped around juicy chunks of meat simmered in its own juice for $1.65 apiece and you'll have one of the reasons La Popular lives up to its name. The main location also serves Mexican pastries. Inexpensive.

Lytle Land and Cattle Co. (325-677-1925; www.lytlelandand cattle.com), 1150 E. S. 11th, on the corner of Judge Ely and S. 11th, a few blocks from the Abilene Zoo. Open 11 AM–10 PM Sunday through Thursday; 11–11 Friday and Saturday. It's a typical Texas non-chain steakhouse: Western decor and atmosphere, varied menu from salads to steaks to seafood. Moderate to expensive. Owner Sharon Riley also has a barbecue restaurant, Sharon's Barbecue (325-672-2229; sharonsbarbeque.com/), at 849 E. US 80.

Selective Shopping

Relics (325-670-9282; www.relics home.com), 1292 N. 1st Street. A 1920s auto-body shop and service station is a cool space for Fair Trade imports crafted by artisans from Mexico and elsewhere: hand-blown glassware, totes fashioned from repurposed burlap sacks, Talavera pottery and tiles, clever little rings made of buttons. Be sure to go upstairs to the warehouse filled with bargains on pottery, wrought iron, furniture, and more. A small cantina serves frozen margaritas to shoppers on Saturday.

Under One Roof (325-673-1309), 244 Pine Street, Abilene. A slew of shopkeepers have their wares under the one roof, selling everything from exquisite hand-blown martini glasses to vintage clothing to I Love Lucy memorabilia. Like most of these large mini-mall arrangements, finding a treasure is a time-consuming affair. If you're not the type to enjoy lots of looking through what you don't want in order to find something you do, this won't be your store.

Texas Star Trading (325-672-9696; www.texasstartrading.com), 174 Cypress Street. This is Texana at its finest—Texas books written by Texas authors, including store owner Glenn Dromgoole; natural soaps and candles made in the state; and the requisite souvenirs like Texas shot glasses, or T-shirts that read FIXIN' TO . . . THE STATE VERB OF TEXAS. If the book selection is overwhelming, look for Dromgoole's list of 10 must-have selections—a books columnist for the Abilene Reporter-News, he's well-versed in the state's wordsmiths as well as its history.

Relics is a fun shop in Abilene with everything from jewelry to furniture.

Jordan Taylor and Co. (325-672-9792; www.jordantaylorandco.com), 201 Walnut Street. This is the kind of furniture store I can remember going into with my mom as a child—locally owned, with tons of pricey pieces arranged throughout a huge building. But travelers will find a few gifts, candles, and the like, at the front section of the store near the entry.

Vletas (800-725-6933; www.candies byvletas.com), R.E.A. Baggage Depot, 1201 N. 1st Street. The word *chocolate* keeps screaming at you every time you reach 1st Street on a walk downtown. The source, up on the hill, is this candymaking operation started in 1912 by two brothers from Greece. You will not regret climbing the steps. Pretty chocolate truffles, fudge, divinity, and sugar-free candies all made on the premises are worth the walk. Inexpensive to expensive, depending on your willpower.

5D Western Hats and Leather (325-673-9000; www.5dhats.com), 3742 A Butternut. You can get a cowboy hat made just for you here, but it won't be cheap—they run from $200 to $475. 5D also sells hand-tooled leather goods, such as cell-phone holders, notebooks, and the like.

Luskey's/Ryon's Western Stores (325-793-9953; www.luskeys.com), 3402 Catclaw. In business since 1919, and with five Texas locations (corporate offices are in Abilene), Luskey's/Ryon's can create custom boots for you, and saddles, too, if you're in the market. They carry all the big boot brands—Lucchese, Anderson Bean, Tony Lama, etc.—in all kinds of hides, colors, and sizes. Or, if you want real customization, they'll inlay your logo or brand into a pair of Luskey's/Ryon's own brand for around $675.

James Leddy Boots (325-788-7811), 1602 North Treadaway. James Leddy was one of the most famous bootmakers in Texas, as was his father before him. Leddy died in 2003, but his wife and children are continuing the tradition. These are serious custom boots—your foot is hand-measured, and the boots are built from scratch just for you. Or, for Texas governors, or country singers such as George Jones, Buck Owens, and Jerry Lee Lewis. The boot workshop is in full view. Prices can range into five figures.

Bell Custom-Made Boots & Repair (325-677-0632), 2118 North Tread-away. Alan Bell was a friend of James Leddy, and he still maintains a work-shop near the Leddy operation. The turnaround time for a pair of these babies is about 16 months. Prices can range into the thousands.

Lankford's Texas Mesquite and Cedar Products (325-670-9888; www .mesquite-lumber.com). Mesquite, considered a nuisance by farmers trying to clear land, but used as shelter by Native Americans in earlier times, has become a chic furniture statement, particularly in Southwest decor. The rich auburn wood is gnarled with intricate grain. Lankford's makes furni-ture, lamps, mantels, and the like.

Special Events

May

Western Heritage Classic Ranch Rodeo (www.westernheritage classic.com). This three-day event in May of each year is much more than a rodeo. It began in 1985 with five events: team roping, team penning, bronc riding, wild cow milking, and calf branding. Now the activities include all those plus a children's rodeo, cowboy poets, vendors, a bit and spur show, Western artisans, horse clin-ics, a parade, and a chuck wagon cookoff, among other things.

Buffalo Gap

Bypassed by the railroad and then dethroned as county seat of Taylor County by Abilene, little Buffalo Gap has emerged as a dining destination known all over Texas because of Perini Ranch Steakhouse (800-367-1721; www.periniranch.com), 3002 Farm-to-Market 89. Open for dinner Tuesday through Sunday; lunch Friday through Sunday. Wealthy ranchers have been known to fly private planes to the area to dine here, and the ranch also has well-appointed cabins for guests who want to relax for a few days. The beef is prepared as it should be—seasoned simply, seared on the outside, and melt-in-your mouth delicious on the inside. Make plans to eat here early, and call for reservations—they're generally com-pletely booked on weekend evenings. Expensive. At Perini Ranch Guest Quarters (800-367-1721; www.periniranch.com), 3002 Farm-to-Market 89, two houses are a comfortable but luxe blend of antique art and quilts with modern amenities like high-def TV. The Main House sleeps five; the Camp House sleeps three. Expensive, but bear in mind the number of

The interiors are inviting at the Perini Ranch Guest Quarters.

people that will fit. WiFi is available at both, and the rates include continental breakfast.

While you're in town, check out Buffalo Gap Historic Village (325-572-3365; www.buffalogap.com), 133 N. William. Hours from Memorial Day to Labor Day are 10–6 Monday through Saturday and noon–6 Sunday. Otherwise, hours are 10–5 Monday through Saturday, noon–5 Sunday. Expect to spend around 45 minutes, depending on crowds, at a complete village fashioned from historic buildings from the 1800s, 1905, and 1925. Adults, $7; 65 and older and military, $6; students, $4; 5 and under, free.

Lodging nearby is The Parsonage (325-572-3365; www.buffalogapvillage .com/parsonage), 426 North Street, Buffalo Gap. It's a three-bedroom, two-bath 1920s house decorated with antiques but providing conveniences like a washer and dryer and cable television. Moderate.

Stop at Buffalo Gap Pottery and see if the owner will demonstrate his special egg cooker.

Finally, stop in at Buffalo Gap Pottery (325-572-5056), 534 Vine Street. Open daily. Proprietors and potters George and Wanda Holland have filled their small gallery and retail space with stoneware and raku pottery.

Special Events

April

Buffalo Gap Wine & Food Summit (www.buffalogapsummit .com). Names as big as Jacques Pepin have appeared at this annual April event at Perini Ranch.

San Angelo

This city divided by the Concho River is a lively, colorful counterpoint to neighboring Abilene's more serious, unchanging feel. It lies nearly on the edge of the Hill Country, and the Austin influence is tangible: live music, funky shops, a thriving arts community.

Angelo State University draws about 6,000 students from here to Fort Worth and beyond, many of them first-generation college students with scholarships from a foundation set up by an oilman in the '70s. The university was among 371 named best in the nation by *The Princeton Review* in 2010.

The city began in 1867 with the establishment of Fort Concho, and a great deal of the fort still stands, one of the main attractions to visit. The town grew up alongside the fort as merchants set up businesses to support it. The military is still a key player in San Angelo—Goodfellow Air Force Base is its largest employer. The painted sheep as public art and sheep T-shirts you'll see on occasion are here because sheep growers contribute significantly to the economy.

Like Abilene, it's not a destination city but a good stop in Central West Texas for history, a little shopping and, if you're staying overnight in San Angelo, some live music. Check out the Concho pearl at area jewelry stores—early Spanish explorers named the river Concho, the word for shell in Spanish, because of the pink and purple "pearls" produced by mussels in area waterways.

Guidance

The soaring Visitors Center building at 418 W. Avenue B is open 9–5 weekdays; 10–5 Saturday; noon–4 Sunday. Phone or Web: 800-375-1206; www.visitsanangelo.org.

Call 911 in an emergency. Otherwise, Shannon Medical Center (325-653-6741; www.shannonhealth.com), 120 East Harris Street; and San Angelo Community Medical Center (325-949-9511; www.sacmc.com), 3501 Knickerbocker Road.

To See and Do

Fort Concho National Historic Landmark (325-481-2646; www.fortconcho.com), 630 S. Oakes Street. Open 9–5 Monday through Saturday; 1–5 Sunday. Twenty-three original buildings from the 1800s still line the parade grounds, including enlisted men's barracks where soldiers lived, a chapel where they worshipped, the post headquarters, the hospital, and officers' quarters. The interiors are roped off so visitors can't tramp through them, but there's still plenty to see, including an exhibit of cannons and other relics of 19th-century soldiering, plus the Museum of Telephony, with antique telephones and directories. Special events take place all year, including the National Cavalry Competition in September. Self-guided tours, adults $3; seniors and military, $2; children 6–17, $1.50; 6 and under, free. Guided tours are Tuesday through Friday every hour on the half-hour from 10:30 to 3:30: adults, $5; seniors and military, $4; children 6–17, $3; 6 and younger, free.

San Angelo Museum of Fine Arts (325-653-3333; www.samfa.org), 1 Love Street. Open 10–4 Tuesday through Saturday; 1–4 Sunday. Closed Monday, major holidays, and between exhibits. At first glance, visitors will wonder whether the saddle-shaped roof of this striking contemporary building is intended to evoke cowboy heritage, or perhaps a covered wagon. It's not. The original design by New York architects included a peaked roof so that it would follow the slope of the land and stand out over other structures in the area; a local committee modified it to its current rounded shape. The permanent collection focuses on contemporary ceramic art, American painting and sculpture, and Mexican and Mexican American art from all eras. Adults, $2; military, Angelo State and San Angelo students, free; seniors, children 12 and under, $1.

Alleyscapes (800-375-1206; www.visitsanangelo.org). Various locations. More than 30 local artists have turned alleys into artspaces using old windows, doors, and the sides of buildings as canvases. The works range from a folk art cityscape to more intimate portraits to patriotic. They're a little hard to find—no signs point the way—but worth the effort. Paintbrush Alley, also called Alley Flats, is in the alley between Twohig and Concho Streets and from Irving to Chadbourne Streets. Secret Garden is between the Wells Fargo Bank building and the Farmers Insurance building at 31 W. Beauregard. Art Opens Doors is at 215 S. Oakes, in the alley between the Federal building and JB Automotive. Free.

Chicken Farm Art Center (325-653-4936; www.chickenfarmartcenter.com), 2505 Martin Luther King Drive. Open 9 AM–5 PM Tuesday through Saturday. You can't help but think of the 1960s upon seeing this laid-back compound, which includes spaces for some 15 artists and artisans (painters, potters, carvers, and blacksmiths who work in iron); a bed-and-breakfast inn; and a restaurant. Started in 1971, the Chicken Farm bills itself as THE BEST LITTLE OLD ART CENTER IN WEST TEXAS. A regular event on the first Saturday of the month includes live acoustic music, blacksmith demonstrations, and free clay for kids.

Historic Orient-Santa Fe Depot and Railway Museum of San Angelo (325-486-2140; www.railwaymuseumsanangelo.homestead.com), 703 S. Chadbourne Street. Open Saturdays only, 10–4. Railroad buffs will want to stop in and see lanterns, track hand tools, silverware used in luxury dining cars, and more, all housed in an old depot. The museum also has two locomotives, a caboose, and a boxcar. Free.

Miss Hattie's Bordello Museum (325-653-0112; www.misshatties.com), 18½ E. Concho. Tours are at the top of the hour from 1–4 Tuesday through Thursday. Velvet drapes and lace curtains on the windows, and bedrooms named after the working women provide a glimpse into a turn-of-the-century bordello that operated until the Texas Rangers closed it down in 1946. Admission, $5.

OUTDOORS

San Angelo State Park (325-949-4757; www.tpwd.state.tx.us/spdest/find adest/parks/san_angelo). More than 7,000 acres on the shores of O. C. Fisher Reservoir, much of it undeveloped, the state park is a place for camping, hiking, mountain biking, and horseback riding. The lake also is open to swimmers (at your own risk, wear shoes if the lake level is low because the bottom is not considered safe), fishers, and boaters. Other uses of the park include an orienteering course, as well as hunting. Scheduled tours give visitors a look at Permian animal tracks, Indian petroglyphs, part of the Texas Longhorn herd, and bison. Stargazing parties are also a regular event. Adults, $3; 12 and under, free.

Pick Your Spot

Best places to stay in and
around San Angelo

The Blues Inn at Sealy Flats in San Angelo
has a historic feel.

Blues Inn at Sealy Flats (325-653-0437; www.sealyflats.com), 204 S. Oakes. Dennise and Rod Bridgeman created this blues-themed, three-suite boutique hotel from a columned brick home in the historic district and were still ironing out a few kinks when I stayed there (my morning cinnamon roll was in my room when I arrived, then disappeared, never to return). But character and live blues just steps away made up for any minor deficiencies. The overall feel is like some of New Orleans' smaller lodgings—exposed brick inside, wood floors and window frames. The suites have a kitschy-cool feel, with framed vinyl records and caricatures of artists. The owners, who live upstairs, greet you on arrival and usher you into one of three suites, and you get a key to the front door. Moderate.

Local Flavors

Taste of the town—restaurants,
cafés, bars, bistros, etc.

DINING OUT

River Terrace Restaurant (325-655-5491; www.theriverterrace.com), 800 W. Avenue D. Open for lunch Tuesday through Friday; dinner Thursday, Friday, and Saturday. Chef Earl Mulley, a Culinary Institute of America grad, prepares elegant entrees such as grilled salmon with chili glaze, and lamb persillade au jus at this restaurant with views of the Concho River. Lunch includes a buffet. Lunch, inexpensive; dinner expensive.

Silo House Restaurant (325-658-3333; innattheartcenter.com/rest), 2505 Martin Luther King Drive. Open for dinner Thursday through Saturday, reservations required. Located in the renovated grain silos at the center of the hippie-ish Chicken Farm Art Center, Silo House has two Culinary Institute of America graduates and just 10 tables. Chefs Liz and J. R. Matthews came to live near family after running a successful catering business in Austin. The prix fixe menu includes five courses with varying options and changes weekly. Moderate to expensive.

EATING OUT

The Diner at Sealy Flats (325-653-0437; www.sealyflats.com), 204 S. Oakes. Open for breakfast, lunch, and dinner daily. Right beside the Blues Inn at Sealy Flats, the diner fills up with guests who eat and drink their fill to live music in the evenings on an outdoor patio—you feel as if you've been transported to New Orleans. It's American diner fare. (Bridgeman says they close up by 9:30 PM in deference to guests trying to sleep at their adjoining hotel). Moderate.

Gil's Restaurant (325-655-5080), 837 Knickerbocker Road. Open for breakfast, lunch, and dinner Monday through Saturday, breakfast and lunch Sunday. Tasty Mexican food, well prepared at a low price and attentive service marked my breakfast at Gil's, one of many Mexican food restaurants here. I had migas, which came with fresh flour tortillas. My scrambled eggs were perfectly done and the mix of peppers, tortilla chips, and cheese was just right. On some days of the week entrees are half-price. Inexpensive.

El Hit de Oro (325-481-3130), 1724 S. Chadbourne Street. Open for lunch and dinner Monday through Friday. A Puerto Rican owner who worked in a family restaurant in Puerto Rico runs this small eatery, and gets ingredients from the island. Moderate.

The Grill (888-853-1378; www.thegrillsanangelo.com), 5769 Sherwood Way. Open daily for lunch and dinner. Expect combinations like steak and enchiladas, New Mexico burgers and tacos at this family-run restaurant. An open kitchen lets diners watch as their food is prepared. Moderate.

Entertainment

Being a college town, San Angelo is full of sports bars and pubs, many with live music. And because it's relatively close to Austin, artists from that scene make this a stop on their rounds. Checking out live music is worthwhile—you might just be listening to the next big thing. Or, you might not. Either way, you'll get an earful of something uniquely Texan. The local newspaper, the *San Angelo Standard-Times* stays on top of who's playing where. Check their listings either in print or at www.gosanangelo.com for addresses, artists, times, and cover charges.

Selective Shopping

This town is old-school enough to close shops on a Sunday, but laid-back enough to leave an upright piano out on the street for anyone to play. The downtown shops have everything from retro furnishings to Concho pearls.

House of Fifi Dubois (325-658-3434; www.fifidubois.com), 123 South Chadbourne Street. Open 11–6 Tuesday through Saturday. Mid-century modern fans will want to search through the goods here, but bear in mind this is not a boutique of carefully tailored selections. There's everything from shiny gold plush furniture to blue plastic chairs, not to mention lava lamps.

Shopping in San Angelo runs to the quirky. Here, a shoe chandelier beckons visitors to the Sassy Fox.

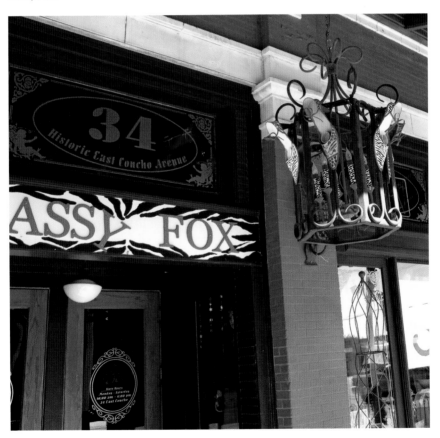

Legend Jewelers (325-653-0112; www.legendjewelers.com), 18 E. Concho Avenue. Open 9–6 Tuesday through Saturday. A fine jewelry store with an in-house designer, the store in one of San Angelo's main downtown shopping areas sells creations made from the lavender-hued Concho pearl.

Concho Valley Farmers Market (325-657-6901), El Paseo de Santa Angela. Open from 7:30 AM until it sells out, Tuesday, Thursday, and Saturday, June through fall. Fresh veggies and fruit, and more—look for healthy car-snacking food here, or put together a picnic for your next stop on the road.

Chicken Farm Art Center (325-653-4936; www.chickenfarmartcenter.com), 2505 Martin Luther King Drive. Open Tuesday through Saturday. This funky compound houses artists' studios (pottery is the most common), classrooms, two galleries, a bed and breakfast, and a restaurant. Studio hours vary. An open house takes place each November.

Public art is part of the scene in San Angelo.

Special Events

February

Annual Writers Conference. This annual daylong event at Angelo State University has readings and features a big-name author for the evening reading and book signing.

April

San Angelo Wine & Food Festival (www.sanangeloarts.com). Pulls in regionally famous chefs from Austin as well as locals, with events in the Museum of Fine Arts and other venues.

Texas Mesquite Art Festival (www.texasmesquiteassn.org). Mesquite, with its rich, reddish brown hue and elaborate grain around frequent knots, has become a popular high-end furniture choice in Southwestern decor. The festival includes furniture makers as well as craftspeople who produce smaller items like highly polished vases and lamps.

December

Christmas at Old Fort Concho (www.fortconcho.com/christmas). This draws some 20,000 people annually for chuck-wagon cooking, cowboy music and storytelling, Native American teepees, and historical reenactments.

3

Big Bend Country

FOR SOME TEXAS TRAVELERS, the Big Bend is the goal, the whole reason for an adventure west through a land called both The Big Empty and *despoblado* or inhospitable.

If you've never been here, you'll understand once you get to Big Bend National Park, to 800,000 acres of unspoiled Chihuahuan Desert at the bottom of Texas, a world of stunning, steep canyon walls plunging straight down to the Rio Grande, layers of deep blue mesas against bluer sky, hardy, adventurous souls who live by the rhythms of the desert . . . I could go on and on, and do in the Big Bend section of this chapter. There is no other place just like it and it's far too much to see on one, two, or even three trips. Many absorbing books have been written just about Big Bend National Park, and those should be your references for detailed study and planning. (See Bibliography.)

What I've done here is make a casual introduction, like sharing my favorite finds with friends who could come to love the place as much as I do.

But as absorbing as the park is, carefully consider your plans from Midland-Odessa onward. It's easy enough to grab a rental and hurtle south for three hours without stopping. You can zip down to the national park by heading south to Fort Stockton, then to Marathon and then the Big Bend in about three and a half hours. But if you take TX 17 to Balmorhea and make several stops along the way, you'll see some of Texas's most beautiful scenery.

Marfa, for example, is a magnet for world-class artists and their work. Davis Mountains State Park is a paradise for cyclists and can reward even

LEFT: The Rio Grande is an easy float through rugged canyons during some times of the year.

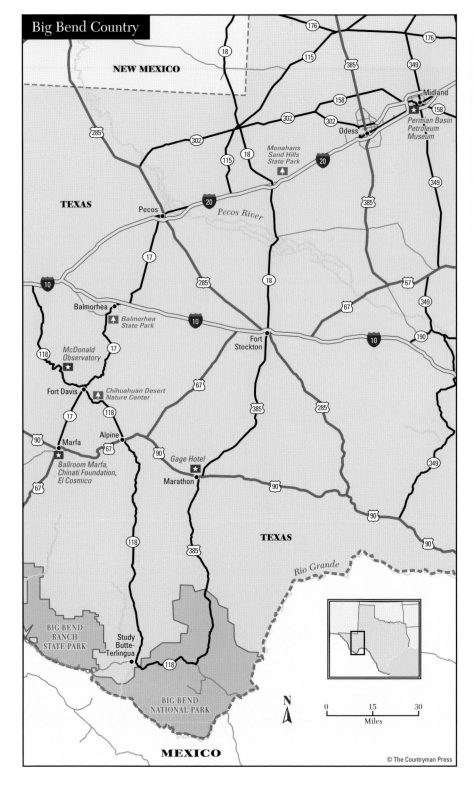

Big Bend Country

NEW MEXICO

TEXAS

Midland

Permian Basin
Petroleum
Museum

Odessa

Monahans
Sand Hills
State Park

Pecos

Pecos River

Balmorhea

Balmorhea
State Park

McDonald
Observatory

Fort
Stockton

Fort Davis

Chihuahuan Desert
Nature Center

Alpine

Marfa

Ballroom Marfa,
Chinati Foundation,
El Cosmico

Gage Hotel

Marathon

TEXAS

Rio Grande

BIG BEND
RANCH
STATE PARK

Study
Butte-
Terlingua

BIG BEND
NATIONAL PARK

N

0   15   30
Miles

MEXICO

© The Countryman Press

Visitors are ready for a sky lesson before the Star Party at McDonald Observatory.

a casual hiker with gorgeous views. Nearby McDonald Observatory gives you the skies as you've never seen them, during regularly scheduled star parties. If you can't spend more than a week down here, I urge you to work at least one of these into your schedule on the way in or out. You'll drive past and wish you had stopped if you don't make plans ahead of time.

On the other hand, the national park has enough surreal beauty to keep an outdoors man or woman busy for more than a week, so if it's desert solitude you crave, by all means speed south.

Area Code

The area code for this region is 432.

Guidance

Convention and visitors bureaus and chambers of commerce are generally great sources of information in the area.

Midland Convention and Visitors Bureau (800-624-6435; www.visitmidlandtexas.com), 109 N. Main, Midland.

Odessa Convention and Visitors Bureau (800-780-4678; www.odessacvb.com).

Fort Stockton Convention and Visitors Bureau (877-336-8525; www.tourtexas.com).

Fort Davis Chamber of Commerce (432-426-3015; www.fortdavis.com).

Marfa Chamber of Commerce (800-650-9696; www.marfacc.com).

Alpine Chamber of Commerce (800-561-3712; www.alpinetexas.com), 106 N. 3rd Street.

Big Bend National Park Service Headquarters, Big Bend National Park: (432-477-2251; www.nps.gov/bibe/index.htm).

Weather

The average high in Big Bend National Park ranges from 93 in July to 61 in January; in Midland, it's 96 and 69. Big Bend lows are from 35 in January to 68 in July; in Midland, 68 and 29. Throughout much of this country you'll find it cools down in the evenings, so come prepared with a sweater, even in the summer. Snow is rare, but fronts can drive the temperatures down below freezing. Precipitation is generally 15 inches a year or less.

Medical Emergencies

Dial 911 anywhere in the area.

Acute care hospitals in the Midland-Odessa area include Midland Memorial Hospital (432-685-1111; www.midland-memorial.com), 2200 W. Illinois Avenue; Odessa Regional Medical Center (432-582-8000, www.odessaregionalmedicalcenter .com); 520 E. Sixth Street, Rolling Plains Memorial Hospital (325-235-1701), 200 E. Arizona, Sweetwater; Scenic Mountain Medical Center (432-263-1211), 1601 W. 11th Place, Big Spring.

In Alpine, the major hospital is Big Bend Regional Medical Center (432-837-3447, www.bigbendhealth care.com), 2600 N. TX 118.

The nearest medical care under an hour from Big Bend National Park is urgent care and family practice services at the Lajitas Infirmary, but

You can pose with a giant jackrabbit in Odessa.

there are no family practice services Monday and Tuesday. Call 432-424-3535 or after hours call the Lajitas resort front desk at 432-424-5000 and tell them you need the health care provider. This is an experienced physician assistant and paramedic.

Odessa American, www.oaoa.com.

Midland Reporter-Telegram, www.mywesttexas.com.

Big Bend Sentinel, 110 N. Highland, Marfa.

Alpine Avalanche, www.alpineavalanche.com.

Getting There

The drive from the Dallas–Fort Worth area takes a little more than eight hours if you head west on Interstate-30E to San Angelo and continue on to Alpine. A quicker option is flying into Midland International Airport, for as little as $99/person on Southwest Airlines booked in advance on the Internet, www.southwest.com. American (www.aa.com) and Continental (www.continental.com) also fly to Midland. The flight takes about an hour; it's another three hours to Alpine, the last pit stop of any size before you get to the Big Bend, which is another two hours from Alpine. If you're coming from elsewhere, Midland International Airport (www.flymaf.com) has non-stop service to Albuquerque, Dallas, Houston, and Las Vegas on Southwest, American Eagle, and Continental Express.

Getting Around

You have no choice. Rent a car, and if you plan on going off-road at all, rent an SUV or jeep. Vehicle rental will run about $200/week—look for coupons.

MIDLAND-ODESSA

You'll likely spend a night in the Midland-Odessa area no matter how you plan a trip to Big Bend country. Some of the nicest people in the world live here in a warm climate with low crime. It's the heart of the oil patch, and if you want to learn all about the inner workings of the industry there's no place better than the Permian Basin Petroleum Museum in Midland.

There are comfortable chain hotels, decent restaurants, and lots of oil wells, in an area that also touts itself as the gateway to the Big Bend—and flying here is a great way to go, shortening the trip from Dallas–Fort Worth by many hours.

These two small cities halfway between Dallas and El Paso rest on the Permian Basin, which contains about 20 percent of the nation's oil and gas. Both cities have the boom-and-bust histories typical of places that rely on the oil patch for a living. When times were good, populations and services soared—for example, 215 oil companies had offices in Midland in 1950 and the population grew from about 21,000 that year to 62,625 just 10 years later. Today, about 129,000 people live in Midland and some 250,000 in the

Don't Miss

The Permian Basin Petroleum Museum

(432-683-4403; www .petroleummuseum.org), 1500 W. Interstate-20. Open 10–5, Monday through Saturday; 2–5 Sunday. If you don't have any idea how an oil well works and would like to know, or if you're fascinated with the hardscrabble life and times of the Texas oil industry and its workers, this is a gold mine of information. The various kinds of drill bits; long, colorful core samples; photos and parts of the early rigs; the story of how it all happened; and

Core samples from oil drilling are on display at the Permian Basin Petroleum Museum in Midland.

much more are on display in more than 32,000 square feet. Adults, $8; 12–17 and 65 and older, $6; children 6–11, $5; under 6, free.

metropolitan area that includes both cities. They're just 20 miles apart, and a bit different in character. It used to be said that the people who ran the oil companies lived in Midland, and the people who worked in the oil fields lived in Odessa, though that's probably changed over the years as both cities have tried to decrease their dependence on oil. You still will see plenty of pumpjacks nodding across the oilfields, though, as you drive through.

Be careful, though, about driving right up to one—they're on private property.

Midland's other claim to fame is as the former home of former presidents George Bush and George W. Bush, now a tourist attraction.

Here, I'll suggest staying at chain lodging. After a week in the Chihuahuan Desert, the brand-name motels in Midland can look mighty comfortable.

CAF Airpower Museum (432-567-3010; www.airpowermuseum.org), 9600 Wright Drive. Open 9–5, Tuesday through Saturday. World War II buffs will enjoy a quick stop here—it's on the way out of the airport. Exhibits include a fun nose-art gallery and other artifacts of aviation during WWII. Adult, $10; seniors 65 and older and children 13–17, $9; children 6–12, $7; children 5 and under, free.

George W. Bush Childhood Home (432-685-1112; www.bushchild hoodhome.com), 1412 West Ohio Avenue. Open 10–5 Tuesday through Saturday, 2–5 Sunday. This is the home where George W. grew up. His father, former President George H. W. Bush, bought the home with his wife, Barbara, in 1951. The building has been carefully restored; many of the items inside—toys, some furniture, etc.—are from the years when Bush was growing up, but were not his. Adults, $5; seniors, students and military, $3; children 5 and under, free.

An outdoor chapel is part of the CAF Airpower Museum in Midland.

Former President George W. Bush's childhood home has been made into a small museum in Midland.

Haley Memorial Library and History Center (432-682-5785; www.haley library.com), 1805 W. Indiana Avenue. Open 9–5 Monday through Friday. Primarily of interest to Western history buffs, the library contains some 25,000 books, manuscripts, and other documents on Western history. Free.

OUTDOORS

Hiking

Odessa Meteor Crater (432-381-0946), Interstate-20, exit 108, about 10 miles west of Odessa. The Thomas Rodman Museum and Visitor Center is open 9–5 Tuesday through Saturday; 1–5 Sunday. Several meteors crashed here some 20,000–50,000 years ago, and left a major hole to admire. It's fun to walk around the Crater Trail and look. Free.

Pick Your Spot

Best places to stay in and around Midland-Odessa

Various chains are available. I stayed at:

Courtyard by Marriott, (432-689-9400; www.marriott.com), 1505 Tradewinds Boulevard, Midland, and found it pleasant, clean, and hospitable. High-speed Internet, breakfast buffet, coffee pot in the room—the usual amenities at a mid-range motel designed for business people. Moderate.

Local Flavors

Taste of the town—restaurants, cafés, bars, bistros, etc.

EATING OUT

The Garlic Press (432-570-4020; www.thegarlicpress.net), 2200 West Wadley, #6 Oak Ridge Square, Midland. Open Tuesday through Friday for lunch, and Tuesday through Saturday for dinner. A popular business lunch spot, this offers a varied menu from steaks and seafood to sandwiches to South-western. The tasty Garlic Press Chile Relleno ($10) was stuffed to overflowing with chicken, mushrooms, and cheese. Moderate.

THE BIG BEND VIA BALMORHEA, FORT DAVIS, MARFA, AND ALPINE

Note: The Fort Davis area was subject to scorching wildfires in spring of 2011. While the attractions and lodging listed here survived, you'll see

The pool at Balmorhea State Park is fed by a natural spring.

burned areas as you travel. Call ahead in case of any temporary closures for renovations.

A favorite route to the Big Bend is to take Interstate-20 west past Odessa to Pecos, and from there, TX 17 south to Marfa.

There are not many towns to worry about stopping in, not for quite a while; but the route will take you right past two of the more interesting state parks in Texas on the way to the renowned, quirky little town of Marfa and finally to Alpine, the place where everyone for hundreds of miles goes for things like prescriptions and groceries.

In Monahans, just half an hour from Midland-Odessa, there are sand dunes spreading toward New Mexico; Balmorhea State Park has a natural spring corralled into a huge swimming pool.

No matter how I traveled west or how long it's taken to this point, I always feel like once I get to Balmorhea, the trip has really begun.

To See and Do

Monahans Sandhills State Park (432-943-2092; www.tpwd.state.tx .us), 6 miles northeast of Monahans off Interstate-20, exit Park Road 41. Open 8:30 AM–10 PM daily, but rented sandsurfing discs must be returned by 3 PM. You may not want to stop so soon after leaving Midland-Odessa, but this is a stunning surprise: 3,840 acres of sand dunes up to 70 feet tall— in fact, this is only a small part of the dunes, which stretch 200 miles into New Mexico. It's a good place to stop and meditate and gaze into the distance. Or, pile out of the car and try sandsurfing. Tips: Surfing is best just

In Monahans, just outside Odessa, the colors and plants of the desert begin.

after a rain, when the sand is packed hard; unfortunately, that's not often, because the annual rainfall is 12 inches (fall and winter are your best bets). Go ahead and leave your shoes in the car. Otherwise they'll just be something else to carry when you're hiking up the dunes. Be sure to take bottled water with you. If you're in a group, especially one with children, agree on a time and place to meet. It's fairly easy to get separated. Visit in the morning to avoid the heat. Dunes are not lighted at night. Adults, $3, under 13, free. Sand disc rentals are around $2 for two hours or just purchase one for $10.

West of the Pecos Museum (432-445-5076; www.westofthepecos museum.com), First and Cedar streets, Pecos. Open 9–5 Monday through Saturday and 1–4 Sunday from Memorial Day through Labor Day; then Tuesday through Saturday 9–5 from Labor Day through Memorial Day. This former three-story hotel built in 1904 is a fun, quick stop, with its bullet hole in the saloon wall and other kitschy old West memorabilia. Adults, $4; seniors, $3; children, $1; under 6, free.

Barbed wire and saddle collections are among the exhibits at Museum of the Pecos in Pecos.

About WiFi and Cell Phones in the Area

Good luck on WiFi. Plenty of places will say it's available, but the reality is that it's not reliable. I found it at Indian Lodge in Fort Davis if I was in the lobby area. Otherwise, don't bet on it.

The good news is you will get a cell signal throughout most of the area, even in Terlingua, although it may be intermittent at times as you drive.

Balmorhea State Park (432-375-2370; www.tpwd.state.tx.us), Toyahvale. The state park opened in 1968, but San Solomon Springs, which feeds the huge pool, was once called Mescalero Springs because the Mescalero Apaches watered their horses here. Today it's a peaceful, 45.9-acre oasis at the foothills of the Davis Mountains. The spring-fed pool is more than 77,000 square feet of water so clear and deep you can snorkel and scuba dive. Don't be alarmed at the slight stinging as you step into the pool—it's tiny fish nibbling. They're endangered species taking refuge here, and they won't hurt you. San Solomon Court, the motel run by the Texas Parks and Wildlife Department, was built of adobe by the Civilian Conservation Corps in the late 1930s to

Buildings at Balmorhea State Park were constructed by the Civilian Conservation Corps in the 1940s.

early 1940s, in Spanish colonial style. The furniture in the historic rooms is heavy, hand-carved wood. Bring your own food and don't expect anything fancy; instead, expect serenity and simple pleasures like starry skies and sparkling water. Inexpensive. Park fees are $7/day per person. Reserve rooms through the TPWD's reservation system—directions are on the Web site or call 512-389-8900.

Fort Davis

TX 17 starts to lope around curves edged with golden hills, and then suddenly you come upon a red brown bluff thrust through a hilltop. The curves tighten as you climb, and you are in the Davis Mountains, up from the prairie. Trees are bright sea foam green against brown rock, all of it sprung from the rich, golden hills.

Some Texans make an annual sojourn to Fort Davis (see Note above) to stay at a favorite hotel, cycle, or hike in the Davis Mountains and just generally soak up the casual scene, mild climate, and copious natural beauty.

The town of around 1,000 people is friendly and quiet. It gets just enough visitors to the area attractions (Davis Mountains State Park and McDonald Observatory) so that the townspeople are welcoming and helpful—not at all tired of talking to curious strangers.

As remote as it is, Fort Davis has tourism history. Back in the early

You don't have to hike forever in the Davis Mountains to get a forever view.

Don't Miss

McDonald Observatory (877-984-7827; www.mcdonaldobservatory .org), 17 miles from Fort Davis on TX 118. Open 10 AM–5:30 PM for self-guided tours. Plan your visit to coincide with a Star Party Tuesday, Friday, or Saturday—these are some of the darkest skies in the continental U.S. Party times vary depending on the season; check the Web site or call. Scientists at the observatory, a research unit of the University of Texas at Austin, use one of the world's largest optical telescopes, the 433-inch Hobby Eberly Telescope. For a Star Party at the public observatory, dress warmly, listen closely, and plan to learn a lot gazing through telescopes in two domes, plus others set up around the domes. Astronomers explain what you're seeing and adjust the telescopes as the night goes on. Families may want to make reservations for the twilight program before each star party, which explains basics of what you'll see, for an additional fee. Bear in mind that the phase of the moon has an important impact on the viewing—if you want great lunar viewing, go when the moon is large in the sky, but it will limit your ability to see faint stars. There's good sandwich and salad-type fare at the Star Date Café. Admission for Star Party only, adults, $12, senior/military, $10, children 6–12, $8. Or, attend a solar viewing, daily at 11 AM and 2 PM, adults $8, seniors, military, children, $7.

McDonald Observatory in Fort Davis is part of the University of Texas.

1900s, well-to-do Gulf Coast residents would flee the stultifying humidity for the cooler, drier air here.

A huge lodging draw is Indian Lodge at the state park. Regulars flood the switchboard each January when reservations become available. But the lovely old Hotel Limpia in town has plenty of fans, too, and some intriguing new accommodations have opened up in the last few years.

The dining choices won't blow you away, but you will be surprised at all the natural and organic foods available in town.

To See and Do

Chihuahuan Desert Nature Center and Botanical Gardens (432-364-2499; www.cdri.org), 4 miles south of Fort Davis on TX 118. Open 9–5 Monday through Saturday. This is more than 500 acres with two fairly strenuous hiking trails, a succulents greenhouse, and an arboretum. Use the nature center as an educational stop to get familiar with the desert plant life you see all around you, and that you will continue to see if you continue on to the Big Bend. Adults, $5; seniors, $4.50; under 12, free.

Davis Mountains State Park (432-426-3337; www.tpwd.state.tx.us), 4 miles north of Fort Davis on TX 118. Open year-round. The elevation here rises to a mile high within the 2,700 acres, making scenic views easy to come by whether on foot or in a vehicle. Even a fairly easy hike will net you views for miles across the valley. And even if you're not the outdoorsy type, you're in for a treat: Indian Lodge is one of the best lodging choices in the area, so popular some Texans come here every year. *See below.* The park also has campsites and RV hookups. Besides hiking, the Davis Mountains offer bird-watching, mountain biking, picnic sites, and two scenic overlooks. Overnight horseback trips also are permitted. You'll begin to truly get a taste of desert

Relax and enjoy the view from a room at Indian Lodge at Davis Mountains State Park.

The Chihuahuan Desert

A high desert (much of it above 4,000 feet) that supports more cacti than anywhere else in the world, the Chihuahuan Desert spills across southern New Mexico and Arizona into far southwest Texas and drops down into six Mexican states.

It is a land of extremes. Winter temperatures here often drop below freezing, while summertime highs can soar over 100. Most of the rainfall is July through October, a wonderful time to visit because thunderstorms make for cool summer evenings.

Newcomers to the desert may have trouble seeing much variety in its vegetation, except for blooming cacti, or the spiky arms of the ocotillo with its brilliant red blooms in the spring. But if you look closer you'll see that the desert scrub is made up of grasses, shrubs, succulents, cacti, and trees. Along the Rio Grande, you'll see cottonwood trees and salt cedars.

The desert also is home to plenty of insects, including desert tarantulas, scorpions, millipedes, and centipedes. Lizards and snakes, including Mexican king snakes, rattlesnakes, and

The ocotillo blooms a brilliant red-orange in the early spring.

Trans-Pecos rat snakes, also live here, as do many bats.

You may see desert bighorn sheep, which once had all but disappeared from the desert, climbing along ridges. Mule and white-tailed deer also live here as do coyotes and an increasingly large population of javelinas (wild hogs). Mountain lions and black bears are occasionally seen. Parks will post warnings and have directions on how to react should you see one.

wildlife here. Javelinas regularly forage in the park, and mountain lion sightings are not unheard-of. If you're lucky enough to come in spring during a rainy year, you'll see lots of wildflowers. Snow falls occasionally in winter. Fees vary according to which part of the park you're using. Call or check the Web site for details.

Fort Davis National Historic Site is part of the Texas Forts Trail.

Fort Davis National Historic Site (432-426-3224; www.nps.gov/foda), along TX 17 and 118 at the foot of Sleeping Lion Mountain. Open 8–5 except holidays. Military buffs will enjoy this 474-acre fort with buildings partially and fully restored. Some of the buildings have period furnishings. The tours are self-guided. Admission, $3.

Pick Your Spot
Best places to stay in and around Fort Davis

Indian Lodge (512-389-8982 for reservations; www.tpwd.state.tx .us/spdest/findadest/parks/indian _lodge). This pueblo-style hotel at Davis Mountains State Park is a stunning complex of white adobe walls, and heavy, simple wood furniture. The older part of the hotel was built by the Civilian Conserva-

Part of Indian Lodge was built of adobe in the 1930s.

Rooms at the Harvard Hotel in Fort Davis have a Texas feel.

Hotel Limpia in Fort Davis is a favorite place to stay for Texans who love the area.

tion Corps in the 1930s. Indian Lodge can get booked up for the entire year in January, when the operators begin taking reservations for the year to come—and once you stay, you'll understand why people come back year after year. The views from some rooms or attached patios can be amazing, and some of them are beautifully secluded. The attached restaurant is a serviceable, no-frills diner. Moderate.

Harvard Hotel (432-426-2500; www.sproulranch.com), 109 State Street. This is a newer hotel—built in 2005—with Texana-style decor including wood ceilings, Texas stars on the walls, and leather furniture. Moderate.

Hotel Limpia in Fort Davis (www.hotellimpia.com; 432-426-3241), at 100 Main Street. This is another spot where vacationing Texans tend to return year after year. It's an island of calm with rockers on the front porches and rooms filled with antiques. The 41-room historic hotel was built in 1912, and the decor is quietly Victorian, so that the feel is more genteel than period. Moderate.

Stone Village Tourist Camp (432-426-3941; www.stonevillage touristcamp.com), 509 State Street. The Hotel Limpia purchased this motor court in 2006, with 14 motel rooms supplemented by 6 camp rooms, which are screened-in and share bathrooms a few doors down. Camp rooms are $44/night for two twin beds, cold running water, and WiFi, plus linens. The small motel rooms retain their comfy motor court feel with chenille bedspreads. Inexpensive.

Local Flavors

Taste of the town—restaurants, cafés, bars, bistros, etc.

Hotel Limpia Dining Room (432-426-3241; www.hotellimpia .com), 100 Main Street. Open daily. Serves regional favorites, like steak and biscuits. Moderate to expensive.

Cueva de Leon (432-426-3801), 611 N. State Street. Open for lunch Monday through Saturday, Sunday for dinner. There's noth-ing fancy here, but it's decent Mexican food—the salsa is spicy and garlicky—and friendly waitstaff in a simple setting. Inexpensive.

Murphy's Pizza, Subs and Pasta (432-426-2020), 107 Musquiz Drive. Open Monday through Friday for lunch and dinner. This busy lunch spot serves pizza made from scratch and baked in a brick-lined oven, as well as salads, spaghetti, calzones, and subs. Inexpensive.

Marfa

Marfa has been heralded as a world-class art town, a magnet for East Coast art figures, a second Santa Fe, the place where *Giant* was filmed, a surprising home to great cuisine . . . and it has elements of all that. But if you look closer, it's also a little town on the high desert where you can hear the choir singing through open church house doors on a Sunday, where the railroad stopped and made a town in the middle of nothing (a railroad engineer's wife named the town after a character in Dostoevski's *The Brothers Kara-mazov*), where the adobe houses, restored though they may be, were originally built of mud because that was what the early settlers had to build with.

Don't Miss

The Chinati Foundation (432-729-4362; www.chinati.org), 1 Cavalry Row. Open by guided tour only. The tour of the contemporary art museum's collection is 10–2 with a lunch break, Wednesday through Sunday. A tour of 100 of Donald Judd's aluminum works only is at 3:45 PM Thursday through Sunday, admission $5. A tour of the complex where Judd lived and worked also is available at times, check the Web site or call for details. His private quarters and the grounds are a study in balance and proportion, carefully put together with meticulous detail.

The museum collection of world-class minimalist art works is inside former barracks and artillery sheds on 340 acres that once were Fort D. A. Russell. Besides pieces by Judd, there are works by Dan Flavin, John Chamberlain, and nine more artists. The tour includes walking outdoors, in the desert, so dress accordingly—don't forget sunblock, hats, and shades. Adults, $10; students and seniors, $5; under 12, free. Reservations are recommended three days in advance during most of the year, and required at holidays and spring break—call 432-729-4362.

It's free twice a year: Community Day (check the Web site for the date this year) and during Chinati Weekend in October. Again, check the Web site for exact dates this year. If you decide to visit then, plan ahead. People flock from miles around to Marfa for this event.

The little town of about 2,000 changed forever in the 1970s when New York sculptor Donald Judd came to town. Originally a watering stop for the steam railroad, Marfa later became a military town but languished after World War II. Judd came with art, money, and connections. He bought up property and eventually created the Chinati Foundation, a contemporary art museum, in 1986.

This drew a lot of attention, and attracted more artists, along with attendant galleries—and restaurants and shops—to support them and the art collectors who followed.

It's all good for travelers today, who can stay in sleek minimalist lodging, dine on some of Texas' most sophisticated cuisine, and take in world-class art literally in the midst of beautiful desert terrain—Donald Judd's cement cubes look, at first, like construction plans gone bankrupt. You have to step back and see the works against the mountains and the desert sky to begin to understand. Like many of Marfa's attractions, they don't work for everyone.

But the odd combinations in the art and in the town exert a rare kind of pull that sticks with you—if you stop, breathe, and try living on Marfa time.

Enjoy the big sky, the lack of traffic, and the sunshine. Take a walk, or, if you want to feel like a Marfan, rent a bike and ride it around town.

Marfa also is a good jumping-off point for starting to explore Big Bend National Park, or can serve as a base for trips to the Davis Mountains if you're into returning to fine dining and lodging at the end of the day.

To See and Do

Marfa Gliders (800-667-9464; www.flygliders.com), at the Marfa Airport on TX 17, 18 miles south of Fort Davis and 3 miles north of Marfa. No, I haven't actually done this, but I have it on good authority that it's spectacular if you're game. A basic glider ride—by appointment only—is $119, subject to change.

A note about galleries: They are plentiful in Marfa considering its size, but they have tended to open and close over the years. Here's a listing of some that have been around for a while in my experience. You'll find more when you visit.

Arber & Son Editions (432-729-3981; www.30x30cmproject.com), 128 East El Paso. Call ahead for hours. There aren't necessarily extensive displays up all the time, but this is a fascinating shop. Master printer Robert Arber moved to Marfa in 1998 after founding his fine-art litho print shop in New Mexico in 1976. Now he produces works for Chinati Foundation artists in residence as part of the 30x30cm Project—each artist's work is in a 30-cm-square portfolio, in editions of 40. The work in various stages is on view at the shop.

Ayn Foundation (432-729-3315; www.aynfoundation.com), 109 N Highland. Open odd hours, call ahead. Andy Warhol's *Last Supper* and Maria Zerres' *September Eleven* are on display here at Brite Building.

exhibitions 2d (432-729-1910; www.exhibitions2d.com), 400 S Highland. Open 11–6 Wednesday through Sunday and by appointment. Here since 2003, the gallery exhibits work by nine artists from across the U.S., generally minimalist drawing and sculpture.

Galleri Urbane (432-729-4200; www.galleriurbane.com), 212 E. San Antonio. Open 10–6 Monday through Saturday; 11–4 Sunday or by appointment. The gallery has works by new and established contemporary artists.

inde/jacobs gallery (432-386-0044; www.indejacobs.com), 208 E. San Antonio. Open 12–5 Wednesday through Saturday or by appointment. Shows works by Donald Judd, Dan Flavin, and others involved with the Chinati Foundation.

Marfa Studio of Arts (432-729-4616; www.marfastudioofarts.org), 106 East San Antonio. Open to the public 3:30–6 Monday through Thursday; 1–5 Saturday and Sunday, and by appointment. The studio provides arts programs for local children, and visiting kids are encouraged to create a piece of art during weekend visits.

Prada Marfa, 37 miles northwest of Marfa off US 90 and about 1.5 miles from Valentine. An art installation, this is a faux Prada store in the middle of nowhere by the artists Michael Elmgreen and Ingar Dragset.

Pick Your Spot

Best places to stay in and around Marfa

Arcon Inn B&B (432-729-4826), 215 N. Austin Street. This two-story Victorian has three rooms in the main house (bathrooms in the hall) and a casita in back. Inexpensive.

Cochineal Guest House (646-491-2412), 115 W. San Antonio Street), next to the restaurant Cochineal and run by its owner, this one-bedroom guesthouse has gorgeous concrete floors, white-slipcovered furniture, and a full kitchen. Expensive.

El Cosmico (www.elcosmico .com; 432-729-1950), 802 S. Highland Avenue, Marfa. There's nothing quite like this, really, anywhere. It's an assemblage of yurts, safari tents, a teepee, camping spots, and meticulously restored vintage mobile homes on 18 acres at the edge of town. Bathtubs and showers are outdoors, the better to see

the stars, but it's not for the luxury-minded. Be aware you have to park at the lobby and haul your luggage out to your trailer in a little wagon. Inexpensive to moderate.

Chinati Hot Springs (432-229-4165; www.chinatihotsprings .com), outside Presidio. It's hard to say which is more meditative: the remote setting in an already-remote

The trailers at El Cosmico in Marfa have been carefully refurbished.

land, or the ancient, soothing hot springs themselves. The locals may tell you to go ahead and take Pinto Canyon Road, which is one of the most beautiful drives in Texas, traveling through creeks and around the edges of deep canyons. You should only do this if you have a little experience with off-roading and a vehicle with high clearance. The road crosses creeks and includes huge, sharp rocks. The alternative is to take US 170 to Ruidosa and on up to the hot springs—longer in miles, but both take roughly an hour. This is not a fancy resort. It's nearly primitive and all the more beautiful because of it. Little casitas are stocked with Mexican blankets, and your private tub is outside, as is the public pool. There are hiking trails, and a large, separate kitchen for food preparation. Bring your

own food and drink, there is none for sale here. Inexpensive. Camping also is available.

Cibolo Creek Ranch (www .cibolocreekranch.com; 866-496-9460). At the other end of the spectrum, this ranch resort outside Marfa in the foothills of the Chinatis is so exclusive and private that the guests aren't even issued room keys—there's no need. Hunt, fish, go for a ride in one of the Hummers. The pretty rooms are filled with Spanish colonial and Mexican touches. Very expensive.

Hotel Paisano (866-729-3669; www.hotelpaisano.com), 207 N. Highland. This is the hotel where James Dean stayed when *Giant* was filmed in West Texas in 1956. The Paisano is a lovely old hotel with a great patio, a wide-ranging gift shop (from beautiful $64 pencil

Cibolo Creek Ranch outside Marfa is an upscale resort.

The Marfa Lights

I've seen them. They were yellowish lights that popped up in the night sky just above where the horizon would have been if I'd been able to see it. I'd have said they were car lights in the distance, since we were facing the road to Presidio, but then they faded away and one reappeared high in the sky. Another waved around in circles. It was seriously eerie.

This has been going on every clear night for more than a century. The first record of them is in 1883, when a young cowboy spotted the lights and thought they might have been Apache Indian campfires. Settlers said they'd seen the lights but found no evidence of camp-fires. Again in 1919, cowboys saw the lights and this time they rode over the Chinati Mountains to investigate—but came up empty-handed.

The investigations grew more serious during World War I, when people were afraid they were signals for an invasion, and during WWII, pilots searched for the source from the air, to no avail.

The explanations have ranged from swamp gas to a mirage—or dis-tortion caused by the atmosphere, considered the most likely.

Whatever they are, the state Highway Department has built a very nice roadside area for viewing them in the desert about 9 miles east of Marfa on US 90. Go around dusk and wait for darkness. (I didn't see the lights from this viewing area, but from a nearby private road. Sorry, but I'm sworn to secrecy on the exact location.)

sets to kids' books that let you "comb the Mona Lisa's hair"), and a separate shop with all the *Giant* memorabilia you could ever want. The hotel's Greasewood Gallery exhibits traditional art. Jett's Grill serves traditional steakhouse fare. Moderate.

Marfa Guest Quarters (432-729-4599; www.themarfaquarters .com), 109 W. San Antonio Street. There are five properties from one-bedroom, one-bath quarters to a two-bedroom, one-bath house.

Nothing fancy, but if you're really in Marfa as a jumping-off place to explore Big Bend, these have kitchens, which come in handy if you're late getting back from the park. Inexpensive.

Riata Inn (432-729-3800; www .riatainn.com), 1500 US 90 East. If you want a motel room, plain and simple, this is your best bet. Inexpensive.

Thunderbird Hotel (432-729-1984; www.thunderbirdmarfa.com), 601 W. San Antonio. This is a very

The patio at Jett's Grill at the Hotel Paisano in Marfa is a nice spot for a cold drink.

cool mid-century modern motor court restored in the minimalist style that pervades Marfa. The 24 rooms are elegantly simple, in a Western (cowhides on the floor) contemporary way, with malin+goetz toiletries. Enjoy the pool, outdoor fireplace, bicycles, record players, gift shop, lounge. Moderate.

Local Flavors

Taste of the town—restaurants, cafés, bars, bistros, etc.

DINING OUT

Cochineal (432-729-3300), 107 W. San Antonio Street. Open Thursday through Sunday for breakfast and brunch; dinner nightly. The ever-changing menu in this gorgeously simple eatery has included duck confit, blue marlin, and interesting sides like lime mashed potatoes. The wine list is extensive, and the date pudding is a favorite dessert. The green chile sauce on the migas for breakfast is divine. Reservations recommended. If you see owner Tom Kapp, ask him about the name of the restaurant. Moderate to expensive.

Jett's Grill at the Hotel Paisano (432-729-3838; www.hotelpaisano .com/pages/jetts.html), 207 N. Highland Avenue. Open Friday through Monday for breakfast and lunch; daily for dinner. The restaurant in the historic hotel where the cast of *Giant* stayed during filming serves up basic steakhouse fare for dinner. The patio is a nice spot to sip a drink on a cool evening. Moderate.

Maiya's Restaurant (432-729-4410; www.maiyasrestaurant.com), 103 N. Highland Avenue. Open Tuesday through Saturday for dinner. This bistro-style Italian restaurant that opened in 2002 is the one that put Marfa on the fine-dining map. Lots of grilled and roasted meats, homemade breads and desserts, plus pastas and salads on the seasonal menu. Reservations recommended. Expensive.

EATING OUT AND NIGHTLIFE

Austin Street Cafe (432-729-4653; www.austinstreetcafe.com), 405 N. Austin Street. Only open for break-fast and brunch 8 AM–2 PM Sundays, but make it a point to get there. Austin Street is run by Jack and Lisa Copeland, who lov-ingly restored the 1885 adobe where they live, and serve some of the best breakfasts in town, from quiches to frittatas. A huge favorite is the Curried Green Eggs. Inexpensive.

Food Shark (281-386-6540; www.foodsharkmarfa.com), between Marfa Book Co. and the railroad train tracks (it's a food truck), open Tuesday through Friday for lunch. A changing menu offers everything from falafel to brisket tacos to braised short rib stew over mashed potatoes. Inexpensive.

frama@tumbleweedlaundry (432-729-4033), 120 N. Austin Street. Open daily 8 AM–9 PM. Frama, inside a very nice laundry, serves espressos and other coffee beverages made from Big Bend Coffee Roasters' coffee, plus hot

The dining room at Cochineal in Marfa is as beautiful as the food is imaginative.

chocolate, tea, snacks from the Food Shark, and Blue Bell (native to Texas) ice cream. If you haven't tried Blue Bell to this point, make sure and grab a scoop. A big favorite is Homemade Vanilla, but I like Vanilla Bean if I can get it. Inexpensive.

Padre's Marfa (432-729-4425; www.padresmarfa.com), 209 W El Paso Street. Open Wednesday through Saturday. This is where at least some of Marfa comes to party, with live music, hardwood dance floor, game room with pool, shuffleboard, jukeboxes and pinball, and an outdoor patio. Also serves burgers and other casual eats. Inexpensive.

Pizza Foundation (432-729-3377; www.pizzafoundation.com), 100 E. San Antonio Street. Thin-crust, New York–style pizza made from scratch is served in an old gas station converted to a restaurant. The pizza is great, but if you're not in the mood, try the tomato bread salad, it's to die for. Inexpensive to moderate.

Squeeze Marfa (432-729-4500; www.squeezemarfa.com), N. High-land Avenue at W. Lincoln Street. Open 9–4 Tuesday through Satur-day. This spot right across from the courthouse serves healthy options such as smoothies and freshly squeezed juices, along with paninis and Swiss chocolate. Inexpensive.

Squeeze Marfa serves (of course) fresh juices.

Selective Shopping

Christophers (432-729-4571; www
.christophers.net), 114 E. El Paso
Street. Open 9–5:30 Monday
through Friday. This is an old-
school furniture store that's been around for generations.

El Cheapo Liquor (432-729-4682; www.elcheapoliquorstores.com), 1309
W. San Antonio Street. Open 11:30 AM–8:30 PM Monday through Thursday;
10 AM–9 PM Friday and Saturday. Just what it sounds like, this is the liquor
store in town.

Fancy Pony Land (432-729-1850; www.fancyponyland.com), 203 E. San
Antonio Street. Call for hours. The goods include Western wear made to
order and off the rack, plus jewelry made from pennies squashed by the
train, among other things.

Hotel Paisano Gallery & Gifts (see the Hotel Paisano entry in *Pick Your
Spot*).

JM Dry Goods (917-548-7606; www.jmdrygoodsmarfa.com), 107 S. Dean
Street. Open noon–6 PM Friday and Saturday. You'll find glasses made from
Mexican soda bottles cut in two and polished; Mexican blankets; Virgin
Mary window decals; cowboy hats; textiles; used boots; a $400 holster and
a $10 canteen; Moroccan hand towels; and all sorts of other goodies in a
century-old adobe.

Little Liberty—Revolutionary Rags & Renegade Relics (432-300-0046),
200 S. Abbott Street. Open noon–6 Thursday through Sunday. Take a look
at refurbished home goods, flowered dresses, naturally dyed clothing,
locally made items. You can leave dressed like a Marfan.

Marfa Book Co. (432-729-3906; www.facebook.com/pages/Marfa-Book
-Company) Open 10–7 Wednesday through Sunday. This has gone through
some changes over the years, but remains an interesting bookstore with an
ever-changing gallery attached. It's fun to grab a book and enjoy it in the
sunshine, if the tables have been put out front.

Moonlight Gemstones (432-729-4526; www.moonlightgemstones.com),
1001 W. San Antonio Street. Open 10–6 Monday through Saturday, noon–4
Sunday. A lapidary shop that primarily sells local agate, it's been open for
more than a decade.

Tienda M (432-729-4440), 108 S. Highland Avenue. Call for hours. Minimalist and eclectic even for Marfa, this feels more like a gallery than a
store, with its carefully edited stock of textiles and jewelry. When I was last
there, most of the elegant goods on the shelves were from Oaxaca.

The Get Go (432-729-3335; www.thegetgomarfa.com), 208 S. Dean
Street. Open 9–8 daily. The town grocery stocks Big Bend Coffee Roasters

Coffee, some local beef, and some organics.

Thunderbird Hotel Gift Shop (see Thunderbird Hotel under *Pick Your Spot*).

Wild-Woolies Marfa (432-729-1850; www.wild-woolies.com), 203 E. San Antonio Street. Open 11–6 Wednesday through Saturday; noon–6 Sunday. Stocks yarns from around the world.

Wool & Hoop Ltd. (432-729-1850; www.woolandhoop.com), 203 E. San Antonio Street. This is a crewel embroidery shop with kits featuring original designs.

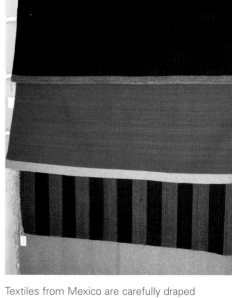

Textiles from Mexico are carefully draped at Tienda M in Marfa.

Alpine

Alpine is the last major outpost before you spin out into the open country with little but the mighty beauty of the desert for companions. The town of about 6,000 can be just a gas and supply stop, but really it's worth more of your time.

There are great food choices, one even legendary; unique shopping; a couple of great hotels; and a museum you have to see before heading into Big Bend National Park.

Alpine has an Amtrak depot downtown.

To See and Do

Museum of the Big Bend, Sul Ross University (432-837-8143; www.sulross.edu/museum), enter from US 90 or Harrison Street and follow the small, brown signs. Open daily. The museum is full of historic and prehistoric artifacts that shed light on who occupied this land over the millennia; collections of maps and *retablos* (devotional folk-art paintings);

Museum of the Big Bend is on the Sul Ross University campus in Alpine.

and an exhibit called Big Bend Legacy that winds through natural and human history. A visit sets the stage for a trip into the Big Bend—you'll understand how this land was made, who has lived here, who explored it before you. Free.

Pick Your Spot

Best places to stay in and around Alpine

Holland Hotel (800-535-8040; www.thehollandhoteltexas.com), 209 W. Holland Avenue. This historic downtown hotel, built in 1928, was recently restored to its original, Spanish colonial style. It is under new ownership the past several years, and looking sharp. Moderate.

Maverick Inn (432-837-06281; www.themaverickinn.com), 1200 E. Holland Avenue. This is another restored motor court, which kept its pretty adobe walls and added

Holland Hotel

saltillo tile floors. The rooms are pretty and clean, and stay true to the Southwestern style of the exterior. Moderate.

The Maverick Inn in Alpine is a renovated motor court.

Local Flavors

Taste of the town—restaurants, cafés, bars, bistros, etc.

EATING OUT

Alicia's Burrito Place (432-837-2802), 708 E. Gallego Avenue. Call to check hours. This is a longstanding institution beloved especially for big breakfast burritos (try the chorizo). Inexpensive.

Talgar's (432-837-5101; talgarsrestaurant.com), 102 W. Murphy Street, Open 11:30–2 and 5:30–9 Thursday through Saturday. This relatively new addition serves Mexican (not Tex-Mex) specialties like *tortas* (Mexican sandwiches) and grilled tilapia tacos with chipotle cream sauce. Inexpensive.

Texas Fusion (432-837-1215), 200 W. Murphy Avenue. The fusion is one of Mexican food, burgers, Texas homestyle cooking, and of course, barbecue. Inexpensive to moderate.

Don't Miss

Reata Restaurant (432-837-9232; www.reata.net), 203 N. 5th Street. Open for lunch 11:30–2 daily; dinner, 5–10 Monday through Saturday. The Reata is a legendary restaurant (this is the first one; a second version is in Fort Worth) that has, over the years, employed some of Texas's finest chefs—Tim Love, Grady Spears, Brian Olenjack. Though it's primarily a steakhouse with a cowboy atmosphere, the menu takes liberties with the genre, serving up favorites like beef tenderloin tamales. The restaurant is famous for its pecan biscuits, served at dinner only. Moderate to expensive.

Selective Shopping

Kiowa Gallery (432-837-3067), 105 E. Holland Avenue. Call for hours. Check out exquisite desert pastels by Lindy Severs and locally made jewelry with skulls and angel wings.

Catchlight Gallery (432-837-9422; www.catchlightartgallery.com), 107 E. Holland Avenue. Open Wednesday through Monday. This co-op sells regionally produced work in a multitude of media from paintings to lapidary pieces.

Front Street Books (432-837-3360; www.fsbooks.com), 121 and 201 E. Holland Avenue. Open daily. This happy find is a stellar independent new and used bookstore with tons of Texana and Big Bend titles, as well as out-of-print and collectible books. There are so many books, the titles continue in a second building across Fourth Street.

Ringtail Records (432-837-1055; www.ringtailrecords.com), 203 E. Holland Avenue. Open 10–6 Monday through Friday. This is a store full of vinyl and the memories that come with it. Owner Michael McCollum led me outside to check out some art painted in the alley, which just shows you how friendly West Texans are.

Murphy Street Raspa Co. (432-837-5556; www.raspaland.com), 100 W. Murphy Street. Open Monday through Sunday. A raspa is shaved ice made on an amazingly old and noisy machine and then soaked in crazily flavored syrups like hurricane, dill pickle, tamarindo, dulce de leche, and buttered popcorn. Be adventurous. My cherry raspa with chile and limon was tart, sweet, and salty all at once. The rest of the store is . . . well, you have to see it. The merchandise includes hammocks, potholders painted with likenesses of macho men, melamine plates in Mexican patterns, lucha libre greeting cards—things you'd never thought you'd see.

Try an icy cold raspa in Alpine.

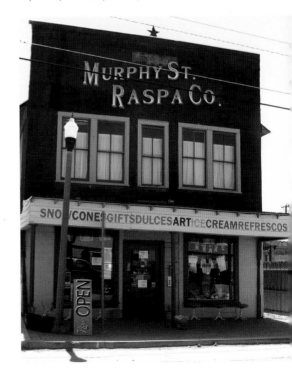

Avoiding and Coping with Emergencies in the Desert

IN A VEHICLE

As you drive into increasingly desolate terrain, make sure you have everything you'll need for the hours and days ahead. Desert dwellers learn to stock up on water at every stop to ensure they have it no matter what.

Watch your vehicle's gauges—it may be hours until the next gas station, and if an empty tank or overheated engine strands you, the wait for help could be hours-long, assuming you have cell signal.

In case of car trouble, for repairs and towing try Terlingua Auto Service, 432-371-2223. For motorcycles or ATVs, Cycletek in Terlingua, 432-371-2560.

You may not run into a functional ATM after Alpine, so stop for cash as you head into Terlingua, just in case. If you need medical care of any kind, or a prescription called in, Alpine is the last place before Big Bend National Park for either one. If you're staying in Terlingua or on the park, bear in mind that you won't find grocery stores or drugstores of any size after Alpine. If you need anything from cold medicine to toilet paper, get it in Alpine.

A cactus blooms in Big Bend National Park.

ON FOOT

The Chihuahuan Desert can be dangerous for walking if you're not aware and prepared. Among the creatures it harbors are rattlesnakes, mountain lions, and poisonous spiders. The cacti and yucca are sharp and spiny, and the terrain can acquire a confusing sameness. Don't venture far into the desert off-trail if you don't have hiking experience, carry a compass and know how to use it.

Make sure to use sunscreen, but also wear a hat and take light, long-sleeved clothing to help stay cool. Always, always carry plenty of water even if you think you're only planning a short hike. Read park service warnings about unusual animal activity and follow directions—they're serious.

The giant roadrunner is one of the attractions in Fort Stockton.

TERLINGUA AND THE BIG BEND
VIA FORT STOCKTON AND MARATHON

Fort Stockton

This is another Texas city that grew up around a fort, which is still probably the major tourist attraction. Fort Stockton Historical Museum (432-336-2400; www.tourtexas.com), 301 E. 3rd Street, is open 9–5 Monday through Saturday. Adults, $3; 65 and older, $2.50; 6–12, $2; free under 6.

There's also the Annie Riggs Memorial Museum (432-336-2167; www.tourtexas.com), 301 S. Main Street, open 9–5 Monday through Saturday, with artifacts from early pianos to mammoth tusks. Adults, $3; 65 and older, $2.50; 6–12, $2; free under 6.

The other big sight in town is Paisano Pete, the giant roadrunner, about 20 feet long and 10 feet or so high. You can go see him at the corner of US 285 and Main Street. Free.

Marathon

There are at least two excellent reasons to come to Marathon: the Gage Hotel, and Shirley's Burnt Biscuit Bakery. The little town 26 miles southeast of Alpine has its share of quirky, artsy characters, and has always been interesting even by West Texas standards. For example, Marathon's first jail reportedly was a windmill; drunks and other petty types were chained to a leg. More serious criminals were taken in to Alpine. In any case, Marathon

Rooms in the Gage Hotel are rich with Southwest textures and colors.

is definitely worth a stop if you're up this way, and a little detour even if you're not.

The last time I was here, many of the stores were closed but had telephone numbers to call if you were interested in seeing what they had to offer. Some of this may have been the slow time of year; some of it the economy; and some of it the freedom and easygoing nature of the area.

Don't Miss

Shirley's Burnt Biscuit (432-386-4008), 109 NE 1st Street. Open 7–1 Monday through Saturday. I have never, ever eaten an apricot fried pie as good as the one I ate while sitting on a yellow vinyl chair at this bakery. It was still warm, with a melt-in-your-mouth flaky crust and tangy-sweet filling. I can only assume and hope that the rest of the baked goods are just as amazing. Inexpensive.

Pick Your Spot

Best places to stay in and around Marathon

Gage Hotel (432-386-4205; www .gagehotel.com), 102 NW First Street. The Gage originally was designed by El Paso architects Trost and Trost as a ranch headquarters, and completed in 1927. Unfortunately, the rancher died only a year after it was finished. More recently, the building was restored in 1978 and became the beautiful hotel it is today. The 20 rooms—10 of them with kiva fireplaces and all of them simply but beautifully done, smelling of cinnamon and draped in Navajo rugs—surround a courtyard. The restaurant, 12 Gage, serves Texas specialties like buffalo rib eye steaks and shrimp with tomatillo sauce. The White Buffalo Bar also serves bar snacks, like venison nachos. Hotel rates, expensive; restaurant prices expensive.

The Gage Hotel in Marathon is an oasis of luxury in the desert.

Local Flavors

Taste of the town—restaurants, cafés, bars, bistros, etc.

DINING OUT

See 12 Gage at the Gage Hotel (under *Pick Your Spot*).

EATING OUT

Famous Burro (432-386-4100; www .famousburro.com), 100 North East First Street. Open 5–9 Thursday through Sunday. Serves a variety of entrees: steaks, meatloaf, and tilapia, along with desserts including homemade ice cream. Full bar. Moderate.

Johnny B's (432-386-4233), 109 W. Highway 190. Open 7–3 daily. Regular old-fashioned soda fountain serving hamburgers and fries, malts, shakes, banana splits, etc. Inexpensive.

Selective Shopping

Baxter Gallery (432-386-4041; www.baxtergallery.com), two blocks east of the Gage Hotel. Open most weekends, many weekdays, call ahead. The gallery with the jackrabbit painted on the front is a source for scenic Big Bend landscapes as well as some sculptures.

The French Co. Grocer (432-386-4522; www.frenchcogrocer.com), 206 N. Avenue D. Open 7:30 AM–9 PM Monday through Friday; 8 AM–9 PM Saturday; 9–9 Sunday. A true general store, French Co. Grocer stocks everything from organic meats and gluten-free foods to camping gear, including mosquito netting.

Evans Gallery (432-386-4366; www.jameshevans.com). Photographer James Evans has captured this high desert landscape and its peoples for decades—it's hard to find a bookstore in Texas that doesn't stock a copy of his big, beautiful coffee-table book, *Big Bend Pictures*. The gallery is open 10 AM–6 PM many days, but then again Evans might be out shooting or in the darkroom. Someone else might let you in, or call ahead to see if he can open. Evans's latest book, *Crazy from the Heat*, was released in fall 2011.

The French Co. Grocer stocks supplies in Marathon.

Front Street Books (432-386-4259; www.fsbooks.com), 105 TX 90 W. Open 9 AM daily; closes 6 PM every day except Sunday and Wednesday, when it closes at 1 PM. This is the Marathon branch of the wonderful independent bookstore in Alpine.

Terlingua/Study Butte

Quite a few people have cruised out to Terlingua thinking they have an idea of what it might be like. Sometimes these are people who know about the old Jerry Jeff Walker album *Viva Terlingua!* and that might give them the idea the town is a kind of musical concern. In other cases, the preconceived notion comes from publicity about how Terlingua is the Chili Capital of the World, so named by the Chili Appreciation Society.

The fact is, there's not much of anything in Terlingua by most peoples' standards—and the resident Terlinguans are good with that. It's a few minutes from Big Bend National Park and Big Bend Ranch State Park, a place to grab an extremely basic motel room to sleep in, in between rafting, kayaking, jeep tours, or otherwise enjoying the parks (the outfitters are based here). But if you love the desert and enjoy being around the sort of folk who like living off the grid, you'll also be at home hanging out here. For one thing, the views from certain high spots are drop-dead gorgeous.

Terlingua is an old quicksilver mining town—some of the buildings are

Leapin Lizard is one of the shopping options in Terlingua.

still standing, hence the name Terlingua Ghost Town. A gift shop occupies the former company store, and a bar/dinner theater is in the old movie theater. Ruins of rock mining shacks are scattered around the area. Sometimes people camp in them. This is the type of town (population, about 257) where people who'd rather not connect to the power company will rig up a car battery to run the VCR one night and watch a movie; where flushing the toilet more frequently than absolutely necessary is frowned upon.

Not to worry, though. There are motel rooms that have power and running water (not always actually in your room), and a few restaurants.

Study Butte (pronounced *stoody byoot*), 5 miles east of Terlingua, is little more than two convenience/general stores: the Cottonwood Store, and the Study Butte Store, which is a liquor store and gas station with WiFi.

Pick Your Spot

Best places to stay in and around Terlingua/Study Butte

Big Bend Motor Inn, and Big Bend Mission Lodge (432-371-2313; foreverlodging.com), TX 118 at TX 170—these are across the street from one another. Basic hotel rooms, nothing fancy. They do have kitchenettes, and two-bedroom suites, handy for a group or a family. Pets are allowed, and there are RV hookups on the property. Rates start at $69.95 for a room with one queen-sized bed.

Where to Stay, for Daytime Park Explorers

Deciding where to sleep while you explore the reaches of the Big Bend can be tough when you're just looking at a map. The obvious solution is Chisos Mountains Lodge, a hotel inside Big Bend National Park, beautifully situated and well priced. I have never found a room available there, but I seldom can plan a trip more than three or four months ahead of time. If you have the lead time, are interested in exploring the national park, and find a room available at the lodge, book it. No question. It's not fancy, but you cannot beat the location and scenery. For those who aren't so lucky, you'll be weighing distance versus access to amenities and necessities. Here's a quick guide by town to help you choose. (Mileage is to headquarters at Big Bend National Park.)

Alpine: 117 miles away, one fine-dining restaurant, many inexpensive choices for dining and lodging; considerable shopping, including a good-sized grocery.

Fort Davis: 140 miles away. Moderate dining and lodging.

Lajitas: 60 miles away. Upscale resort with lodging and dining.

Marfa: 148 miles away, several fine-dining choices, eclectic lodging, shopping, art.

Marathon: 86 miles away, one upscale hotel with upscale restaurant; moderate dining options available, some shopping.

Terlingua: 49 miles to headquarters, but you're on the park in about 20 minutes out of town. Very basic lodging and decent, but limited, dining.

Blue sky peeks between an overhang and a cliff on the Rio Grande in the Big Bend.

Chisos Mining Co. Motel (432-371-2254; www.cmcm.cc), TX 170. This is very basic lodging for people who want to enjoy the outdoors. I wouldn't suggest trying to sleep two in the room with the double bed for $57.23, although you do get a full bath and it's a bargain compared to some rates in town. Inexpensive.

El Dorado Hotel (800-371-3588; www.eldorado-hotel.net), TX 170, 5 miles east of the junction with TX 118. One more time: Nothing fancy. Our room had a huge hot tub, but you had to turn on a switch near a sink outside the bathroom to warm up the water first. Inexpensive.

La Posada Milagro (432-371-3044; 432-386-6496, cell; www.laposadamilagro.net), on Terlingua Ghost Town Hill. This is a rustic compound built six years ago on the foundations of old buildings. The least-expensive room is the Bunkroom, and that means four bunk beds crammed into a tiny space. The shared bathroom is next door off a courtyard that looks out over gorgeous desert views. Expensive. The attached coffee shop makes great espresso.

Local Flavors

Taste of the town—restaurants, cafés, bars, bistros, etc.

EATING OUT AND NIGHTLIFE

Kathy's Kosmic Kowgirl Kafe (432-371-2164; kathyskosmickow girlkafe.blogspot.com), off TX 170; you can't miss the hot pink trailer. Decent breakfasts, plus burgers and barbecue for lunch. Inexpensive.

Starlight Theatre Restaurant & Bar (432-371-2326; www.star lighttheatre.com), 100 Ivey Street. Open all week for dinner and for brunch on Sundays. Everyone hangs out in front and drinks beer in the evening. Then they go inside and eat burgers, drink, and dance to live music as the night wears on.

Kathy's Kosmic Kowgirl Kafe in Terlingua makes a mean barbecue sandwich.

Inexpensive to moderate.

La Kiva Restaurant and Bar (432-371-2250; www.lakiva.net), on TX 170 at Terlingua Creek. Open daily, 5–midnight, and until 1 AM on Saturdays. This subterranean bar/restaurant is dark and spooky, but they have an extensive menu including barbecue, ham soup, chicken-fried steak, and more. Moderate.

Selective Shopping

Terlingua Trading Co. (432-371-2234; www.historic-terlingua.com). Open 10 AM–9 PM. Find tons of books; clothing, including souvenir T-shirts; chili sauces and powders; and Day of the Dead accessories. This also is the source for the usual shot glasses and other souvenirs.

Lajitas

General John J. Pershing's troops established a cavalry post here in 1916 after Francisco "Pancho" Villa came through. In the 1970s, Lajitas was famous for a beer-drinking goat that eventually was elected mayor. By the 1980s, it was a resort town, and was sometimes used for filming movies and television (the movie *Contrabando* was filmed nearby, and the TV mini-series *Streets of Laredo*, starring James Garner, was filmed here.

The population has never been much more than 50 to 75, and today the town is mostly the 27,000-acre Lajitas Golf Resort and Spa, which has its own airport.

Pick Your Spot

Best places to stay in and around Lajitas

Lajitas Golf Resort and Spa (432-424-5000 or 877-LAJITAS; www.lajitasgolfresort.com). Lajitas is attractively designed and well maintained, but irregularly open shops and spotty service keep it off the A list of exotic destination resorts. That said, everyone was most helpful to me when I took a quick tour, though not too much was open. The many resort activities include backpacking, biking, ATV rentals, bird-watching, fishing, climbing, horseback riding and lessons, jeep tours, mountain biking, nature tours, river excursions, hunt-ing, and skeet shooting. Golfers can check out Black Jack's Crossing Golf Course (www.blackjackscrossing.com), an 18-hole championship course designed by pro golfer Lanny Wadkins. The par-72 course has a 500-yard driving range with 25 stations; putting green; a nine-hole par-3 course; a short game practice facility; and a GPS system. The old Lajitas trading post is the pro shop and the Longhorn Museum, which has a large collection of cattle horn specimens, including many from longhorns.

The small boardwalk at the resort offers an antiques store, bakery, the Cowboy Art Gallery, a Western tack and saddle store, and Christina's World, which has international clothing and jewelry.

The resort also has its own air-

The Badlands Hotel is part of the Lajitas Resort.

port, Lajitas International Airport, and an RV park, Maverick Ranch RV Park.

Local Flavors

Taste of the town—restaurants, cafés, bars, bistros, etc.

The nearby Lajitas General Store stocks groceries and essentials.

The Candelilla Café serves breakfast, lunch, and dinner, at prices that range from moderate to expensive.

Scenic Drive

The Camino del Rio or River Road between Lajitas and Presidio is more than 30 miles of TX 170 within Big Bend Ranch State Park. It's stunning and a little scary if you're not used to going up and down steep (but paved) hills alongside canyon walls. The road can be narrow with little or no shoulder. The *Contrabando* movie set is along the road, just west of Lajitas.

Presidio

The remote little town on the Rio Grande sits on land that's been farmed since 1500 B.C. and has a population of about 7,000. In 2010, it was featured in *National Geographic* magazine for having a giant battery for storing electricity, to help cope with frequent fluctuations and failures. Aside from that and a few gas stations, the only thing of note for a visitor to Presidio is Fort Leaton State Historic Site. The 23.4 acres once were home to a fortified trading post. The site also serves as a place to pick up permits and passes for Big Bend Ranch State Park.

Special Events

The Globe Theatre in Odessa stages Shakespeare each year.

Shakespeare Festival (hamlet@globesw.org; www.globesw.org), 2308 Shakespeare Road, Odessa. Each fall, Globe Theater of the Great Southwest.

Terlingua International Chili Cookoff, at Rancho CASI (Chili Appreciation Society International) de los Chisos in Terlingua, on the north side of TX 170, 11 miles west of Study Butte, 7 miles east of Lajitas. First Saturday in November.

Chinati Open House (432-729-4362; www.chinati.org), every October, Marfa. It's a free weekend to see Chinati galleries, with meals, talks, and more. The event fills Marfa with about 2,000 people each year.

Marfa Film Festival (www.marfafilmfestival.org), May in Marfa. Lou Reed was a guest one year.

Big Bend National Park

The land where the Rio Grande changes its mind and turns north before heading back down to the Gulf of Mexico is a desolate fantasyland so powerful and remote that you, like the river, will change from having been here.

The solitude alone is an immense force that sweeps away everything your senses know. The sights climb up and down through desert, grasslands, mountain woodlands, and floodplain; the sounds of the familiar world are gone, left far behind and replaced, mostly, with silence; smells are of damp river bottom, pines in the heights, and desert whipped clean by winds and briefly wet with fresh summer rains; touch with caution, because the life here is necessarily spiny and sharp for survival; and you'll develop a taste for water—a gallon a day is necessary for survival. Thrust into this other world, physically and mentally taken aback, visitors tend to either wish they could go home to the familiar, or find themselves eagerly overwhelmed at the possibilities, already planning the next trip when the first has scarcely begun. I've made three trips here and barely scratched the surface. I hope to come every year for the rest of my life.

There are basically three ways to take in the park: by car, on the river, or by hiking. There are enough explanations at pull-overs to keep you busy for more than a day just driving. River outfitters will take you on trips that range from a quick half-day to several days at a time, both roughing it and in luxury. There's enough easy hiking to take children on very short hikes (with plenty of water) and enough tough ones to suit the most extreme experienced hikers.

I like to combine all three on a single trip: Driving to get my bearings and perhaps see something new; rafting for the surreal canyons; and hiking to get close to the lonely, lovely desert.

Guidance

The National Park Service (www.nps.gov/bibe/index.htm) is the key source of information for anything you want to do here. They can keep you updated on road construction, mountain lion sightings, crowds, and anything else you

Staying Safe

The plain old common sense you brought from home isn't enough here. Heat can kill very quickly. In 2004 a man who didn't take water along died on a 2-mile trail after he apparently became disoriented. Even though I grew up in the desert and know to look for landmarks in the terrain (which tends to look the same after a while), I once became turned around hiking down around the river and took longer than I would have liked to get back to a parking spot. I did have water, though. Again, the rule of thumb is a gallon of water per person per day. Other pointers from the park service:

- Ask about conditions, check the weather forecast, get the maps you need.

- Tell someone where you're going, whether it's camp hosts or family.

- Don't leave your car if it breaks down. It's easier to find than a person walking alone.

- Don't count on a cell phone to get help. Horns, a mirror, or flares are other options. Wood fires are banned.

want to know before you leave home or after you arrive. Call 432-477-2251 or for just the weather information hotline, 432-477-1183.

The park is open 24/7 all year. The main visitor center, Panther Junction Visitors Center, is open 8–6, but can be closed on Christmas Day. Chisos Basin Visitor Center is open 8–3:30 PM daily November through March and closed for lunch. April through October it's open 9–4:30 daily. The other three visitor centers typically are open only October through April. Rio Grande Village Visitor Center, 8:30–4:30; Persimmon Gap Visitor Center, 9–4:30; Castolon Visitor Center, 10–5. All are closed for lunch, and all these times are subject to change.

The entrance fee is $20 per vehicle for a seven-day pass.

Getting Around

The only choice is whether to use a four-wheel drive so you can check out the primitive and dirt roads, or if you'd rather rent a vehicle at the airport that works only on pavement. I've chosen cars for budgetary reasons, but usually wished I had something with more clearance, because I hesitated to go down roads I wanted to investigate.

To See and Do

DRIVES

You can see by looking at a map that the park has few paved roads, mostly linking the visitor centers with entrances, but that doesn't mean you can't see a lot of stunning scenery this way. Just don't be tempted to keep driving when you see a pull-over. Sometimes a quick walk can be a lot of fun and teach you a lot about where you are. The speed on all park roads is 45 max, and they're serious about this. It's both to protect wildlife and visitors on the two-lane blacktop.

Persimmon Gap to Panther Junction: This is a good start to get you inside the park. During the 28-mile drive, you'll see the Rosillos Mountains to the west and Dead Horse Mountains to the east. The cool hoodoos (rock spires) at Tornillo Flat are visible along this road. Get out and look around the visitor center. There are rangers here to answer your questions, cold beverages, and lots of books and maps at the good-sized center.

Panther Junction to Rio Grande Village: The Rio Grande Village is a developed campground. This road also takes you to Boquillas Canyon, the park's longest and widest canyon. From here you can look across and see the village of Boquillas, Mexico. (See Boquillas sidebar) This drive also takes you past Dugout Wells picnic area and nature trail and the Hot Springs Historic District.

Maverick Entrance Station-Panther Junction: This comes to Panther Junction from the west, and has roadside pull-overs telling you what kinds of wildlife you might see. You'll see turnoffs for the Ross Maxwell Scenic Drive and **Chisos Basin Road:** This short one, 6 miles roughly in the center of the park, is a must. The views of rocky peaks coming up into the Chisos from the desert are amazing. The sharp curves and steep grades prohibit RVs longer than 24 feet and trailers longer than 20 feet.

Ross Maxwell Scenic Drive: The 30 miles from Burro Mesa down to the river are gorgeous. You can pick up a hiking trail and take a closer look at the canyon at the end (see sidebar). Flash flooding can close the section from Castolon to Santa Elena Canyon.

Dirt and Primitive Roads: Some of the dirt roads are navigable most of the time in a two-wheel drive car, but not always. Check with the park service if you're thinking about trying one, and heed any warnings. Whatever else you do, make sure you have plenty of gasoline, plenty of water, and a fully inflated spare.

OUTDOORS

Bird Watching

More than 400 species of birds have been spotted here, from peregrine falcons around the Chisos to greater roadrunners, which I've seen all over the park. The Colima warbler, which lives only in the Chisos Mountains, is the Holy Grail here for serious birders.

Camping

Rio Grande Village, Chisos, and Castolon: In a cottonwood grove next to the river, Rio Grande is the biggest developed campground, with 100 sites. All three of these campgrounds have picnic tables, grills, flush toilets, and running water for $14/night. Some sites can be reserved November 15 through April 15, call 877-444-6777. There are also group campsites available only by reservation by calling the same number.

Rio Grande Village RV Campground: This is run by Forever Resorts (not the park service, like the other campgrounds) and is the only one in the park with RV hookups, 25 of them. Call 877-386-4383.

Backcountry Camping: Both zoned sites for backpack camping and primitive campsites are available. Backcountry use permits, $10 each, are required, and you must follow park rules regarding food storage (Not only bears, but javelinas and kangaroo rats are interested in your food.) Check www.nps.gov/bibe for details.

Geology

The lack of vegetation here makes the geologic forces easier to see than in many parts of the world—and the forces that twisted and thrust through this land were many. I'm not a geologist, but I've summarized here the National Park Service's comprehensive explanation of how it all worked (if you want to read the complete story, you'll find it at www.nps.gov/bibe):

A deep-ocean trough stretched from what are now Arkansas and Oklahoma to the Big Bend for about 200 million years. Beginning about 300 million years ago, in the Paleozoic Era, a continent to the south collided with the sandstone and shale beds that had formed in the trough, to create the early Ouachita Mountains. Those mountains were eroded over 160 million years, and some of what was left is visible near Persimmon Gap. The limestone layers we see now at Santa Elena, Mariscal, and Boquillas canyons, the cliffs of the Sierra del Carmen in Mexico, visible from Rio Grande Village, and elsewhere in the park were created some 135 million years ago during the Cretaceous Period, when a warm, shallow sea lay over the Big Bend. That sea retreated to where it lies now, in the form of the Gulf of Mexico. Some interesting fossils were left behind, including a giant flying reptile called *Quetzalcoatlus northropi.* You can see a replica of the bones of one wing at Panther Junction Visitor Center.

As that period ended, mountain building began, including the uplifting that formed the Rocky Mountains—Mariscal Mountain in Big Bend is an extension of the Rockies.

The Rio Grande

The Rio Grande, or the Rio Bravo del Norte on the Mexico side, suffers as it winds its way down more than 1,000 miles from the San Juan Mountains of Colorado to the Gulf of Mexico. Irrigation to the north pulls out a lot of water, and it's slowed by the Elephant Butte and Caballo dams. Salt cedar, or Russian tamarisk, introduced to stabilize the banks, slurps up water and has crowded out much of the other vegetation that used to thrive. So by the time the mighty Rio makes it to the Big Bend, it can be pretty slow going at some times of the year—in 2003, the river actually stopped flowing through the park. But not to worry, rafting or canoeing or kayaking the river is still very doable and lots of fun. Just check the flow with your outfitter if this is a crucial part of your trip—and it should be—and plan accordingly. Unless you're an experienced river runner, you'll need an outfitter. All three of these outfitters offer a variety of tours besides river rafting, and also rent equipment.

Things were fairly quiet for the next 10 million years, but then volcanic activity began. Some 38–32 million years ago, eruptions took place below the South Rim of the Chisos Mountains, and then at Pine Canyon, Burro Mesa, near Castolon, and elsewhere. These caused the brightly colored layers you see at lower elevations.

Sometimes the magma didn't make it to the surface, and spread in layers of rock, lifting them up and then cooling. Erosion has exposed some of these, which today are Maverick Mountain, the Grapevine Hills, Nugent Mountain, and Pulliam Ridge.

In another 10 million years (or about 26 million years ago), the earth's crust started to stretch, leaving fractures where blocks of rock slid down. The Chisos Mountains, from Sierra del Carmen to the Mesa de Anguila, are such blocks.

You can see the faulting at the tunnel near Rio Grande Village, where the limestone layer over the tunnel is the same layer that makes the skyline of the Sierra del Carmen.

The volcanic activity still takes place—a 5.6-magnitude earthquake was recorded near Marathon in 1995.

Meanwhile, the Rio Grande only made it to the Gulf of Mexico within the last 2 million years, making it the youngest major river system in the U.S. The river continues to carry material caused by erosion (from runoff and flash-flooding) out of the park.

Far Flung Outdoor Center (800-839-7238; www.ffoc.net), Terlingua. Valynda Henington, who co-owns Far Flung with Greg Henington, will help you figure out anything about your trip. Greg was more than patient when I lost a notebook and had to have a garage unlocked well after hours. Besides being nice, they've been doing river trips and jeep tours around here for most of two decades. Their guides know their stuff. We took a one-day trip down Colorado Canyon in Big Bend Ranch State Park and were blown away by what we saw. Far Flung also offers every-thing from half-day to 10-day river trips, including specialty journeys like music trips, gourmet trips (these luxury floats with menus including beef Wellington and fine wines were featured in *Texas Monthly* and *Southern Living*), and family adventure trips. From $66/person for a half-day family float. Also offered: jeep and ATV tours, guided educational hikes, and wilderness medicine instruction.

Desert Sports (888-989-6900; www.desertsportstx.com). The smallest of the three outfitters in town, Desert Sports touts that as an advantage, since they guide more intimate groups and the same crews return year after year. From $125 per person with four people, $135 with two or three. Also available: hiking and camping trips, mountain biking trips.

Big Bend River Tours (800-545-4240; www.bigbendrivertours.com). Their Web site calls them the oldest full-service outfitter in the area, with lots of options on the river and off. Half-day river tours start at $64 for groups of 21 people and more. Also offered: horseback tours, guided hikes, and driving tours by van.

Hiking

The park has more than 150 miles of hiking trails, from very easy to very difficult. The easiest trail of all is the paved, handicapped-accessible Window View Trail—do this if you don't take another hike the entire trip. You can walk up the .3-mile trail from the Chisos Basin trailhead and rest on benches. The reward for very little effort is a great view of the sunset through the Window, a gap in the rock formations, so head out in the early evening.

Otherwise, you have a choice of trails at every skill level. The park rangers will take the time to mark maps and give you directions to the ones that are within your capabilities, so the most important stop you make will be the visitor center if you want to hike but don't know much about the park.

Jeep Tours

You'll learn a lot during the interpretive jeep tour offered by Far Flung Outdoor Center, but here's a tip: You'll learn almost as much on a rafting trip with the same outfitter. Their river guides are highly knowledgeable about the desert flora and fauna, as well as the history of the area, and you'll spend a long time with them on a rafting trip. You don't necessarily need to book both, unless you want the thrill of repeatedly cresting the rugged, rocky hills and plunging down in a four-wheeler, which is a little like a roller-coaster ride. And you will get to spend time looking at cacti, etc., close-up, which is a must whether you do it this way or by hiking.

Kids

The Big Bend is like any outdoors experience with kids—you'll have to choose age-appropriate activities and keep busy to prevent boredom. Unless you're into family camping and are fully prepared for it, the easiest way to see the park with kids would be to book a room at Chisos Mountain Lodge. That avoids long car trips from other towns and potentially sketchy motel rooms in Terlingua. Children don't usually care much about a beautiful view

Santa Elena Canyon

One of the most extraordinary sights in the park is among the easiest to see via a hiking trail. I climbed it as I was getting over a (poorly timed) case of the flu, so the hike shouldn't prove too hard for most people. The steep canyon walls rise some 1,500 feet above the Rio Grande. The Santa Elena Canyon trail starts at the end of Ross Maxwell Scenic Drive. It's about 1.7 miles round-trip. After crossing Terlingua Creek, you climb up short switchbacks and then begin to descend to the river, amid huge boulders, until you're finally at the bottom. The feeling of being so small at the bottom of the vertical limestone cliffs is awe inspiring.

Steep canyon walls rise above the Rio Grande in Big Bend National Park.

from the car, but they'll get into interesting rocks and rock formations; an easy rafting trip (make it a half-day if they're small—the younger kids on a full-day trip I took may have been a little too exhausted by the end); or horseback riding. Definitely bring lots of water and plenty of sunscreen, no matter where you're going, plus hats and light, long-sleeved clothing. Families will want to pay special attention to trip timing, to ensure they come during cooler months of fall or early spring. Kids may enjoy completing the

Boquillas

For years, one of the great Texas traditions for Big Bend regulars was a boat trip across Boquillas Canyon to the Mexican side of the river, where the little town of Boquillas welcomed visitors with beer, tequila, and tacos. It was a happy reciprocal arrangement that provided a little tourist money for Boquillas, where it went a long way, and a little fun for park visitors. That all ended with the September 11, 2001 terrorist attacks, when the tiny border crossing was closed.

The official word is that the crossing was to be reopened in April 2012, so ask the rangers, and be sure to check it out if you like a little adventure. The river tends to be quieter in Boquillas Canyon, so it's a favorite spot for a float trip.

Junior Ranger Program. Pick up a Junior Ranger Activity book for $2 at any visitor center and take a look—children can attend ranger programs (divided into age groups) and complete learning activities about history, wildlife, and plant life to earn Junior Ranger status. Junior Rangers get a badge or patch, a certificate, and a bookmark.

Mountain Biking

I am not a cyclist, at least not devoted enough to bring a bike traveling, but I can see why the park is a favorite place for it. Few vehicles, more than 100 miles of paved roads and 160 miles of dirt roads, on terrain from flat to mountainous—it offers something for every skill level. You'll find the least traffic in summer, but it's hottest then. Beware spring break and the holidays, when cars are all over the park. No single-track cycling is allowed, nor is off-road, to protect the desert.

Of the three outfitters in Terlingua, Desert Sports offers mountain-bike trips. If you're bringing your own bike, get advice about the best routes and difficulty from them and from rangers, and pick up a road map. To get a feel for what's there, check out the park service Web site, which lists nine rides, with mileage, difficulty, and description, www.nps.gov/bibe/planyourvisit/biking.htm.

Pick Your Spot

Best places to stay in and around Big Bend National Park

There's only one motel in the park, the spectacularly located Chisos Mountains Lodge (877-386-4383, reservations; 432-477-2292, lodge; www.chisosmountainslodge.com).

The 72-room motel sits in the center of the park, the Chisos looming overhead, trailheads nearby. Plan a year ahead of time if you want to stay here—the lodge stays booked. The most crowded times are spring break, Easter weekend, Thanksgiving weekend, and the week between Christmas and New Year's. The lodge has a restaurant that opens at 7 AM, and a gift shop. Moderate.

Food, Gasoline, Supplies

Again, the only restaurant is at the Chisos Mountains Lodge. Otherwise, you can stock up on snacks off the park when you stop for gas (call ahead to make sure they're open).

Panther Junction Chevron (432-477-2251), Panther Junction.

Stillwell Trailer Park (432-376-2244), Farm-to-Market 2627.

The view from certain cabins at Chisos Mountains Lodge is stunning.

Big Bend Ranch State Park

The state park is more than 300,000 acres, with 23 miles along the Rio Grande. During one of my trips we took a rafting trip down Colorado Canyon in the state park because of low water conditions elsewhere. The state park reaches from Lajitas to Presidio and has more than 66 miles of trails and about 49 campsites.

For information and permits: Sauceda Complex in the park (432-358-4444); Barton Warnock Visitor Center (432-424-3327), Lajitas; Fort Leaton State Historic Site (432-229-3613), Presidio.

Lodging is at the Sauceda Complex (reservations, 512-389-8919, from 9 to 6 Monday through Friday), which can sleep eight. Rates vary according to the number of people, but start at $100/room for 1 or 2 people. There's also a bunkhouse that accommodates men and women separately for $35/person.

You can rent mountain bikes and horses at the complex. Or, for a real Wild West experience, come to the state park for the longhorn roundup, a four-day event that takes place twice a year. Call 432-358-4444 for roundup information.

The daily entry fee for the park is $3 per person per day.

Big Bend Resort & RV Campground (800-848-BEND), Junction of TX 118 and FM 170.

Study Butte Store (432-371-2231), Study Butte, TX 118.

Big Bend Resort Convenience Store (432-371-2218), TX 118, Study Butte.

The Terlingua Store (432-371-2487), FM 170, Terlingua.

Terlingua Springs Market (432-371-2332), FM 170, 0.5 mile west of junction with TX 118.

Learn More

BOOKS

Hiking

Glendinning, Jim. *Adventures in the Big Bend: A Travel Guide*. Iron Mountain Press, 2010. The author has lived in the area for more than a decade.

Parent, Laurence. *Hiking Big Bend National Park*. Falcon Press, 1996. A very detailed hiking guide.

Parent, Laurence, and Joe Nick Patoski. *Big Bend National Park.* University of Texas Press, 2006. A picture book with good hiking info from an experienced hiker.

History

Ragsdale, Kenneth B. *Big Bend Country, Land of the Unexpected.* Texas A&M University Press, 1998. Gives a sense of the area through stories.

Smithers, W. D. *Chronicles of the Big Bend.* Texas Historical Association, 1999. An essential collection of documentary historical photos, with narrative.

Tyler, Ronnie C. *The Big Bend, A History of the Last Texas Frontier.* Texas A&M Press, 2007. A comprehensive history.

Coffee Table Books

There are many, but my favorite remains:

Evans, James, and Robert Draper. *Big Bend Pictures.* University of Texas Press, 2003.

4

Far West Texas

EL PASO

EL PASO SITS against the Franklin Mountains, their deep blue flanks a backdrop for the city's sprawl over the Chihuahuan Desert, south to the Rio Grande and the border with Mexico.

The teeming city of 700,000 is separated only by the river from more than a million people in Juarez. Cultures have clashed and meshed here for centuries. Native Americans were in the area since before recorded time; the Spanish passed through in 1598, and founded Guadalupe mission in 1659 in what they called El Paso del Norte, now Juarez. Texas, and therefore El Paso, became part of the U.S. in 1845, and the Mexican War in 1848 finally settled the question of where the border lay—mostly. The meandering Rio Grande caused squabbling that was finally settled with the signing of the Chamizal Convention in 1963.

The economy here is driven largely by Fort Bliss (the U.S. Army post), and government jobs including U.S. Customs and the Border Patrol.

If it's sophistication you're after, this is not the place. But El Chuco, as it is fondly known by residents, has many charms. The city is safe—violent crime is low—despite several years of violence across the border. Its long history of Native American, then Spanish settlement, and proximity to Mexico mean cultural diversity is a given. The population today is more than 70 percent Hispanic, so you'll hear Spanish spoken as often as English.

The climate is lovely in winter and fall, and intensely hot (100 degrees and higher) in late spring and summer, making it fine for outdoor activity year-round.

LEFT: Madrone trees grow in Guadalupe Mountains National Park.

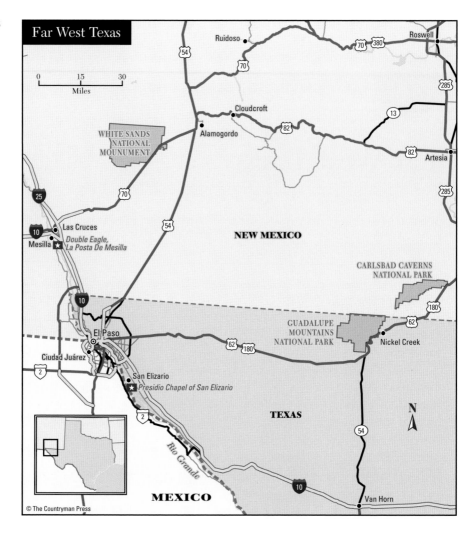

Far West Texas

0 15 30
Miles

Ruidoso
Roswell
70 · 380
54
70
285

Cloudcroft
13
82

WHITE SANDS NATIONAL MOUNUMENT
Alamogordo
82
Artesia

70
25

285
NEW MEXICO

Las Cruces
10
54
Mesilla · Double Eagle, La Posta De Mesilla

CARLSBAD CAVERNS NATIONAL PARK
180

10
GUADALUPE MOUNTAINS NATIONAL PARK
62
El Paso
62 · 180
Nickel Creek

Ciudad Juárez
2

San Elizario
Presidio Chapel of San Elizario

TEXAS
N

2
54

10

Rio Grande

MEXICO
© The Countryman Press
Van Horn

El Pasoans also love to make music, from the summertime Music Under the stars at the Chamizal National Memorial to mariachi bands you'll occasionally hear in restaurants.

Mexican food aficionados are in heaven—everyone has a favorite restaurant or three, and almost all of them are very reasonably priced. If it's something more cosmopolitan you crave, you'll find some of that too, particularly on the West Side, where increasingly sophisticated eateries are serving up the likes of fusion dishes and more.

You also can see a lot for very little money here—most of the museums and attractions are free.

Key Spanish Phrases

You'll hear a lot of Spanish spoken in El Paso, although everyone also speaks English. If you want to join in on the Spanish, or if someone looks confused, here are a few sentences to get you by in an emergency:

Where is the bathroom? *¿Dónde esta el baño?*

One more beer, please. *Uno mas cerveza, por favor.*

How are you? *¿Cómo está usted?*

The check, please. *El cheque, por favor.*

Excuse me (for use in a line or crowd). *Con permiso.*

El Paso is not a city of great architectural beauty, but the tall Franklins are beautiful against the blue desert sky, and the peaks take on tinges of pink and orange at sunset. (They also make it easy to navigate the city if you're directionally challenged.)

Most of all, the cultural diversity developed over four centuries makes this a place with a heart—a place where, for centuries, travelers have stopped for a day or a year, or stayed despite the differences they may have brought with them. This openness continues today.

Area Codes

El Paso's area code is 915. The area code in southern New Mexico is 575.

Guidance

El Paso Convention and Visitors Bureau (800-351-6024; www.visitelpaso .com), One Civic Center Plaza, can steer you to what you need to know.

Getting There

It's a long drive from the Dallas–Fort Worth area—10 to 12 hours—and there's not a lot to look at on the way without drastic detours down to Big Bend or up to Carlsbad Caverns in New Mexico. So flying may be your best bet. There are plenty of flights daily on both American Eagle and Southwest Airlines, starting at around $300 round trip from the DFW area. Southwest offers two free checked bags and departs from Love Field in Dallas. American Eagle flies from Dallas–Fort Worth International Airport. El Paso International Airport is small and easy to navigate.

Like much of West Texas, renting a car is really the only option. El Paso does have a bus system, but you'll be wanting to travel outside the city while you're here.

The Sun Metro Bus Service (915-534-5816; ww.ci.el-paso.tx.us/ sunmetro) covers the city well, and it's a bargain at $1.50 standard fares, but be aware the buses are often quite crowded.

Medical Emergencies

The major hospitals are Providence Memorial Hospital (915-577-6011; www.sphn-pmh.com), 2001 N. Oregon Street; Sierra Medical Center (915-747-4000; www.sphn.com), 1625 Medical Center Drive; University Medical Center (915-544-1200; www.umcelpaso.org), 4815 Alameda; Del Sol (915-595-9000; www.delsolmedicalcenter .com), 10301 Gateway Boulevard West; and Las Palmas (915-544-5203; www.laspalmashealth.com), 1801 N. Oregon Street.

About Juarez, Mexico

For years, shoppers went across the border to Juarez for barhopping, shopping, and dining. No more. The border city of 1.3 million people to the south is no longer safe. The annual number of homicides has been in the thousands for several years running as warring drug cartels battle for control of U.S. trafficking routes.

Surprisingly, the opposite has been happening in El Paso over the same time period. In 2010, Juarez murders numbered 2,500, while in El Paso there were 5— down from 12 in 2009.

People who live and work here feel extremely safe. They just don't cross into Juarez anymore.

Media

The *El Paso Times* is the daily newspaper here. *El Paso Scene* is a free monthly arts and entertainment publication.

Web sites:

www.visitelpaso.com

www.elpasohistory.com

www.elpasotexas.com/downtown

Tours

By bus: Amigo Shuttle Tours (915-355-1739; www.amigoshuttle.info), 6869 Enid Court, #11, has long provided tours in the city as well as out to Carlsbad Caverns, White Sands Missile Range, and more.

By foot: The convention and visitors bureau can supply you with a comprehensive pamphlet on a self-guided walking tour through the downtown historic district. It takes about 90 minutes. If the weather's nice (not too hot) and you don't have young ones who will get tired, this is worth your while. There are some pretty old buildings, and you have to see the Luis Jimenez alligator sculpture at San Jacinto Plaza, as well as sites of famous gunfights, including the spot where John Wesley Hardin was killed.

To See and Do

Downtown

Camino Real Hotel (915-534-3000; www.caminoreal.com/english), 101 S. El Paso Street. An historic hotel originally built in 1912, the Camino Real is El Paso's finest downtown hotel. The property has changed hands over the years and currently is owned by a Mexican company (unless you read Spanish be sure to add /English to the Web site address). The likes of Pancho Villa and Blackjack Pershing have stayed here. A must-see that a lot of visitors miss is the gorgeous, 80-year-old Tiffany glass dome at the Dome Bar. It's a laid-back, quiet place to have a drink. Moderate.

El Paso Museum of Art (915-532-1707; www.elpasoartmuseum.com), One Arts Festival Plaza downtown. Closed Monday. The striking contemporary building opened in 1998, but the museum was founded in 1959. The permanent collections hold more than 5,000 works: American (including a Gilbert Stuart painting of George Washington), European masters, works on paper, and more. In a tribute to the area's history, there's also a Spanish Viceroyal collection as well as Mexican colonial, and a nice collection of *retablos*. The gift shop contains a good collection of Diego Rivera and Frieda Kahlo items. Free, except for selected exhibitions.

The Camino Real downtown is El Paso's fine hotel.

Don't Miss

Wyler Aerial Tramway (915-566-6622; www.tpwd.state.tx.us), 1700 McKinley. The schedule changes somewhat for summer and winter, but the tram is closed Tuesday and Wednesday all year, and open noon–6 most of the rest of the week all year. The Swiss-made tram sways a little, providing a real thrill if you're afraid of heights. You'll drive up the mountain from the East side to the parking lot at 4,692 feet, where the view of the city is impressive. The tram takes you to the top of Ranger Peak, at 5,623 feet. From there, you can see about 7,000 square miles—into three states (Texas, New Mexico, and Chihuahua state in Mexico) and two nations (the U.S. and Mexico).

El Paso Museum of History (915-351-3588; www.elpaso.gov/history), 510 Santa Fe Street. Built in 2007, this downtown museum takes you through 400 years of the colorful history here at the Pass of the North, covering everything from the Spanish presence to the Mexican Revolution to present times. Free except for selected exhibitions.

Fray Garcia Monument, Pioneer Plaza at El Paso and San Francisco streets. The sculpture by John Houser remembers the priest who founded the first mission in the area.

Insights-El Paso Science Museum (915-534-0000; www.insightselpaso .org), 505 N. Santa Fe. This is the fun one for the kids, with fossils, bubbles, and wonders like a Tesla coil and centrifugal force spinner. Adults, $8; students, military, and seniors, $6; ages 4–11, $4; 3 and under, free.

A Luis Jimenez sculpture greets visitors at the El Paso Museum of Art.

Plaza Theatre (915-231-1100; www.theplazatheatre.org), 125 Pioneer Plaza. Originally opened in 1930, the Plaza almost was razed to make room for a parking lot in 1986. Supporters, including singer Rita Moreno, rallied to

Best of El Paso

Wyler Aerial Tramway

Franklin Mountains State Park

Plaza Theatre

Mission Trail

El Paso Saddleblanket

raise money and saved the old building. It was restored and re-opened in 2006. Now the building is a beauty again, and it's a lively venue that brings in Broadway productions, and is the home of the El Paso Symphony Orchestra. The Plaza Classic Film Festival is an increasingly popular event each year.

San Jacinto Plaza, at the center of downtown, bordered by Mills, Mesa, Oregon, and Main Streets, sits where Spanish explorer Ponce de Leon once had corrals. At one time, three alliga-tors lived in the pond—the source of the nickname La Plaza de los Lagartos (Alligator Plaza)—but they were moved to the zoo in 1967. An alligator sculpture by nationally known artist Luis Jimenez, an El Pasoan, stands there now.

Adair Margo Fine Art (915-533-0048; www.adairmargo.com), 215 Stanton, Suite 602. Stop by to see who's exhibiting—you might see works that will be nationally famous later. Dozens of regional artists have been placed by this gallery into the White House, national museums, and U.S. embassies.

East and West Sides

Chamizal National Memorial (915-532-7273; www.nps.gov/cham), 800 South San Marcial Street. Visitors center open Tuesday through Saturday; grounds open daily. The site of great open-air concerts with dancing to diverse genres from Cajun to Mexican (the free, summertime Music Under the Stars), the 55-acre memorial marks the end of a longstanding border dispute between the U.S. and Mexico. The friction began because the Rio Grande had gradually moved south, taking land from Mexico. The problems were resolved by the signing of the Chamizal Convention in 1963. Because of the treaty, cement was installed in some 4 miles of riverbed to stop the

Fort Bliss

Fort Bliss is a huge Army post on the east side of El Paso that stretches 1.12 million acres (about 1,700 square miles) into the desert for training and tank maneuvers. At any given time at least 60,000 people live on the post, which is home to the First Armored Division.

Ballet Folklorico and Mariachi Bands

You may run into *ballet folklorico* at Chamizal National Memorial and you definitely will see it if you attend a performance of *Viva! El Paso* at McKelligon Canyon Amphitheatre. The traditional folk dancing varies in costume and music by the state in Mexico where it originated. If it's Nuevo Leon, for example, the music will be mostly polkas and waltzes. The female dancers wear white lace dresses if the dance is from Veracruz. Probably the most common style is from Jalisco, where the men wear a big sombrero and the women are dressed in brightly colored swirling skirts.

Jalisco also is where the tradition of *mariachi* bands came from. For the uninitiated, these are bands you may see coming toward you at a Mexican restaurant. There's usually a guitar or two, trumpets, possibly a violin, and lots of singing. They're quite loud, and a lot of fun, but their talents are lost on some people. They are liable to stand there playing until you tip them, and you should—how much is up to you, but don't be insulting. It's fair to wave them off and say "no gracias" the second time they approach.

shifting and straighten that section of the river. Besides the concerts, regular cultural events at the memorial, such as *ballet folklorico* (Mexican dancing) and the Siglo de Oro Spanish Drama Festival celebrate understanding between cultures. Different exhibits rotate through the memorial's three indoor galleries. Rangers provide tours, and you can stretch your legs with a stroll along the 1.8-mile Cordova Island Trail, which encircles the park. Admission to the grounds is free except for groups of 50 or more, which must pay a $25 application fee.

Concordia Cemetery (915-591-2327; www.concordiacemetery.org), 3700 Yandell. Open daily. History buffs will want to make a stop at the Texas State Historical site, the final resting place for some 60,000 people, including Buffalo Soldiers, early Mormon pioneers, Texas Rangers, and John Wesley Hardin. Free. Also, the Paso del Norte Paranormal Society has ghost tours the first Saturday of each month for $10.

El Paso Museum of Archaeology and Wilderness Park (915-755-4332; www.elpasotexas.gov/arch_museum), 4301 Transmountain Road. Closed Mondays. Located in the Franklin Mountains, the city-run museum has 15 acres of nature trails and exhibits telling the history of inhabitants starting in the Ice Age. Free.

University of Texas–El Paso

As you explore the Westside, you'll probably notice a cluster of unusual buildings along the way—tan orange, overhanging roofs capping cream buildings with sloping walls. This is the University of Texas–El Paso campus, and the architecture is Bhutanese.

The story of how the architecture of a country between India and Tibet came to be in El Paso began just after the university was founded, in 1914, when it was the Texas State School of Mines and Metallurgy. The wife of then-Dean Steven Worrell had seen a *National Geographic* photo essay on Bhutan, and convinced her husband that the style would suit the new campus. The first building on campus, Old Main, was built in that style, and it continued as the campus grew.

Today UTEP has semi-annual Bhutan Days to remember its buildings' roots.

Keystone Heritage Park (915-584-0563; www.keystoneheritagepark.org), 4220 Doniphan. Botanic gardens open weekends; desert area open daily for bird-watching until 12:30 PM. Archaeology access requires a guide. A wetlands preserve and botanic garden also includes a village carbon-dated to more than 4,000 years old. Admission, $3.

Lower Valley

The Mission Trail (915-534-0677; www.elpasocvb.com), San Elizario, 15 minutes from downtown: Take I-10 east to the Zaragosa exit, turn south and follow the blue historical signs. Open during daylight hours.

Seeing the three beautiful Spanish missions built in the 1600s and 1700s is a perfect way to spend an afternoon, and get a real feel for El Paso's beginnings. Because the Tigua and Piro Indians helped build the missions, they bear elements of both Spanish and Native American craftsmanship and decoration.

The pretty adobe Ysleta Mission originally was established in 1682, but the current building

Afternoon Excursion

Spend an afternoon looking at the three missions on the Mission Trail; stop off at Licon's Dairy and see the goats; then have a steak at Cattleman's Steakhouse.

The San Elizario Chapel is on El Paso's Mission Trail.

went up in 1851. The Socorro Mission was built in 1682. The San Elizario Presidio Chapel, still an active church today, was built in 1789.

Maps for self-guided tours are available at the El Paso Convention and Visitors Bureau at One Civic Center Plaza Downtown and at the Portales Museum and Information Center (915-851-1682), 1521 San Elizario Road, San Elizario, which has historical exhibits. Admission is free. Guided tours are available at various rates from the Mission Trail Association (915-851-9997; www.themissiontrail.net), 1500 Main Street, San Elizario.

Licon's Dairy (915-851-2705), 11951 Glorietta Road. Pet the goats and buy fresh, white asadero cheese.

OUTDOORS

Hiking, Rock Climbing, Camping

Franklin Mountains State Park (915-566-6441; www.tpwd.state.tx.us), 1331 McKelligon Canyon Road. The park also is accessible from the Canutillo-Transmountain Road exit off I-10 and from Loop 375. Developers were beginning to build roads on the Franklins in the 1970s, and the Texas Legislature acted quickly to stop the carving, designating 37 square miles as a state park. Only two hiking trails are in use (the trailheads are near the entrance from Loop 375), but the park has picnic tables with marvelous vistas—or, if you're not in the mood for a picnic, just pull over and enjoy the view. If you go up toward McKelligon Canyon on a weekend, you might get the urge to join others headed up the mountain for exercise, some of

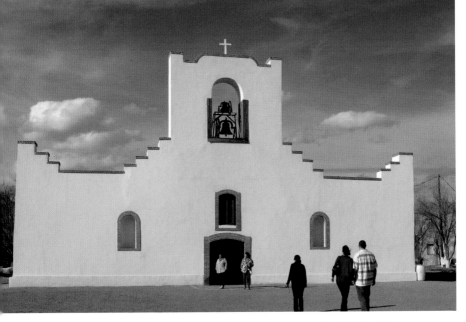

The Socorro Mission was built in the 1800s; the original was founded in 1682.

them soldiers trudging with backpacks. Rock-climbing, mountain biking, and primitive camping also are available at the park. If you go in spring, you'll see acres of brilliant red and yellow Mexican poppies blooming. Admission $4 per person over 13 years of age, per day.

Guadalupe Mountains National Park (915-828-3251; www.nps.gumo). Visitor center hours 8 AM–4:30 PM. The park that contains the highest peak in Texas, Guadalupe Peak, is about a two-hour drive from El Paso, on the road to Carlsbad Caverns. There's a trail to the top of Guadalupe Peak, but you need to be in good shape to get there. One of the most popular hikes (and much easier) is McKittrick Canyon in the fall, when the trees are changing. You can also cool off at Frijole Ranch History Museum, the site of an old ranch headquarters. The park is open year-round. All the hiking areas have easy hikes of less than 1 mile, in addition to the more difficult trails. McKittrick Canyon is a day-use area; the gate at the highway opens at 8 AM and

The view from Transmountain Road stretches for miles.

A hike in Guadalupe Mountains National Park can be easy or strenuous; take your pick.

closes at 4:30 PM. Drive past the McKittrick Canyon and Frijole Ranch turnoffs to stop at the visitors center, where you can get a free, good map with descriptions of the hikes. Adults, $5.

Mount Cristo Rey, off McNutt Road, in Sunland Park, New Mexico. Easter pilgrims climb the 800-foot peak to a 29-foot statue of Christ created by sculptor Urbici Soler. This area has had problems with crime (robberies) in the past, but it's safe to climb in a group.

Aguirre Spring Campground (505-525-4300; www.blm.gov/nm), 45 minutes from El Paso off US 70. Open year-round. This is high in the steep and rugged Organ Mountains just over the state line in New Mexico. As you ascend, you'll see the vegetation change from desert cacti to piñons and juniper. Two trails (4 and 6 miles) lead to spectacular views. There are more than 50 campsites, and just as many picnic areas. It can get crowded with picnicking families on the weekends. Mountain lions are occasionally spotted here. Fees are $3/vehicle days, and $3/night to camp.

Feather Lake Wildlife Sanctuary (915-545-5157), 9500 North Loop Drive. There's not always water in the lake on this small (43.5-acre) sanctuary, but when there is you can see muskrats swimming, and turtles. Bird-watchers have spotted more than 200 species. Free.

Kilbourne Hole, 30 miles west of the Franklin Mountains. A Maar volcanic crater more than a mile wide and 300 feet deep, it's believed to be about 80,000 years old. The directions for getting here (see www.visitelpaso.com) are complicated, and it's a destination that's hard to grasp if you're not a

The First Thanksgiving

Some El Pasoans will argue that the first Thanksgiving wasn't the traditional feast with the Pilgrims at Plymouth Rock that we learned
about in school, but instead a 1598 celebration by exhausted Spanish
explorers at the end of what sounds like one of the most miserable
trips in Texas history.

Don Juan de Oñate that year led some 500 people from San Pedro,
Mexico, to the El Paso area, after an earlier group came back and
failed to tell him about the lack of water on the trail. Early on, they
were rained on for a straight week. The big expedition moved slowly,
burdened as it was with livestock, so food ran out, forcing them to
eat roots. Water also eventually ran out. Partway there, Oñate sent out
an advance patrol that was scared to death when Indians held them
prisoner—and then let them go, saying it was all a joke. By the time
the patrol arrived at the Rio Grande, after about 50 days, they were
so thirsty they all plunged into the river. Two of the horses drank until
they burst, and human members of the party drank so much they
grew waterlogged and lay beside the stream "like foul wretches
stretched upon some tavern floor," say historical records kept at the
time. Once the main body of the expedition joined them, everyone
swapped stories about their scrapes, and the banks of the Rio Grande
looked like "the Elysian fields of happiness, where, forgetting all our
past misfortunes, we could lie beneath the shady bowers and rest our
tired, aching bodies . . ." reported one of the party, Gaspar Perez de
Villegra. They fished the river, shot ducks and geese, built a bonfire,
barbecued, and ate on April 30, 1598. Oñate had a chapel built for
High Mass, and had everyone put on their best clothes.

And that, say some El Paso historians, was the First Thanksgiving,
celebrated since 1989 in April in San Elizario.

A gigantic monument called *The Equestrian* that sits outside El
Paso International Airport was based on Oñate, but the name was
changed because controversy over his treatment of Native Americans.
It is 33 feet tall.

geology buff. Because of its size, you can't see from side to side, so it's
hard to tell you're looking at a crater. Mineral collectors come to look for
olivine. There's no cell-phone signal, and you need a vehicle with high
clearance. You are out in the desert here, so bring hats, sunscreen, and
lots of water. Free.

Hueco Tanks State Park

(800-792-1112; www.tpwd.state.tx.us), 6900 Hueco Tanks Road
No. 1. Take US 62/180 for 32 miles, then turn north on Ranch Road
2775. Open daily, year-round, but visitation is restricted, so make
reservations.

Whether you appreciate the surreal landscape or not, you won't
see anything like this elsewhere. Rugged walls bearing pictographs,
left by the prehistoric Jornada Mogollon people and the more recent
Kiowas and Mescalero Apaches, drop to deep basins, called *huecos*,
which collect rainwater. Thirsty travelers have stopped at these watering holes for centuries, including 49ers headed for California and the
Butterfield Overland Mail Route.

Today's travelers bring a picnic and spend the day hiking, rock-
climbing, bird-watching, and looking at the pictographs. There's also
an historic ranch house and the ruins of a stagecoach station.

Visits are limited and restricted, for protection of the pictographs,
so be sure to make reservations. Adults, $5, which includes tours;
camping fees are an additional $12–16 per night.

Golf

Golf legend Lee Treviño was born here. Courses now include: Painted
Dunes Desert Golf (915-821-2122; www.painteddunes.com), 12000
McCombs Street; El Paso-Coronado Country Club (915-584-3841; www
.coronadocountryclub.com), 1044 Broadmoor Drive; Vista Hills Country
Club (915-592-6767; vistahillscc.com), 2210 Trawood Drive; Ascarate
Municipal Golf Course (915-772-7381; www.golf.com), 6900 Delta Drive
#2; Lone Star Golf Club (915-591-4927; www.lonestargolfclub.net), 1510
Hawkins Boulevard; El Paso Country Club (915-584-1111; www.elpaso
countryclub.com), 5000 Country Club Place #B; Butterfield Trail Golf
Club (915-772-1031; www.butterfieldtrailgolf.com),1858 Cottonwoods
Drive.

Pick Your Spot

Best places to stay in and
around ElPaso

El Paso has plenty of lodging, most
of it low- to mid-priced hotel and
motel chains. The historic Camino
Real downtown (see To See and Do)
is considered the city's finest hotel.

Local Flavors

Taste of the town—restaurants, cafés, bars, bistros, etc.

A note about prices in El Paso: Because of the abundance of inexpensive good Mexican food, what's moderate in the rest of West Texas probably seems expensive in El Paso by comparison. The pricing in this chapter still follows the guidelines shown in The Way This Book Works.

DINING OUT

Billy Crews Fine Dining and Cocktails (505-289-2071; www .billycrews.com), 1200 Country Club Road. Open daily. Technically in New Mexico, but people drive here for the extensive wine list and imported beers, as well as steak, prime rib, lamb, and seafood. The cellar has more than 23,000 bottles, and if you go Wednesday through Saturday there's live entertainment. Moderate.

Café Central (915-545-2233; www.cafecentral.com), 109 N. Oregon Street. Open Monday through Saturday. From appetizers like beef carpaccio to entrees like crispy duck breast with confit-fingerling potatoes and Medjool-date puree, this is the upscale choice in El Paso for innovative dishes today, with a changing seasonal menu. Originally opened in Juarez in 1918, it was Miguel's Central Café before it languished in the 1980s. It was brought back under new ownership in 1991, and has been one of few bistro-style eateries in the city. The signature cream of green chile soup is a creamy, spicy delight. Expensive.

Don't Miss

Cattleman's Steakhouse (915-544-3200; www.cattlemanssteak house.com), about 35 minutes from Downtown El Paso—I-10 east, left at Fabens exit 59, 5 miles north. Open daily for lunch and dinner. It's worth the drive, but even more so if you're already in the Lower Valley. Besides steaks, Cattleman's has hayrides, donkey rides, a children's zoo, a movie set to view, and much more. Expensive.

Donkeys are kept as pets as often as they're used for work purposes around rural West Texas.

The Garden (915-544-4400; www.thegardenep.com), 511 Western. Open Monday through Saturday. The extensive menu covers everything from sushi to pasta to steak to ribs, plus it's a cigar bar with a full menu of fine smokes. The bar has a scotch menu. In the downtown Union Plaza district, there are both indoor and outdoor spaces. Moderate to expensive.

Shogun Japanese Steak House (915-775-1282), 1201 Airway Boulevard. Open for lunch Monday through Friday, dinner Monday through Sunday. If you're in the mood for flaming showmanship and airborne knives, this is your choice—food is prepared in front of you including steak, lobster, chicken, and seafood. Serves sushi, as well. Moderate.

The Sushi Place (915-838-8088; www.thesushiplace.com), 2604 N. Mesa Street. Open daily for lunch and dinner. Expect a full complement of sushi—sashimi, nigiri, and all. The extensive menu includes lots of rolls and combinations to try for those who aren't ready for plain raw fish, as well as filet mignon and cheesecake. Moderate.

EATING OUT

There are an untold number of Mexican restaurants in El Paso, and you can't necessarily tell by the outside how good the food will be inside. In fact, the inside isn't a good indicator, either—the tiniest hole in the wall with smeared windows can have some of the best tacos you ever tasted. El Pasoans develop their favorites over years of trial and error, but some places are solid standbys for almost everyone— for a great dish, overall good food, or interesting atmosphere. For your convenience, I've organized the Mexican restaurants by area of the city, so you won't have to interrupt your sightseeing to drive across town for a good one.

Most recently, high-end Juarez restaurants have begun popping up around the city—a little-known fact of border life used to be that you could dine in high style (five-course meals, waiters with towels draped over their arms, etc.) in Juarez. That was before the drug violence, but the new restaurants are making some of the upscale choices available in El Paso.

Mexican

Downtown
Azulejos (915-534-3020), 101 S. El Paso Street in the Camino Real Hotel downtown. Open daily and best known for its Sunday brunch, which includes smoked salmon, carved beef, peel and eat shrimp, and more. Moderate.

West Side
Avila's Mexican Food (915-584-3621), 6232 N. Mesa Street. Open daily. The chile con queso here is a favorite, and you'll have reliably decent food at a good price from a large menu. Inexpensive.

Red or Green? A Chile Primer

You'll order enchiladas and immediately be confronted with the question: Red or green? Well, it depends. Generally speaking, green is hotter, especially if you're eating New Mexico-style enchiladas, which are different from almost all of those served in El Paso (you'll occasionally run across them on a menu).

Restaurants in El Paso typically make green sauce from tomatillos, which gives them a tangy flavor. Sometimes they'll also include jalapeños, which add the fire. You probably won't be able to tell, because the sauces are blended. If you're squeamish about eating hot, spicy food, it's best to ask your server whether it's hot. But remember, it's all relative. What's hot to an El Pasoan would probably ruin a meal for an uninitiated visitor.

Green enchiladas, served in New Mexico or in that style, are almost always stacked, not rolled, and are made from chopped long green chiles, rather than blended. The flavor can vary from very mild to a mouth-burning heat that will have you repeatedly sending for more water. In fairness, that will happen very rarely. If it does, try drinking milk, sometimes that quenches the flames faster.

Red chile, on the other hand, is almost always milder. Personally, I'm not a fan of red in El Paso. It's usually made from powdered red chile and, in my view, it's bland, although many, many people prefer it. Red New Mexico-style has a deep, rich flavor made from blending whole red chile pods into a sauce that is simmered with garlic and whatever secret spices the cook chooses to add (coriander and cumin are two possibilities).

In short, if you're worried at all, get red.

Casa Jurado (915-833-1151), 4772 Doniphan Drive. The food here is closer to New Mexican than most others in El Paso (which makes sense, because the restaurant is near the state line). For one thing, they serve enchiladas norteños, or northerner's enchiladas, which means stacked, New Mexico–style instead of rolled, and topped with an egg if you want it. You'll usually find real green chile in season in the green sauce (ask about extra chile if you want it), and a rich chile con queso that has the creamy tang of Monterey Jack. While I cannot resist a stacked enchilada, the flautas here also are especially good—thin, crispy, and ungreasy, topped with queso and served with guacamole and sour cream. Moderate.

Lucy's Restaurant (915-544-3922), 4119 N. Mesa. I am a fan of the machaca here, although I like it better at Kiki's (see below). Lucy's is often packed at lunchtime, and I found that's when the food tastes freshest and best (I lived within walking distance). The enchiladas and tacos are OK—not bad, not outstanding. Inexpensive.

Central

Forti's Mexican Elder Restaurant (915-772-0066; www.fortis-restaurant.com), 321 Chelsea Street. Open daily. Forti's is the go-to place for both ambiance and reliably good food—it's somewhat higher-priced than many of the Mexican restaurants in town, so locals often reserve it for weekends out, or bring in visitors who might not be comfortable at a hole-in-the-wall. The restaurant is pretty, with Spanish clay tile, lots of Mexican tile, and arches inside and out. The menu includes seafood and many versions of steak, along with the usual combination plates, tacos, enchiladas, etc. Moderate.

H & H Carwash (915-533-1144), 701 E. Yandell. Open Monday through Saturday. Yes, you really can get your car washed and eat good Mexican food all in one stop. H & H is known for serving up some of the best in town. Inexpensive.

L & J Café (915-566-8418; www.landj.com), 3622 E. Missouri. The L & J, aka THAT PLACE BY THE CEMETERY (it sits near Concordia Cemetery) first opened as Tony's Place in 1927, during the Prohibition. Fans of the place today usually rave about the green enchiladas. In an unusual twist, the L & J has a good list of "carb specials," for those counting carbs, and will also prepare your enchilada without frying the tortillas, and with less cheese. Inexpensive.

Los Bandidos de Carlos & Mickey's (915-778-3323), 1310 Magruder. Open daily. The food here is reasonably good, but the big draw is the margaritas during a long happy hour from 4 to 7. Be careful. They don't taste like it, but they are powerful. I know more than one person who had to unexpectedly call a taxi to go home after enjoying them. Moderate.

East Side

Kiki's Restaurant and Bar (915-565-6713; kikismexicanrestaurant.com), 2719 N. Piedras. Open daily. Order the machaca. This is an amazing concoction of brisket, chicken, or crab sautéed with green chiles, tomatoes, onions, a little egg, and smothered in an incredible creamy sauce, topped with melted cheese. Other restaurants here serve machaca, but I think this is the best. Large menu also includes enchiladas, tacos, etc. Inexpensive to moderate.

American

Cincinnati Club (915-532-5592; www.cincinnaticlub.biz), 207 Cincinnati Avenue. Open daily.

Chico's Tacos

It's a well-known phenomenon. You leave El Paso and constantly crave Chico's Tacos. People pine for them so that when they come back to El Paso, even after driving for days, they'll go directly to a Chico's before going anywhere else. All the fuss is over three taquitos in a tomato-y sauce with shredded American cheese. If you're not getting sauce on your fingers and possibly on your face, you're not eating them correctly. You get a plastic fork in the bag, but that's used only to pile the cheese onto a taco, and spread around the green sauce that comes in little plastic containers. Then you pick it all up, dripping, with your fingers, and bite into it. I didn't get it, at first. This is some pretty basic cheap food. But after my second visit, I wanted to come back. In fact, I want one right now, just writing about them. It's crazy. You should try them. Chico's has three locations, all on the Eastside: 5305 Montana Avenue (915-772-7777); 4230 Alameda Avenue (915-533-0975); 3401 Dyer Street (915-565-5555). Inexpensive.

Serves burgers and appetizers in an Irish pub-style atmosphere with sports on the tube. Inexpensive.

Geogeske (915-544-4242; www.g2geogeske.com), 2701 N. Stanton. Open daily. Also called G2, this spot serves up contemporary atmosphere and cuisine to match, with trendy favorites like an in-house mac and cheese, Chilean sea bass, and glazed salmon, as well as steaks and ribs. The bar is a popular nightspot. Moderate to expensive.

Crave Kitchen & Bar (915-351-3677; www.cravekitchenand bar.com), 300 Cincinnati Avenue. Open daily. The cuisine here is modern American with out-of-the-box offerings such as a lime-soy cucumber salsa or a turkey, brie, and bacon sandwich with cranberry chutney, and conventional dinner fare with a twist, including steak with a homemade Guinness steak sauce. Moderate to expensive.

Fellini Film Cafe (915-544-5420; www.fellinifilmcafe.net), 220 Cincinnati Street. Open daily. Rent an art-house video and grab sandwiches, espresso beverages, chai tea, frappes, and more. Inexpensive.

Rib Hut (915-532-7427; www.ribhutelpaso.com), 2612 N. Mesa. Open daily. You can't miss the distinctive A-frame on the Westside. Barbecue snobs won't be jumping up and down, but it's fine if you want a taste of Texas-style ribs, sausage, or brisket. Moderate.

The State Line (915-581-3371; www.countyline.com). Open daily. Part of a 10-restaurant Texas and

The Cincinnati District and Downtown

El Paso has a long tradition of dive bars and cheap restaurants, beloved by college students and soldiers. But the Cincinnati District near UTEP has broken that habit with hip bars and restaurants attractive to a more sophisticated crowd. The Mini-Bar/Loft has added variety to the area's nightlife with video mixes, while restaurants like Aroma offer cuisines that were almost unheard-of here a decade ago. The district is small, so parking is a snap, and it's a quick walk from place to place.

The Cincinnati District includes sophisticated eateries like Aroma, a Juarez import.

Like the Cincinnati district, downtown around Union Plaza has more and more to do in the evenings these days. At last count there were 31 clubs in the general area and more than 50 restaurants.

New Mexico chain that started in Austin, this is farther from Downtown, but diehard barbecue fans make the drive regularly. Moderate.

Toro Burger Bar (www.toro burgerbar.com), 2609 N. Mesa, 915-533-4576; 6590 Montana Ave, 915-774-0990; 1700 N. Zaragoza Road, 915-921-8676. Open daily. Named #4 on the list of best burgers in Texas by *Texas Monthly* (which takes food seriously), Toro Burger Bar serves up the expected hamburgers made of Angus beef (finer marbling, hence generally more tender) plus the American Kobe burger, an Ultimate Blue Crab burger, and a salmon burger. Moderate.

Brown Bag Deli (915-591-1414; www.brownbagdeli.biz), 4319 Fred Wilson. Open daily. This is the go-to spot to pick up a sub sandwich, with daily specials of $4.79 for a regular sub. It's no gourmet shop, but you'll get a decent, filling sub. Inexpensive.

Jaxon's Restaurant and Brewing Co. (www.jaxons.com), 135 Airway, 915-778-9696; 7410 Remcon, 915-845-6557. The fare is Southwestern plus seafood, pasta, burgers, and barbecue. The brew-pubs (the brewery is at the Airway location) serve around seven different microbrewed ales and lagers. Inexpensive to moderate.

Fusion

Aroma (915-532-4700), 2725 N. Mesa. Monday through Saturday for lunch and dinner. One of the Juarez restaurants that has relocated to El Paso, the creative menu includes an appetizer of Carioca cheese (panko-crusted Muenster in tomatillo sauce topped with avocado and cilantro). Expensive.

Modern American

The Kitchen by Chef Sai (915-833-7800), 5380 N. Mesa. Open daily for lunch and dinner. The dessert menu includes cheesecake pops frozen with liquid nitrogen. Moderate.

Italian

Ardovino's Pizza (www.ardovinos pizza.com), 206 Cincinnati, 915-532-9483; 1879 N. Zaragoza Road, 915-856-9111; 865 N. Resler, 915-760-6000. Open daily for lunch and dinner. After starting more than four decades ago as one small grocery carrying gourmet and Italian foods along with wines, Ardovino's added a full menu of pizza as well as lasagna and sandwiches and has been a huge favorite for a quick Friday night meal to take home ever since. Both the sandwiches and the pizza are delicious. Even diehard East Coast Italian food fans like it. Inexpensive to moderate.

Cappetto's Italian Restaurant (915-566-93577; www.cappettos .com), 2716 Montana. Open daily. Even the pickiest of eaters should be able to find something to try here. Among other things, you can combine any of five pasta cuts with any sauces available, and also choose from veal, chicken, steaks, and seafood each prepared many different ways. This has to be one of few places where you can have jalapeños sautéed with the vegetables in your rigatoni (in the rigatoni Isabella). Inexpensive to moderate.

Como's Italian Food (915-533-0238; www.comositalianrestaurant .com). Open daily; limited delivery. A West Side staple that's been around since 1958, Como's serves all the Italian classics, plus pizza. Inexpensive to moderate.

Michelina's Italian Restaurant (915-592-1700; www.michelinos .com), 3615 Rutherglen. Open Monday through Friday for lunch, daily for dinner. This is more fine dining than checkered tablecloth, but the prices are not extravagant. A favorite on the East Side, Michelino's serves classic Italian fare plus steak. Moderate.

Sorrento Italian Restaurant (915-565-3937; www.sorrentoitalian restaurant.com), 5325 Dyer Street. Open Monday through Friday for lunch, daily for dinner. Complete with wax-covered Chianti bottles, Sorrento serves daily lunch specials like baked spaghetti; for dinner, it's steak, seafood, and traditional

Italian favorites. Inexpensive to moderate.

Thai

Tara Thai Restaurant (915-533-1300; www.tarathairestaurant.com).

Modern and fresh Thai in a simple setting, this is a change of pace if you grow tired of sampling all the Mexican food. The pad thai is excellent, as is the spicy basil. Moderate.

Entertainment

NIGHTLIFE

El Paso's bar scene for years has been college/Army base dive bars, but there are variations from that theme.

Don't Miss

If you're into the bar scene, pick up *Tiempo*, the *El Paso Times*' weekly entertainment magazine. It has listings with cover charges and the names of the acts playing that week.

Club 101 (915-544-2101; www.club 101.com), 1148 Airway. This Eastside spot has been the big dance club for years. It pulls in acts like the former lead singer of Ratt. Enough said.

The Dome Bar in the Camino Real downtown is a quiet place for a drink.

Old Plantation (915-533-6055; www.theoldplantation.com), 301 S Ochoa Street. El Paso's oldest gay bar and for many years the only one.

Hemingway's (915-532-1881; www.facebook.com/HemingwaysKPT), 214 Cincinnati Ave. A small neighborhood bar in the Cincinnati district with a good selection of beers.

HORSE RACING

Sunland Park Racetrack & Casino (575-874-5200; www.sunland-park .com), 1200 Futurity Drive, Sunland Park, N.M. Just over the state line, the racetrack has been here since 1959. The casino—slot

Sunland Park

Technically, it's in New Mexico but so close to El Paso it feels like part of the city.

machines only—was added in the 1990s. No alcohol is served in the casino, by law. The complex includes two restaurants, one buffet style, and lounges that do serve alcohol.

MUSIC

Music Under the Stars (see Chamizal National Memorial). Free at 7:30 every Sunday night in the summer, with local performers from bluegrass to salsa to plain old rock and roll. All ages dance up a storm at the outdoor venue.

El Paso Symphony Orchestra (915-532-3776; www.epso.org), Plaza Theatre, 125 Pioneer Plaza. Celebrating some 80 years, the symphony has 12 classical music concerts each year, plus youth concerts and other performances at different venues around the city.

Speaking Rock Entertainment Center (915-860-7777; www.ysletapueblodel sur.org/speaking_rock.sstg), 122 S. Old Pueblo Road. Operated by the Tigua Indians of Ysleta del Sur, the center stages free concerts by big-name artists.

THEATER

Plaza Theatre (915-231-1100; www.theplazatheatre.org), 125 Pioneer Plaza. Broadway musicals such as *Chicago* and *Wicked* play here.

AMUSEMENT PARKS

Western Playland (575-589-4410; www.westernplayland.com), 1249 Futurity Drive, Sunland Park, N.M. Open afternoons and evenings daily. This is a smaller amusement park, not on the scale of a Six Flags park, but the price is right. The Bandido roller-coaster is the favorite ride, but the park also has plenty for smaller kids. Adults, $16.70; non-riders, $5; over 60 and under 2, free. Rides are $2 each.

Wet 'N' Wild Waterworld (915-886-2222; www.wetwild.com), 8804 South Desert Boulevard, Anthony, TX. Open daily. Some 20 water rides include the Pirate Plunge and a 16-foot slippery climbing wall, or gentler features for smaller kids. Barbecuing is permitted, and you may bring food, but no glass. Adults, $19.95; seniors, $13.95; kids 4–12, $17.95; toddlers, $2.95; under 11 months, free. Picnic fee for those not using rides, $13.95.

The restored Plaza Theatre is home to musical performances and an annual film festival.

Selective Shopping

El Paso has two large malls (Cielo Vista Mall and Sunland Park Mall) with all the usual retailers if you need a mall. But the real reason to shop here is the huge supply of Mexican and Southwestern goods—everything from wallets to furniture to pottery. Fans of the look can—and do—furnish entire homes with pieces and accessories from El Paso. The prices are generally very reasonable, especially for smaller home goods, and you'll likely take home something nobody else has.

El Paso Saddleblanket (915-544-1000; www.elpasosaddleblanket.com), 6926 Gateway East. Open Monday through Friday. You don't have to leave town feeling as if you've missed out by not shopping in Mexico if you visit this warehouse-like 1-acre store. Mexican rugs in every shape, size, and color from pastels to primaries are stacked all over, along with cowhides, Casas Grandes pottery, leather goods, and more. Prepare to be over-whelmed, but happy about the price tags. Skip the souvenir T-shirts for your friends and family and get Southwestern-patterned woven coasters and other small pieces instead.

Hal Marcus Studio and Gallery (915-333-9090; www.halmarcus.com), 1308 N. Oregon. El Paso–born Hal Marcus is a self-taught artist whose colorful

Boots

El Paso is possibly the best place in the state to buy real Texas cowboy boots economically, because several big-name factory outlets are here. A secret: You can buy flat-heeled, round-toed ropers, be just as authentic, and possibly not feel silly back home if you'd rather forgo elaborate stitching, exotic leathers, and pointy toes. In some cases you can find factory seconds and discontinued boots. Be aware that if you shop the seconds every size is not always available, and fit can vary even within the same pair, so be sure to try them both on. Boot wearers usually have a favorite brand. Here's a selection of different price points and big names, so you can choose yours.

Caboots (915-309-4791; www.caboots.com), 2100 Wyoming Street. If you want a pair of purple lace-up ankle boots, you can find them here, along with more conventional cowboy boots, and costume reproductions. They'll set you back several hundred dollars.

Cowtown Boots (915-593-2929; www.cowtownboots.com), 11451 Gateway West. Open daily. Cowtown manufactures boots and sells brands—lots of brands, in a 50,000-square-foot retail factory store—including Tony Lama, Justin, Acme, Dingo, Dan Post, and Cowtown's own brand. One of the most economical places to buy a pair of kickers.

J.B. Hill Boot Co. (915-599-1551; www.jbhilltexas.com), 335 N. Clark Drive. These are high-end boots made to order—or sold in places like the upscale Stanley Korshak in Dallas. Prices start at $825 and run into the thousands.

Justin Boots Factory Outlet (915-779-5465; www.justinboots .com), 7100 Gateway East. Besides Justin, the company also makes Tony Lama, Nocona, and Chippewa boots. Their low-heeled ropers are a daily wear boot of choice for plenty of Texans.

Lucchese Boots (915-778-8060; www.lucchese.com), 6601 Montana Avenue, Suite. L. Open Monday through Saturday. Lucchese is considered the Cadillac of big-name off-the-rack boots. You can order a custom pair here as well as buy them off the shelf.

Tony Lama Factory Outlet (915-581-8192; www.tonylama.com), 5040 N. Desert Boulevard. Tony Lamas are well-made boots (I've had the same pair for 12 years and seen virtually no wear).

Distances

El Paso is more than two hours from almost anything else in terms of major cities or attractions. Living there can feel a little like you're on an island in that way. Here are some key driving times:

Albuquerque, N.M.—4 hours, 10 minutes

Big Bend National Park—5 hours, 40 minutes

Carlsbad Caverns—3 hours, 15 minutes

Dallas–Fort Worth—10 hours, 50 minutes

Gila Cliff Dwellings National Monument—3 hours, 40 minutes

folk art–style images are on the posters of local charities, and displayed nationwide. His gallery shows his own works, as well as pieces by many other artists.

Galeria San Ysidro, Inc. (915-544-4444), 801 Texas Avenue. Open Monday through Saturday. A three-story gallery houses Mexican primitive and folk pieces as well as items from Morocco and Africa.

Tres Mariposas (915-584-4444; www.tresmariposas.com), 5857 North Mesa. Open Monday through Saturday. If you need a last-minute dress for an event and want to try something other than a mall, this is a good place to start. The upscale boutique is a destination for the perfect party dress or formal for many El Paso women. The lines range from Escada to more affordable labels like Maggy London.

Special Events

January

El Paso Pro-Musica Chamber Music Festival (915-833-9400), various sites. Founded in 1977.

March

Siglo de Oro Spanish Drama Festival (915-532-7273; www.nps.gov/cham), Chamizal National Memorial, 800 S. San Marcial. Plays from Spain's Golden Age in Spanish and English.

April

1st Thanksgiving Celebration (915-851-1682; www.visitelpaso.com), 1500 Main Street, San Elizario Plaza in April. Take I-10 east to the Zaragosa exit, turn south and follow the blue historical signs. Free.

KLAQ International Balloonfest (915-886-2222; www.klaq.com), Wet 'N' Wild Waterworld, 8804 South Desert Boulevard. A three-day hot-air balloon festival.

June through August

Viva! El Paso (915-588-7054; www.viva-ep.org), McKelligon Canyon Amphitheatre in Franklin Mountains State Park; 8:30 Friday and Saturday nights in June and August. The outdoor musical drama covers 400 years of history in four cultures: Native American, Spanish, Mexican, and Western American. Tickets $20–24.

July

Ysleta Mission Festival (915-860-9848; www.ysletamissionlorg), at Ysleta Mission, 131 Zaragoza Street. Three days of food, traditional dances, and carnival rides.

August

Plaza Classic Film Festival (915-533-4020; www.classic.com), 125 Pioneer Plaza. The beautiful, restored old movie palace makes a great setting for classic films plus "best of" other film festivals.

Shakespeare on the Rocks Festival (915-474-4275; http://shakespeareon therocks.com), Chamizal National Memorial, 800 S. San Marcial. Scripts are cut and music added in some cases to make the works more accessible.

September

Fiesta de las Flores (915-533-3730; www.fiestadelasflores.org), El Paso County Coliseum, 4100 Paisano. Beauty pageant, ballet folklorico, golf tournament, more. Founded by LULAC (League of United Latin American Citizens) more than 50 years ago.

October

Concordia Walk Through History (915-591-2326), Historic Concordia Cemetery, 3700 East Yandell Street. Reenactments, gunfights, and more.

Amigo Airsho (915-562-6446; www.amigoairsho.org), Biggs Field, Fort Bliss. The jets, wing-walkers, and aircraft displays attract a big crowd annually.

Hueco Tanks Interpretative Fair (915-857-1135; www.tpwd.gov), Hueco Tanks Historic Park, 6900 Hueco Tanks Road #1. The free two-day fair has Native American, folklorico dancers, a Buffalo soldier camp, and more.

Mexican Independence Day

The annual event at Chamizal National Memorial (915-532-7273; www
.nps.gov/cham/), 800 S. San Marcial, celebrates El Grito de Dolores,
the cry that started the Mexican War of Independence from Spain.

A lot of people are under the misconception that Cinco de Mayo,
the 5th of May, is Mexican Independence Day. Actually, that is Dieciseis de Septiembre, the 16th of September.

Cinco de Mayo marks the day Mexico defeated the French in Puebla,
Mexico, in 1862. The celebration is about their bravery and victory in
the face of terrible odds. The Mexican militia led by General Ignacio
Zaragoza was poorly armed and had 4,500 men, while Napoleon III's
army was well equipped and numbered 6.500. The French invaded
again later and took control of Mexico, but the surprising defeat at
Puebla was a proud moment in Mexican history.

Dieciseis de Septiembre celebrates the beginning of the Mexican
War of Independence in 1810. It began with El Grito de Dolores, or
the cry of Dolores, a literal call to revolt by Father Miguel Hidalgo in
the small town of Dolores, Guanajuato, on September 16.

SOUTHERN NEW MEXICO ITINERARIES

Of course New Mexico isn't West Texas, but I'm including it in this book for
several reasons. First, El Paso is the largest city for about six hours in any
direction, and the airport makes it a departure point for travelers both in
and out of Texas who are planning trips to southern New Mexico. The city
puts you in driving distance to truly amazing natural wonders, great New
Mexican food, and cool, refreshing mountain country. A third consideration
is that the drug wars in Mexico (see sidebar in this chapter) have ruled out
Juarez as a tourist destination. Traveling north instead of south opens up a
world of new options once you're done exploring the city.

Just 45 minutes away, you can hike the Organ Mountains or take the
back road to Mesilla to get a taste of New Mexican culture without the
crowds of Santa Fe. In Las Cruces, you'll find New Mexico State University, a downtown that's being renewed, and COAS/My Bookstore, which
carries rare and out-of-print books and is a favorite for collectors. An hour
away from El Paso, you can climb the gleaming dunes at White Sands Missile Range. Two or three hours toward the east, explore the surreal world
of Carlsbad Caverns, retreat to the pines in Ruidoso or Cloudcroft, or
cut across New Mexico back into Texas and hike Guadalupe Mountains
National Park.

McKittrick Canyon offers some of the easiest hiking and best scenery at Guadalupe Mountains National Park.

I've divided the trips into day trips and overnights for ease of planning. (While I mentioned a few New Mexico destinations in the first section of this chapter, those are just across the state line; these are trips that involve a drive.)

Day Trips
Mesilla/Las Cruces

It would be a real shame to take the interstate to Mesilla. I spent years driving up and down NM 28, first from college at New Mexico State University in the 1970s, and then a decade later, when I lived in El Paso. The 40-mile drive is a good one for a lazy trip, stopping off at wineries, eating home-made *gorditas* (crispy cornmeal crust folded over spicy meat or beans), and stopping to buy local pecans. Once you arrive in Old Mesilla, with its adobe buildings around a central plaza, take in New Mexican food, unique shopping, and live music. I've included a hotel in case you want to stay a while.

Local Flavors

Taste of the town—restaurants, cafés, bars, bistros, etc.

The Little Diner (915-877-2176; www.thelittlediner.com), 7209 7th Street, Canutillo, TX. Closed Wednesday. Do not hesitate. It's off the beaten path (see directions on the Web site), but it's well worth your time to stop here on your way to Mesilla. The atmosphere is orange plastic booths in a smallish dining room, but it doesn't matter. Good *gorditas* are hard to find anywhere, and these are the real thing. The restaurant grinds and processes its own corn. Use your odometer to follow the directions on the Web site. It's a short detour, but former President George W. Bush and actor Tommy Lee Jones have made the trip. Inexpensive.

Chope's (505-233-3420), off NM 28 in La Mesa. Closed Sunday and Monday. Hours can vary. The tiny bar/restaurant is a local favorite that's frequently packed with all sorts of diners, from bikers to families. Order the chile relleno plate. You'll get a fresh, long green chile from a local farm, stuffed with melted cheese, coated with a fluffy egg batter and fried. These are not the heavy, stiff rellenos you find at Tex-Mex places. Residents also come here for the green chile enchiladas, also made with fresh green chile, and stacked, New Mexico style. A tip: Green chile is freshest and best in the fall right after harvest. Diners who aren't used to spicy food should proceed with caution here—the chile can be hot. Inexpensive.

Café Don Felix (575-527-0008; www.cafedonfelix.com), 2290 Calle Parian, Mesilla. Open daily for lunch and dinner. Right on the Mesilla Plaza, the café has an outdoor patio that sometimes has live music and offers a menu of traditional New Mexico fare (stacked enchiladas, tacos, etc.) as well as sandwiches. Inexpensive to moderate.

La Posta de Mesilla Restaurant, Cantina & Chile Shop (575-524-3524; www.laposta-de-mesilla .com), 2410 Calle de San Albino, Mesilla. La Posta, with its aviary and maze of dining rooms in an old Butterfield Stage building, is a destination for families celebrating a special night, or couples looking for a New Mexican dining spot that's more of a fine dining experience than the smaller cafés. It's best known for its *tostadas compuestas*—corn tortilla cups

filled with beans, red chile, cheese, lettuce, and tomatoes—but serves a full menu of New Mexican food plus steaks. Moderate.

Double Eagle de Mesilla and Peppers Café (575-523-6700; www .double-eagle-mesilla.com), 2355 Calle de Guadalupe, Mesilla. Open daily for lunch and dinner. Aged steaks in a fine-dining atmosphere are served at the Double Eagle, while Peppers Café entrees include salmon and barbecued ribs. Peppers also claims to serve the world's largest green-chile cheeseburger, which is on its lunch menu. There are seatings at 11 and 1:30 on Sunday for a champagne brunch. Moderate to expensive.

A kiva-like fireplace is flanked by red chile ristras at Café Don Felix in Mesilla, N.M.

WINERIES

Rio Grande Vineyards and Winery (575-524-3985; www.riogrande winery.com), 4 miles south of the Mesilla Plaza on NM 28. Open noon–5:30 Friday through Sunday. The tasting room has floor-to-ceiling windows that look out over the desert. Produces a small selection of varietals.

La Vina Winery, Inc. (575-882-7632; www.lavinawinery.com), 4201 S. NM 28, La Union/Anthony, N.M. Open noon–5, closed Wednesday. This is probably the oldest winery in the area, and it has a wine list to prove it: chardonnay, cabernet sauvignons, syrah, and more.

Zin Valle Vineyards (915-877-4544; www.zinvalle.com), 7315 Canutillo La Union Road, Canutillo, TX. Open noon–5 Friday through Monday. Makes the Rising Star brand, including Gewürztraminers, a Chianti, and a rosé.

Selective Shopping

Bowlin's Mesilla Book Center (575-526-6220), 2160 Calle Principal. Call for hours. An independently owned bookstore, the center stocks a good selection of New Mexico and Southwest titles, with Chimayo, N.M., and Navajo rugs in back.

COAS/My Bookstore (575-524-8471; www.coasbooks.com), 317 N. Main Street, and 1101 S. Solano Drive, Las Cruces, N.M. Open daily. Buys, sells, and trades used books, CDs, DVDs, VHS tapes, audio books, and games, with more than 450,000 books in stock.

La Mariposa (575-647-2636; www .lamariposa.com), 2470 Calle De Guadalupe, Mesilla. Call for hours. Offers a selection of clothing from Moroccan to unique scarves. A good place to get something light to take home.

General information about shops: www.oldmesilla.org.

Stahmann Farms (800-654-6887; www.stahmanns.com), 22505 NM 28 South in La Mesa and

Everything that can be made with pecans is available at the Stahmann Farms store on NM 28.

2030 Calle de Parian in Mesilla. Open daily. You'll know you're in Stahmann country when the canopy of trees envelopes the highway. Everything pecan is here, at one of the largest pecan farms in the world, from candies to pies to the plain, meaty, easy-to-shell pecans. The Zias, a rich concoction of pecans, caramel, and milk chocolate, are hard to pass up. Stahmann's ships, if you don't want to carry them home.

Pick Your Spot

Best places to stay in and around Mesilla

Josefina's Old Gate (575-525-2620), 2261 Calle de Guadalupe, Mesilla. A 100-year-old adobe hacienda, Josefina's has two pretty suites with high-thread-count sheets, flat-screen TVs and a comfortable spot outside to sit and enjoy the pretty plaza. Expensive.

The café inside Josefina's Old Gate is small and welcoming.

To See and Do

White Sands National Monument and White Sands Missile Range (Trinity Site)

The gleaming white gypsum sand dunes covering 275 square miles off US 70 are a stunning sight. They're surprisingly easy to walk on—the sand is only loose for the top couple inches, because the gypsum dissolves and sticks together when it rains. A day here amid the dunes is almost otherworldly. The National Park Service schedules full-moon bike rides and sunset strolls on White Sands National Monument (575-679-2599; www.nps.gov/whsa), along with a tour of Lake Lucero, the playa (dry lake bed) that explains how the sands were formed. Stop at the visitor center and decide what you want to do. There's an 8-mile drive through the monument, along with four hiking trails. You can also buy snow saucers for sledding. Park admission is $3.

Trinity Site (575-678-1134.www.wsmr.army.mil, click on Public Affairs), where the first atomic bomb was exploded, is a designated National Historic Landmark on White Sands Missile Range. Tours of Trinity Site are available

A Note about Las Cruces

It's a fun college town, and I lived there for four years—a long time ago. Unfortunately, I didn't have the resources to investigate what's there today for this book, which actually focuses on West Texas. I know a day trip to Mesilla will keep you plenty busy. I've included a good bookstore on the recommendation of a book-collecting friend. If you want to explore Las Cruces further, check in with their visitors and convention bureau (575-541-2444; www.lascrucescvb.org), at 211 North Water Street.

only twice a year, in April and October, with no reservations. The missile range is still an active test range—traffic on US 70 is occasionally stopped during tests.

Overnight Trips
Cloudcroft

About three hours north of El Paso on US 70 West, you're in a mountain retreat. Here are the Sacramento Mountains and the Lincoln National Forest, birthplace of the original Smokey the Bear. Temperatures are cooler (cold in winter, this is snow country) and even in the summer, evenings drop to sweater weather. Whereas Ruidoso (see below) is the tourist spot, Cloudcroft is the quiet, simple mountain town in the Sacramentos. Camping is available, as is a small selection of cabins. Many New Mexico natives prefer to come here to get away from the touristy vibe in Ruidoso, but it's too much peace and quiet for others. The town has few shops and about seven restaurants, including fine dining at The Lodge Resort and Spa (www.thelodgeresort.com). The historic lodge also comes with its own ghost, Rebecca. Rates here start at $91. The Lodge's nine-hole golf course at 9,000 feet above sea level is open April through October. The Lincoln (www.fs.usda.gov) is the playground, with cross-country skiing, hiking, snowmobiling, fishing, and mountain biking. Alpine skiing is at Ski Cloudcroft, (575-682-2333; www.skicloudcroft.com). More information about Cloudcroft, www.cloudcroft.com.

Ruidoso

This charming, busy little vacation town, also about three hours north of El Paso, is a destination for many Texans, who keep cabins in the mountains

Books

El Paso's history is fascinating and action-packed. Two of the best resources:

Pass of the North (Texas Western Press) by C. L. Sonnichsen. The two volumes of history, written in 1968 and 1980, are lengthy but not at all difficult reading. One of Texas' favorite historians, Sonnichsen was not without a sense of humor. Unfortunately, they're hard to find. I did find copies at www.bookfinder.com.

El Paso: A Borderlands History (Texas Western Press) by W. H. Timmons. Order from Texas Western Press at www.twp.utep.edu.

and enjoy the skiing and horseracing. If relaxing beside the gurgling creek (the town was named for it—*ruidoso* means noisy in Spanish) isn't your thing, there is a horseracing track/casino, Ruidoso Downs (575-378-4431; www.btkcasino.com); or, you can stay outside town at Inn of the Mountain Gods Resort and Casino (575-464-7777; www.innofthemountaingods.com), 1287 Carrizo Canyon Road, Mescalero, N.M., a resort run by the Mescalero Apaches that also has a casino. Rooms start at $79/night. If you want to make a day trip to the casino, All Aboard America and New Mexico Coaches leave El Paso at 7 and 8 AM Tuesday through Thursday, and return at 6 PM (915-751-2219; www.allaboardamerica.com). The small ski mountain is Ski Apache (575-464-3600; www.skiapache.com). Cruise the main drag, Sudderth Drive, for a place to eat—you won't find a gourmet experience, but a plethora of casual spots keep visitors full.

The best lodging experience is renting a cabin, and there are plenty of them, plain and fancy (www.ruidoso.net), at different prices. An afternoon's worth of shopping is here, including the souvenir-shop variety and galleries that stock mostly New Mexico art. Here, too, the Lincoln National Forest is filled with hiking and biking trails in several wilderness areas, and also offers fishing, snowmobiling, and cross-country skiing. Horseback riding and hunting also are permitted in parts of the forest. Campgrounds, open May through early October, are abundant. For more about Ruidoso, www.ruidoso.net.

Carlsbad Caverns

Carlsbad Caverns National Park (575-785-2232; www.nps.gov/cave) is 150 miles northeast of El Paso. The caverns are an underground wonderland of stalactites and stalagmites. You can walk down into the caverns through the natural entry (last entry at 2 PM September through Memorial Day weekend, 3:30 PM Memorial Day weekend through Labor Day weekend) or descend in an elevator (last entry times are 3:30 and 5). If you have kids (see age limits below), consider taking the Big Room tour rather than the long and steep Natural Entrance tour, which can be tiring. If you have small children, take the elevator down. Self-guided tours for adults are $6, children 15 and under, free. Be sure to bring a sweater. The temperature in the caverns stays at about 56 degrees. Unless you're a cave aficionado, you may want to take a ranger-guided tour to better understand what you're seeing. Check the Web site for the fee schedule on these; they vary widely according to the destination. Children under 3 are not permitted on any of the guided tours. Strollers are not permitted in the caverns. Another attraction here is the evening bat flight, when hundreds of free-tailed bats leave the cavern entrance to fly through the night for food. The females give birth in June and July, and fly south in October for the winter.

5

The Panhandle
and South Plains

THOUGH THEY'RE JUST about two hours apart, Lubbock is in what's known as the South Plains, while Amarillo is the largest city in the Panhandle.

The South Plains is considered habitable by the rest of the state, but the Panhandle is generally looked upon as a place where only the hardiest can survive. After all, it does snow up there once in a while.

In all seriousness, Amarillo does have its charms, having been named one of the 20 best places to live in the West by *American Cowboy* magazine.

Both cities have an addictively slow pace; wide streets; a refreshing lack of traffic; and friendly people who say hi as if they mean it. You'll feel like you're really in the West here, and you are. People make a living farming and ranching and living a simple life—the streets are quieter on Sunday, for example, until after church lets out.

Come and explore the walls of Palo Duro Canyon, or spend some

Deep green, rosy orange, and blue sky are nature's palette at Palo Duro Canyon.

LEFT: The Wind Power Museum in Lubbock is dedicated to all things windmill.

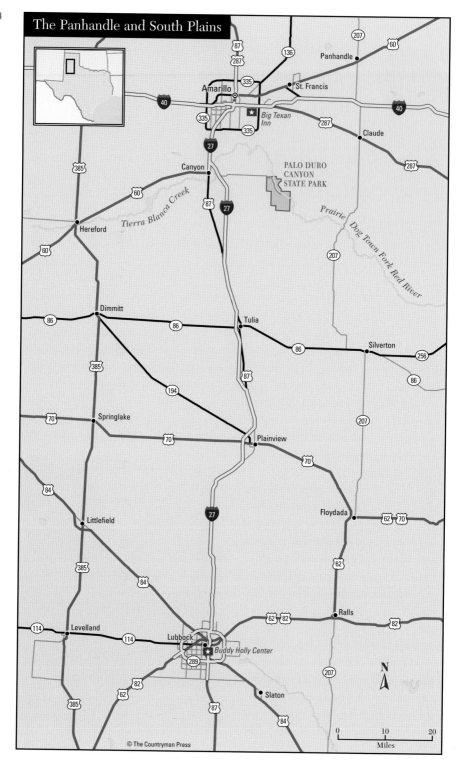

The Panhandle and South Plains

© The Countryman Press

Contrasting colors wind across a mesa at Palo Duro Canyon.

time puzzling over Cadillac Ranch. Or, maybe you'll want to investigate the three universities for a son or a daughter, or yourself.

This tends to be a love it or hate it kind of place. Spring dust storms and tumbleweeds the size of a Volkswagen (well, almost) might scare you away. Or the space and the rugged, flat beauty might lure you to stay a while.

LUBBOCK

Often called the Hub City because it's the economic, education, and health care hub of the South Plains, Lubbock has a population of about 270,000 people. The three universities—Texas Tech, Lubbock Christian, and Wayland Baptist—play a big part in the economy. In fact, Tech is the biggest employer.

The area also is one of the biggest cotton-growing regions in the world, drawing water for irrigation from the massive Ogallala Aquifer.

The mild, dry climate (only 18 inches of rainfall a year, and an average temperature of 80 degrees in July) make the Lubbock area comfortable for outdoor activities year-round.

Three universities create something of a college-town atmosphere in parts of the city, but remember this is the Bible Belt and one of the more conservative parts of a conservative state. The universities also help keep the city young—more than 60 percent of the population is younger than 35.

The health care part of the hub comes from Covenant Health System, the second-largest employer, as well as Texas Tech University Health Sciences Center.

Guidance

The Lubbock Convention and Visitors Bureau (800-692-4035), 1500 Broadway, 6th floor, Wells Fargo Center, has maps and information to get you on your way. They're also the ones to contact if you're interested in getting a tour of one of the area ranches.

Getting There

It's about a five-hour drive from the Dallas–Fort Worth area. Both American Eagle (www.aa.com) and Southwest Airlines (www.south westairlines.com) offer flights, which take about 50 minutes, to Lubbock Preston Smith International Airport (806-775-2035; www.flylia.com), 5401 N. Martin Luther King Boulevard.

Getting Around

The best mode of transportation is driving. Traffic is minimal and it's easy to get around.

Medical Emergencies

Dial 911. Covenant Health Systems (806-725-0441; www.covenanthealth .org) has a medical center, a women and children's hospital, a separate children's hospital, and care clinics. Also, University Medical Center Health System Hospital (806-775-8200; www.umchealthsystem.com), 602 Indiana Avenue.

Media

The *Lubbock Avalanche-Journal* (www.lubbockonline.com) is the newspaper. Besides all the things you'd expect from a newspaper, it maintains a Buddy Holly archive here: www.buddyhollyarchives.com.

To See and Do

American Wind Power Center (806-747-8734; www.windmill .com), 1701 Canyon Lake Drive. Open Tuesday through Saturday; and Sundays from May to September. A fantasyland of windmills, from modern wind turbines to the iconic West Texas version to one old-school Dutch windmill, spin outside on 28 acres. Indoors, a huge collection of motors, blades, and parts of all kinds from innumerable manufacturers are

Don't Miss

The **Museum of Texas Tech University** (806-742-2490; www.depts
.ttu.edu/museumttu), 3301 4th Street, open Monday through Friday,
is a wonderful surprise after you've been scaling cliffs in Palo Duro
Canyon (see Amarillo) and taking in the other outdoor sights. Founded
in 1929, back when Texas Tech University was Texas Technological
College—Texans still refer to it as Tech for short instead of TTU—the
museum umbrella includes the Lubbock Lake Landmark site, Moody
Planetarium, and other research divisions. The main museum building
on 4th Street has nearly 5 million objects. Kids will wonder at the life-
sized replicas of giant prehistoric animals, such as the Columbian
mammoths. Adults who enjoy fine art will love the intriguing pieces
in the permanent collection, including Polaroids Andy Warhol shot
as sketches for his trademark silkscreened prints. Permanent
galleries include African art, pre-Columbian, Southwest Indian, Taos/Southwest Gallery, and Ethno-
history. A small Asian section contains an elephant tusk more than
5 feet tall that is carved so intricately you'll wonder how it holds
together. Free.

The Helen Jones Auditorium and
Sculpture Court Wing were added
to the Museum of Texas Tech in
2001.

on exhibit in row after row of a big, warehouse-like structure. The gift shop
has windmill replicas, T-shirts, hats, and the like. Admission $5, active-duty
military and family, free.

Lubbock Lake Landmark (806-742-1116; lubbocklake.musm.ttu.edu),
north of the intersection of Loop 289 and US 84 on Landmark Lane,
across from Burl Huffman Athletic Complex. Closed Monday. The ancient
lakebed, which contains some 12,000 years of history, has been explored
since 1939, when bison kills were discovered. It's still excavated every year,
and you can watch during summer months. There's also a learning center
that offers daily tours. Free.

Don't Miss

Buddy Holly Center (806-767-2686; www.buddyholly.org), 1801 Crickets Avenue. Open Tuesday through Sunday. A giant pair of the late musician's black-framed glasses sit in front of the restored railway depot, the perfect backdrop for the best kind of kitschy tourist photos. Inside, a guitar-shaped gallery holds a more poignant pair—the ones Holly was wearing on February 3, 1959, when the Beechcraft Bonanza that carried him crashed right after takeoff outside Clear Lake, Iowa. Holly, J. P. "The Big Bopper" Richardson ("Chantilly lace, and a pretty face . . ."), and Ritchie Valens had just finished a gig and were headed to another on the day the music died. The Lubbock-born singer was just 22, his career barely begun. He and the Crickets had recorded the mega-hit "That'll Be the Day" in 1957.

A neon Buddy Holly sign greets visitors at the Buddy Holly Center in Lubbock.

Buddy Holly and the Crickets were considered pioneers in many ways. His trademark chorded, rhythmic guitar strumming, use of layers of sound (before overdubbing existed), and willingness to experiment with sound were all techniques that shaped rock 'n' roll.

The museum is small, but packed with endearing relics including the Gibson guitar on which he recorded his last songs; the Stratocaster that was in the bus, headed to the next gig when the plane crashed; a replica of his bedroom; pairs of his shoes; a leisure suit. Recording buffs will be interested to see the Ampex recorder from the Norman Petty studio in Clovis, New Mexico, where Holly got his recording start. His music plays while visitors browse the exhibits and read the extensive discography and biographical displays.

Don't skip the film; it's one of the best experiences of the visit. Holly's brothers talk about growing up with him; Paul McCartney discusses his influence on the Beatles' music; and there are some hilarious bits of The Big Bopper making what must have been the first music videos with a mannequin. Don McLean provides some insights, too, about his song "American Pie," with the famous lyrics THE DAY THE MUSIC DIED. Was he really talking about that fateful day in 1959? You'll have to visit and see. Adults, $5; seniors, $3; children and students, $2; under 6, free.

National Ranching Heritage Center (806-742-0498; www.nrhc.ttu.edu), 3121 4th Street. Open daily. You'll take a self-guided tour of 48 restored, furnished buildings: bunkhouse, dugouts (in-ground homes), and more on 16 acres. Free.

OUTDOORS

See Palo Duro Canyon.

Best of Lubbock

Museum of Texas Tech University

Buddy Holly Museum

La Diosa Cellars

Pick Your Spot

Best places to stay in and around Lubbock

Lubbock has more than 50 lodging establishments, including chains and bed and breakfasts. I stayed at one of the La Quinta Inns and found it clean and reasonable. Your best lodging option, though, is to rent one of the small cabins at Palo Duro Canyon if possible—there are only three, so reserve early. See sidebar.

Local Flavors

Taste of the town—restaurants, cafés, bars, bistros, etc.

DINING OUT

La Diosa Cellars (806-744-3600; www.ladiosacellars.com), 901 17th Street. Open Tuesday through Saturday. Spicy, bohemian decor (red-painted walls, tufted antique sofas, plenty of art on the walls) entice visitors to sit down and enjoy a relaxing conversation over, perhaps, a plate of gourmet olives and a glass of wine in the afternoon. Later, live music keeps the scene busy Thursday through Saturday, and diners

La Diosa Cellars has a warm, boho-chic feel.

may want to turn to the interesting menu of entrees, which includes smoked oysters with chimichurri, and empanadas filled with shredded beef, golden raisins, and caramelized onions topped with crème fraiche. La Diosa produces about 2000 cases of wine a year, all from West Texas grapes. Moderate.

Café J (806-743-5400; www .cafejlubbock.com), 2605 19th Street. Open daily for dinner; Sunday and Tuesday through Friday for lunch, Sunday for brunch. Paintings by Santa Fe artists line the walls, setting the stage for exquisitely prepared food, some with Southwestern touches. The rib eye steak, for example, comes with a red-chile glaze, while a zucchini fritter appetizer arrives with jalapeño béarnaise. Everything I tried was delicious. There's also a martini bar and a patio for dining outside. Expensive.

Manna Bread & Wine (806-791-5600; www.mannabreadand wine.com), 2610 Salem Avenue in Cactus Alley. Open Monday through Saturday for lunch and dinner. A tiny restaurant tucked into what appears to be a small apartment complex turned into a little shopping plaza turns out remarkably sophisticated fare in a cozy room with fabrics draped over beams in the ceiling. The menu includes steak, but the standouts are tapas, like the goat-cheese croquette, or Napoleons of whipped blue cheese with pecans and an apricot glaze. More than 50 wines are served by the glass. Moderate to expensive.

EATING OUT

Home Café (806-687-1466; www .our1home.com), 3131 34th Street. Open Tuesday through Friday and Sunday for brunch. Lubbock natives love this happy mix of mismatched tables and chairs and homemade food in a strip center, adorned with photos hung from clothespins. Sunday brunch, especially, gets a "divine" rating from a journalist friend of mine who's dined around the globe. Lunch entrees include vegetarian, pizza and pasta specials, salmon salad, and smoked pork loin chops. Moderate.

Spanky's (806-744-5677; www .spankys.com), 811 University Avenue. Burgers and cheese sticks are the staples at this college-crowd favorite—it's the kind where you wait in line to order and they call your name over a loudspeaker. Inexpensive.

Triple J Chophouse and Brew Co. (806-771-6555; www.triplej chophouseandbrewco.com), 1807 Buddy Holly Avenue. If hunger and thirst strike while you're out touring the Buddy Holly Museum, you'll find burgers and sandwiches on the menu for lunch, steaks and seafood for dinner, all to be washed down with handcrafted beer. Moderate.

WINERIES

West Texas has been making a name for itself in the world of wine for years—since Franciscan missionaries near El Paso started making it in 1662. The Lubbock area, though, has taken off as a grape-growing region in the past 20 or so years. The cool evenings and hot, dry summers are ideal for the vines, and the Ogallala Aquifer provides irrigation water. One of the smaller producers, La Diosa Cellars (806-744-3600; www.ladiosacellars.com), 901 17th Street, offers a menu that's perfect for wine-tasting amid the boho-chic decor and friendly service. Across the street, McPherson Cellars Winery (800-687-9463; www.mcphersoncellars .com), 1615 Texas Avenue, and its tasting room are inside an historic Coca-Cola bottling plant.

One of the oldest and biggest in the state, Llano Estacado Winery (800-634-3854; www.llano wine.com), which started in the '70s, is a short drive out of town at 3426 E. Farm-to-Market 1585. Another oldie, Pheasant Ridge Winery (806-746-6033; www .pheasantridgewinery.com) also is a little drive out of town at 3507 E. County Road 5700.

A newer addition, Cap°Rock Winery (806-686-4452; www.cap rockwinery.com), is to the south at 408 E. County Road 7600.

McPherson Cellars is a winery in an old Coca-Cola bottling plant in Lubbock.

Entertainment

Some of the best restaurants double as some of the best places for cocktails, seeing, being seen, etc. Those include Café J, Manna, and Triple J Roadhouse and Brew Co.; see Where to Eat, above.

There also are sports bars and a few dance clubs (the dance scene also runs to two-stepping and country swing). And, as a college town, Lubbock gets its fair share of big-name concerts. To keep an eye on all the action, go to the *Lubbock Avalanche-Journal's* entertainment site, www.events .lubbockonline.com. For highbrow entertainment, look to the Lubbock Symphony Orchestra, www.lubbocksymphony.org.

Selective Shopping

If you're in need of something quick in a store you recognize, Slide Road is your best bet—most of the retail chains are here, as is the South Plains Mall (806-792-4653; www.southplainsmall.com), Slide Road and South Loop 289.

Almost any small city or large town in Texas has an antiques mall, where dozens of vendors set up shop in one big location (for those who love the hunt only). Here, it's Antique Mall of Lubbock (806-796-2166; www.antqmall.com), 7907 19th Street.

Get your Western look on with gear from Boot City (806-797-8782; www.bootcity.com), 6645 19th Street; Cavender's Western Outfitters (806-785-7400; www.cavenders.com), 5620 W. Loop 289; and Luskey's-Ryon's Western Wear (806-795-7106; www.luskeys.com), 5034 Frankford Avenue.

The upscale choice for big-name labels in men's and women's clothing (Missoni, Valentino, etc.) is Malouf's (806-794-9500; www.maloufs.com), 8201 Quaker Avenue, #106.

Special Events

March

Flatland Film Festival (806-762-8606; www.flatlandfilmfestival.com), Louise Hopkins Underwood Center for the Arts, 511 Avenue K.

April

Lubbock Arts Festival (806-744-2787; www.lubbockarts.org), Lubbock Memorial Civic Center, 1501 Mac Davis Lane.

Apple Blossom Festival (800-765-70550 www.applecountryorchards.com), Apple Country at Hi-Plains Orchards, 12206 E. TX 62, Idalou, TX.

June

Wine & Clay Festival, Llano Estacado Winery (806-745-2258; www.llano wine.com), 3426 East Farm-to-Market 1585.

June through August

Moonlight Musicals (806-770-2000; www.lubbockmoonlightmusicals.org), at Mackenzie Park, 600 Broadway at the Wells Fargo Amphitheater.

August

Harvest Festival and Grape Crush, Cap°Rock Winery (806-686-4452; www.caprockwinery.com), 408 E. Woodrow Road.

September

National Cowboy Symposium (www.cowboy.org), Lubbock Memorial Civic Center, 1501 Mac Davis Lane.

December

Carol of Lights (www.housing.ttu.edu/carol.php), Texas Tech University, 2500 Broadway.

Candlelight at the Ranch (www.depts.ttu.edu/ranchhc), National Ranching Heritage Center, 4th Street and Indiana Avenue.

AMARILLO AND CANYON

In a region filled with quirkiness, the Panhandle ranks right up there with the best. Only here would a billionaire rancher hire three San Francisco artists in the 1970s to stick 10 Cadillacs nose-down in the dirt near Amarillo and call it art. Stanley Marsh 3 (he eschews the Roman numerals because he considers them pretentious) has also erected odd street signs around the city and calls his ranch home Toad Hall.

Amarillo, with about 173,000 people, is the biggest city in this part of the state, but 26 counties over 25,610 square miles make up the Panhandle. The climate is cooler than Lubbock's, with average highs up to 91 in July and lows dipping to 22 in January.

Geologically speaking, the Panhandle Plains are part of the Llano Estacado, a name given it by Spanish explorers and usually interpreted to mean staked plains. A more accurate interpretation is believed to be palisaded plains, to describe the line of cliffs, or palisades, the early explorers found. Francisco Vasquez de Coronado was dumbfounded when he came across this country in 1541, writing to the King of Spain, "I reached some plains so vast, that I did not find their limit anywhere I went, although I travelled over them for more than 300 leagues . . . with no more land marks than if we had been swallowed up by the sea . . . there was not a stone, nor bit of rising ground, nor a tree, nor a shrub, nor anything to go by."

Members of his expedition are believed to have been the first Europeans to see Palo Duro Canyon (see sidebar), which had been a campsite and watering hole for prehistoric peoples and Native American tribes for tens of thousands of years.

Nearby Canyon, population 13,000, is home to West Texas A&M University, and once was home to Southwestern artist Georgia O'Keeffe.

Guidance

The Amarillo Visitor Center (806-374-8474; www.visitamarillotx.com), 401 S Buchanan, Suite 101, Amarillo Civic Center Entrance #2, has brochures, suggestions, maps, and travel guides.

Getting There

American Eagle, Continental Express, and Southwest airlines service Rick Husband Amarillo International Airport. The drive from the Dallas–Fort Worth area is about six hours.

Getting Around

Rent a car at the airport—most of the major rental agencies are here.

Medical Emergencies

Dial 911. Major hospitals are BSA Health System (806-212-2000; www .bsahs.org), 1600 Wallace Boulevard; and Northwest Texas Healthcare System (806-354-1000; www.nwtexashealthcare.com), 1501 S. Coulter. Urgent care clinics are located around the city as well.

Media

The *Amarillo Globe-News* (www.amarillo.com) is the local daily.

To See and Do

* Alibates Flint Quarries National Monument (806-857-3151; www .nps.gov/alfl), 35 miles north of Amarillo in Fritch, see Web site for directions. Evidence indicates peoples from as early as the Ice Age quarried the brightly colored Alibates stone for tools and weapons. Tours of the site,

The Panhandle-Plains Historical Museum is in Canyon, right outside Amarillo.

filled in over the years from the effects of wind and rain, take place twice a day at 10 AM and 2 PM for the 1-mile walk. Call ahead to confirm times. Free.

American Quarter Horse Hall of Fame & Museum (806-376-5181; www .aqha.com), 26011 I-40 East at Quarter Horse Drive. Open 9–5 Monday through Saturday. The quarter horse has been a part of the national culture in movies, books, and is still part of daily life for a lot of people in the Panhandle. Adults, $6, seniors, $5, youth, $2, children under 5, free.

Livestock Auction (806-373-7464; www.amarillolivestockauction.com), 100 Manhattan, Amarillo. If you're here 9–5 on a Tuesday, you can watch cowboys, businesspeople, and cattle on the auction floor and rub elbows with them at the Stockyard Café next to the arena.

Panhandle-Plains Historical Museum (806-651-2244; www.panhandle plains.org), 2503 4th Avenue, Canyon. Open daily. Cattle brands decorate the entrance of pretty Pioneer Hall, made of Texas limestone in 1932. The museum sits on the West Texas A&M University campus, and is filled with an interesting variety of galleries. The most notable artifact of the 2 million stored here is the full-length headdress of Comanche Chief Quanah Parker. Fine art focuses on Southwestern pieces. One Georgia O'Keeffe painting hangs here—the artist lived here in Canyon for several years. She taught

Palo Duro Canyon State Park

One of the greatest reasons for visiting this part of Texas is a trip to **Palo Duro Canyon** (806-488-2227; www.palodurocanyon.com), 1450 Park Road 5, Canyon. If you can, call ahead and make a reservation for one of the rock cabins perched right at the edge, so you can wake up and gaze across the second-largest canyon in the U.S., after the Grand Canyon. Two of the three rustic cabins built by the Civilian Conservation Corps have just two rooms each plus restrooms and shower, and can accommodate only four people per night. But you won't be concerned about the cozy accommodations inside Goodnight and Lighthouse, because you'll want to spend time sitting outside looking over the canyon. The third cabin, Sorenson, is slightly larger and has a rooftop deck, for an even better view. If you don't get a cabin, don't worry. The best view is from almost anywhere, even from your car. The canyon is 120 miles long and 20 miles wide in spots. Deep green juniper contrasts sharply with the rosy canyon walls against the blue West Texas sky, and the whole scene changes color subtly as the sun crosses from east to west.

The canyon was formed by erosion from the wind, and by the Prairie Dog Fork of the Red River. Humans have lived here for some 12,000 years, starting with nomadic hunting tribes. Comanche and Kiowa lived in the canyon until 1874. Charles Goodnight of Goodnight-Loving Trail fame once kept some 100,000 head of cattle here. The name Palo Duro, which means hard wood in Spanish, is thought to have been coined when Spanish explorers found abundant mesquite and juniper in and around the canyon.

Today, you can drive, stopping to wade in cool streams; picnic at tables set up roadside; camp; backpack; mountain bike; or ride horseback. Just on a driving tour you're liable to see wild turkey, and a roadrunner or two, maybe even deer. However you choose to take it in, you'll leave Palo Duro in a more peaceful mood than when you

elementary school art here from 1912–14, and then returned to head the art department at what is now West Texas A&M University from 1916–18, when she was still in her 20s.

The museum also looks at ways of life in its Pioneer Town and People of the Plains sections. The oil patch gets its due with good, detailed explanations of oil-well drilling and examples of the tools used to do it. Adults, $10; seniors, $9; children, $5; under four, free.

Turkeys at Palo Duro Canyon don't hesitate to amble along the road.

started—the size and beauty of the natural wonder have a way of making everything else, including your troubles, seem small. **Note:** Leashed pets are allowed on the park, but can't be crated or kept in a car or otherwise allowed in the cabins. The Lubbock Convention and Visitors Bureau Web site (www.visitlubbock.org) has a long list of pet lodgings. Adults, $5, children, free. Visit the Web site for details and fees for camping and other uses.

MORE WAYS TO SEE THE CANYON
Elkins Ranch Jeep Tours (800-658-2613; www.theelkinsranch.com), 11301 E. TX 217 at Palo Duro Canyon. Start out with a chuck wagon breakfast and then take one of five jeep tours ranging from $25 to $65 to get up close to features of Palo Duro Canyon you'd never see otherwise. There's also a Western nights tour that includes a chuck wagon supper, jeep drive afterward, and relaxing under the stars with cobbler and cowboy coffee. Elkins is a third-generation working ranch, besides being a purveyor of tours. Reservations required. If you're into horseback riding, **Palo Duro Riding Stables** will hook you up. They've been at it since 1962, providing mounts for both experienced and inexperienced riders and guides to take you to see spring waters at other sites. Call for prices and hours.

OUTDOORS

River Breaks Ranch (806-553-4400; www.riverbreaksranch.com), 612 South Van Buren Street, Amarillo. This is more a destination for events like birthday parties, corporate retreats, weddings, etc. Guests can ride in covered wagons, watch cowboys roping steers, and even get serenaded around the campfire, if you choose. Breakfast and dinner are available. Call or email through the Web site for booking and rates.

Cadillac Ranch

Today it's pigeonholed as the car for fairly well-to-do older people, but in the 1950s, the Cadillac stood for having arrived. To have one was to be successful, able to afford the best. The Cadillac's hallmark then was the tailfins, which kept getting larger and larger through the '50s. Twenty years later, wealthy rancher Stanley Marsh (The *Amarillo Globe-News* has referred to him as "Amarillo's leading eccentric") suggested to a San Francisco art collective called the Ant Farm that they make a proposal for an art installation on a wheat field of his. The artists, Chip Lord, Hudsen B. Marquez, and Doug Michels (all are still alive today except for Michels, who died in 2003), chose the Cadillac for their work. In Lord's book, *Autoamerica,* he writes, "So the latent tailfin image became a roadside attraction, a monument to

Cadillac Ranch, a row of 10 half-buried Cadillacs in a cow pasture near Amarillo, is an art installation and famous roadside attraction.

Wildcat Bluff Nature Center (806-352-6007; www.wildcatbluff.org), 3 miles north of I-40 west on Loop 335, just west of Soncy Road. Open Tuesday through Saturday; visitor center, 9–5, trails open sunrise to sunset. Easy trails of 1 mile or less, one of them wheelchair-accessible, take you across country dotted with cottonwoods and grassland, where you might see a horned lizard or a hawk. Adults, $3; children, $3; under three, free.

Pick Your Spot

Best places to stay in and around Amarillo

Amarillo has four bed-and-breakfast inns and some 50 motels. Check in with the Visitors and Convention Council for locations and phone numbers.

the rise and fall of the tailfin. It would be, we decided, ten Cadillacs planted alongside Route 66 on Stanley's ranch. We drew up an artist's conception of how it would look, and a budget. Stanley liked the idea." They collected old Cadillacs, and hired a backhoe driver to dig holes and lift the cars into them. Writes Lord, "Stanley arrived with fried chicken, beer and instructions not to talk to the local press. Work went pretty fast, despite curious motorists who would stop and walk out to the job site with increasing regularity."

In 1997, the whole thing was moved to a cow pasture 2 miles west, after Amarillo city limits got too close. The Cadillacs gained thick coats of spray paint over the years, an intentional part of the installation. They were once painted pink in honor of Marsh's wife's birthday and once black, perhaps in honor of Michels' death, and also to give visitors a fresh canvas.

Motorists are still stopping. When I visited one spring day there were four or five carloads of people walking around, scratching their heads, and another four or five showed up as I left. Cans of spray paint are scattered around the ground, and visitors are encouraged to pick them up and add their own touches to the spectacle. Stop and add your own. Take photos. It will make you smile. To get there, take exit 60 off I-40 heading west. Drive south to the frontage road and turn left, then left again (turn around). Cadillac Ranch is 1 mile east; you'll see the partially buried Caddies sticking up in the distance. You can park along the side of the road and walk. The gate is unlocked. It's free. More information: www.libertysoftware.be/cml/cadillacranch/crmain.htm.

Local Flavors

Taste of the town—restaurants, cafés, bars, bistros, etc.

DINING OUT

Big Texan Steak Ranch (806-372-7000; www.bigtexan.com), 7701 I-40 East (take exit 75). Open daily for breakfast, lunch, and dinner. The Big Texan is legendary for its 72-oz. steak—it's free if you can eat it in an hour, and people actually have succeeded. Of course, other sizes are served for lesser appetites. A motel and a horse hotel are on-site, so you won't have to waddle far after dining. You also can get a ride in the longhorn limo, swim in the Texas-shaped pool, browse the gift shop for souvenirs, and eat free prime rib or chicken-fried steak on your birthday. Here's your chance to sample Rocky Mountain oysters (hint: they don't come from the sea) and fried rattlesnake, too. Moderate.

Kabuki Romanza (806-358-7799; www.kabukiromanza.com), 8130 I-40 West. Open daily. Despite the odd blending of Asian and Italian in the name, I have it on good authority from my brother, who grew up around cattle and knows beef, that they do a good teppan-style steak. Plus, the dining area looks like a boat and there's a rain and light show about every 45 minutes. Moderate.

Selective Shopping

The Georgia Street Mall (806-355-5658) at 34th and Georgia streets has more than 150 booths to search through for treasures. For Western wear, there's a branch of the Cavender's Boot City (806-358-1400; www.cavenders.com) open daily at 7920 W. Interstate 40.

Special Events

June, July, August

Texas (806-655-2181; www.texas-show.com), a musical drama depicting pioneer life in the Panhandle, takes place June through mid-August every year.

September

Good Times Celebration and Barbecue Cookoff (amarillo-chamber.org) is yearly, as is the Tri-State Fair and Rodeo (www.tristatefair.com).

October

Pirates of the Canyon Balloon Festival (www.piratesofthecanyon.com). Palo Duro Canyon, where aircraft are usually restricted, opens to the balloons each year.

November

World Championship Ranch Rodeo (www.wrca.org). See how the working cowboys rodeo at the annual event by the Working Ranch Cowboys Association.

Bibliography

THESE ARE BOOKS AND SOME OF THE WEB SITES I used to research this guide (I also used, to one degree or another, every Web site mentioned in the book and more as I checked for accuracy and confirmed details after research trips). All were invaluable, and the books and sites below also form a good reading list for anyone who wants to know more about specifics in West Texas. You'll find a few more details about the books in the Big Bend and El Paso chapters.

BOOKS

Evans, James, and Robert Draper. *Big Bend Pictures.* University of Texas Press, 2003.

Glendinning, Jim. *Adventures in the Big Bend: A Travel Guide.* Iron Mountain Press, 2010.

Parent, Laurence. *Hiking Big Bend National Park.* Falcon Press, 1996.

Parent, Laurence, and Joe Nick Patoski. *Big Bend National Park.* University of Texas Press, 2006.

Ragsdale, Kenneth B. *Big Bend Country, Land of the Unexpected.* Texas A&M University Press, 1998.

Smithers, W. D. *Chronicles of the Big Bend.* Texas Historical Association, 1999.

Sonnichsen, C. L. *Pass of the North.* Texas Western Press, 1968.

Timmons, W. H. *El Paso: A Borderlands History.* University of Texas Press, 1990.

Tyler, Ronnie C. *The Big Bend, A History of the Last Texas Frontier.* Texas A&M Press, 2007.

WEB SITES

www.tshaonline.org, the Texas State Handbook online.
www.texasbeyondhistory.net, by the University of Texas at Austin.
www.texasalmanac.com, the Texas Almanac online.
www.traveltex.com, the state tourism Web site.

Index